Ships That Sail No More

Giles T. Brown

Ships
That Sail
No
More

*Marine Transportation
from San Diego to
Puget Sound, 1910-1940*

UNIVERSITY OF KENTUCKY PRESS
LEXINGTON, 1966

To A.W.B., E.L.K.B., and B.C.B.
who have encouraged

Foreword

THE HISTORY of the West Coast is inextricably tied to the history of shipping along that coast. American ships traded there before 1800, and the first Americans to settle in California and Oregon were dependent upon shipping for much of their contact with the outside world and with each other. In later years, the spectacular career of the railroads in the economy and politics of the Far West diverted public attention from maritime trade. Ships still plied the seas along the coast, however, offering some advantages to both shippers and passengers and providing stiff competition for the railroads. In this scholarly and authoritative volume, Dr. Brown has rescued from undeserved obscurity the story of shipping along the West Coast during the crucial years prior to 1940.

The title, *Ships That Sail No More*, suggests the romance of an age that is gone. There is some romance in these pages, but this book is valuable as a careful and well documented account of the rise and fall of one of the major American steamship companies of this century—the Admiral Line: the manner in which it rose to power, the services it rendered, the competition it faced, the effects of its labor policies, and the factors which finally forced it out of business.

Dr. Brown is well qualified to tell this story. He is familiar with the Pacific Coast and with the history of that fast changing section. He knows ships, and he has had access to the records and papers of the principal steamship companies engaged in the trade. Out of this background, he has written a book which will be a significant contribution to the history of the Pacific Coast and to the economic history of the United States.

Vanderbilt University   Harold Whitman Bradley

Preface

MUCH HAS BEEN written about the American merchant marine, the graceful clipper ships, the first ironclads, the trans-Atlantic steamers, and the trans-Pacific side-wheelers, but the sea lanes along the Pacific Coast of the United States have been somewhat neglected. Long after the sooty steam engine had begun to puff its way from Chicago to San Francisco on regular schedules, the people of the coastal cities and towns of western America depended upon the sturdy steamer for economic, commercial, and intellectual contacts with the outside world. Even after 1890 when a north-south rail line had been completed, the shipping industry was able to offer faster service than the trains for several years.

Just before World War I, the western coastwise shipping industry was involved in a struggle from which emerged the Pacific Steamship Company, the Admiral Line. The pages which follow present the life history of this line, its rivals, its attempts to monopolize the sea lanes, its drive to make the West Coast the hub of a great nautical empire which temporarily reached from Mexico to Canada, from the West Coast to the Orient, and from California to Nome, Alaska, and its eventual defeat. Out of these efforts developed plans for what became the round-the-world service of the Dollar Line and the present American President Line. The history of its almost three decades of aggressiveness includes World War I, wrecks, strikes, rate wars, and the Depression. It is a case study of American initiative, eagerness, success, and failure on a sea frontier. Two families, the Robert Dollars and the H. F. Alexanders, became shipping titans and rivals. In fact, H. F. Alexander once reportedly boasted that he was a bigger man than the Secretary of the Navy. This statement had some validity since Alexander was able to obtain possession of a naval ship, which the Navy did not want to sell, before the bids were opened. The story also includes the rivalry of the Hill and Harriman railroad empires to obtain and to retain a portion of the lucrative coastwise trade. James J. Hill dropped his original plan to extend a rail line into California and instead built two of the fastest ships ever to fly the American flag. They were named, appropriately enough, after the two Hill railroads, the *Great Northern* and *Northern Pacific*.

Today the ships are gone. Many went down in disasters, others served faithfully until sent to the scrap pile, and some helped America to win World War II although their industry had succumbed five years before Pearl Harbor. The zenith and fall of the Pacific coastwise transportation industry make a fascinating chapter in the transportation history of America. No longer do ships carrying passengers and cargo ply the sea lanes from San Diego to Puget Sound. They have vanished and with them a transportation system that did much to make possible the development of the area they served.

Limitations are necessary. The narrative is concerned principally with events which took place between 1910 and 1940, although these dates provide informal guidelines rather than serve as rigid determinants. The geographical limits are San Diego on the south and Puget Sound on the north. Thus the important and fascinating trade between the mainland and Hawaii and Alaska is

excluded. The economic focus has been on those companies which provided a common carrier service vying for
the patronage of the traveling and shipping public

In the field of scholarship, no person works alone. As
has been noted in the following pages, many individuals
have assisted in a variety of ways. In particular, the help,
counsel and inspiration of Professor Harold Whitman
Bradley have been important and deeply appreciated. The
responsibility for the results—both good and bad—obvi-
ously rests on my shoulders alone.

Newport Beach, Calif.   G.T.B.
January, 1966

Contents

Illustrations

ONE

The Beginning
of an Era

WHERE IT DIPS under the waters of the Pacific
Ocean, the continental shelf of the United States
creates a long jagged coastline of almost two thousand miles. Expressive names brighten the map of this
area. Sister Rocks, Crooks Point, Dragon Rocks, The
Turtles, Devils Gate Rock, Hunters Cove, and a host of
others quicken the imagination. Cape Disappointment,
Cape Shoalwater, and Cape Foulweather remind one of
the treachery of the sea. Cape Flattery and Destruction
Island, though close geographically, are distant in connota-
tion. These place names also reveal the mixture of peoples
who dared the elements to settle the West Coast. Cape
Perpetua (everlasting), Cape Fortunas (good luck), Point
Gorda (large), Point Delgada (thin or slender), Point
Sur (south), and Point Arguello (lack of health) are
Spanish. Point Cabrillo, Lopez Point, Coronado Islands,
Point Vincente, and Cape Vizcaino commemorate those
Iberians who sailed from Mexico as far north as Juan de
Fuca Strait and present-day British Columbia. The Rus-
sians have left Fort Ross and Russian Gulch. Drake's Bay
marks the exploits of the daring Englishman. Portuguese
Point adds another nationality and Yankee Point a fifth.
Dana Point became world famous because of a sickly

college student and his book, *Two Years Before the Mast*. Although politically overwhelmed by the Europeans, the Indians have places which serve as reminders of their former supremacy: Tatoosh Island, Point Chehalis, Umatilla Reef, Tillamook Rock, Cape Kiwanda, and Yaquina Head.

By the beginning of the twentieth century, the West Coast not only possessed a colorful history but also had become a tourist attraction of the first rank. California, billed as the "great winter playground," boasted of such varied items as the Golden Gate, the Cawston Ostrich Farm in South Pasadena, palm trees, and sunny skies. Mount Lowe, two hours from Los Angeles, thrilled visitors who reached its Alpine Tavern at an elevation of 5,000 feet by an incline railway. The Glenwood Mission Inn was becoming justly famous for its mission type architecture and bell tower in the heart of Riverside, a city with no navigable river. Other attractions included Catalina Island and its Hotel Metropole, deep sea fishing off the Coronado Islands near San Diego, and Venice, an Old World name for a New World beach. The infant movie industry was soon to make Hollywood known to thousands.

The sea and the land complemented each other in the development of the coastwise shipping industry. White men had first gazed upon the rocky points and undulating hills of what is now the western United States from the ceaselessly tossing decks of ships. To the Spaniard, Russian, Frenchman, Britisher, or American, the Pacific Ocean furnished a natural road upon which he could travel with some degree of safety and ease to the scattered places along the rugged coastline. For decades, no river, railroad, stagecoach, or wagon train competed with the rolling swells of the sea as the north-south highway. Long after the puffing steam engine had become a familiar sight, the people of the cities and towns clustered along the coast depended, to a great extent, upon the faithful steamer to provide contacts with the outside world, to carry away their produce, and to bring their supplies.

In view of the great amount of marine activity along the Pacific Coast, it is surprising to find that so little was known of its physical characteristics. As late as 1918, less than 30 percent of the coast had even been surveyed, which meant that there was many an uncharted reef to gouge a hole in an unsuspecting ship. In sharp contrast to the neglect of the Pacific Coast was the attention given by the government to the waters around the Philippine Islands, which were 64 percent charted by 1918.[1]

Geography has not been kind to western shipping. A glance at an outline map of the United States will show that the central portion of the Pacific Coast bulges into the ocean. In order to avoid the jutting capes and heads, ships had to make an outward movement which added to the length of the journey. Had the western coastline been straight or concave, as is the case with the Gulf Coast and most parts of the Atlantic Coast, distances between shipping points would have been materially reduced. In addition to adding mileage, the convex western shore presented a danger. To reduce the length of a trip, ship captains approached the bulges as closely as possible. At night or in a fog, errors could be easily made which would result in disaster. The fate of the *Bear,* the *Alaska,* and the *Harvard* testifies to this danger.

In addition, the Pacific Coast offers few miles of sandy beaches. Officially the entire length is termed "rocky" by the United States Coast and Geodetic Survey. In contrast, the eastern and southern coasts are composed largely of

---

[1] E. Lester Jones, *The Neglected Waters of the Pacific Coast: Washington, Oregon, and California* (Washington, D. C., 1918), p. 6.

sand, mud, or coral. When a ship went aground on a rocky shore, she was not only apt to become a total loss but casualties were frequent. Another distinctive feature of the Pacific coastline is that the 100-fathom curve lies at an average distance of less than ten miles from land. This condition makes it difficult to secure an anchorage in an emergency. Between ports only a few areas offer shelter.

There are five principal seaports between the Mexican border and British Columbia. Seattle, the farthest north, is the nearest of the five ports to the Orient. Portland, which serves the great Columbia River valley, is located some distance inland but has miles of deep-water frontage. San Francisco is on a landlocked, deep-water bay which has an area of about 450 square miles and a shoreline of more than two hundred miles. The entrance is through the famed Golden Gate whose width varies from one to three miles. The bay is also the tidewater terminus of the drainage from about sixty thousand square miles of tributary area. Most of this is the great central valley of California with its Sacramento and San Joaquin rivers. The harbor of Los Angeles is entirely man-made with three long breakwaters creating an outer area of safe anchorage. The inner harbor has miles of docking space and adequate turning basins. Three transcontinental railroads converge at this key transportation junction; the Santa Fe, the Union Pacific and the southern route of the Southern Pacific. The southernmost of the western ports is San Diego, located ten miles north of the Mexican boundary. Its crescent-shaped bay is about fourteen miles long. Two rail connections provide San Diego with transportation facilities for the transfer of goods and passengers between land and sea. One is a spur line of the Santa Fe from Los Angeles and the other is the San Diego and Arizona Railway which operates about 150 miles of track eastward from San Diego to El Centro, where a connection with the Southern Pacific Railway forms a direct route east.[2]

Of these five principal seaports, only two are readily accessible from the sea. Downtown Los Angeles is 23 miles from its harbor, Portland is 110 miles up a winding river, and Seattle is about 144 miles east and south of the open ocean. Travelers from Los Angeles who planned to board a coastwise vessel had to take a special train to the dock, adding an hour or more to the travel time. Baggage had to be at the Los Angeles downtown station two hours before sailing time. Of the five, only San Francisco and San Diego are located near the sea lanes and even in the case of San Diego, Point Loma makes it necessary for ships to follow a tortuous nine-mile channel before docking.[3]

A serious geographical handicap faced the steamship lines that operated between California and the ports of Oregon and Washington. Since Portland was over a hundred miles inland, it was impracticable to use the same vessel for calls at both Seattle and Portland. The lines, consequently, had to operate two separate routes out of San Francisco that for more than two-thirds of their distance paralleled each other. Had this geographical condition not existed, a shipping company that offered a twice weekly service from Portland and tri-weekly from Seattle could have provided five sailings weekly from both ports with the same amount of equipment. Few companies had a sufficient number of units to offer service to both Portland and Seattle and there was little opportunity of

2 The Port Series published by various governmental agencies and in various years contain a wealth of material concerning the ports along the Pacific Ocean. For the period following World War I, this series was prepared by the U. S. War Department, Corps of Engineers, U. S. Army and the United States Shipping Board.

3 Los Angeles *Times,* Jan. 5, 1922, March 2, 1929; advertising folders in LASSCO Mss, Maritime collection of John H. Kemble, Claremont, California, and in Admiral Mss, in the Honnold Library for the Claremont Colleges, Claremont, California.

establishing a marine transportation service between Portland and Seattle since the distance by land was 185 miles
compared to 415 miles by sea.

With all these peculiarities, it is a wonder that the
shipping industry on the West Coast was able to exist and
yet for some years it not only existed but prospered. A
thriving coastwise industry overcame those hardships and
local pride developed port facilities, sometimes with the
assistance of the federal government.

EARLY COMPANIES

Anyone who attempts to chronicle the life story of steamship lines encounters difficulties peculiar to maritime
history. A vessel, steaming for the last time from a port,
leaves in its wake no trace of its existence. No ties, no
railbed, no ruts, no rails, no rolling stock remain as
evidence of more prosperous days. The ship herself is
probably sold or chartered to run on some remote route;
when she sinks beneath the waves or ends in a scrap pile,
there are few who remember or care. Ship routes easily
can be altered to include or exclude ports, and while this
fluidity can be a boon to the ship operator, it makes the
accurate recording of the past activities of the steamship
lines more difficult. The tenure of shipping companies
over their terminal properties is fleeting, for usually the
offices and piers are merely leased from some third party.
When a steamship line dies, therefore, few physical evi-
dences of its existence remain to help a later generation
reconstruct its glory. The empire builders on the western
sea lanes have therefore had to be content with relative
anonymity.

The record of the first company to furnish passenger
and freight service along the Pacific Coast is obscure.

There are several nominations for the honor. Apparently as early as 1825, the little steamer *Telica* began to trade along the California coast. Eleven years later the better-known *Beaver*, also a steamer, arrived on the coast from the Thames River in England. Some maintain that she was the first to establish a regular service. In 1848, the pioneer Pacific Mail Steamship Company decided to furnish monthly coastwise service from Astoria on the Columbia River to the Isthmus of Panama, with calls at San Francisco, Monterey, and San Diego. In the contract signed with the American government, the company agreed to deliver mail for an annual compensation of $199,000. The new service was inaugurated in 1848. Despite this earlier activity, the title of the "great-grand-mother of Pacific Coast carriers" is sometimes given to the *Goliah*, a side-wheeler which had been built in New York originally as a tug. In 1850, the *Goliah* left San Francisco for San Diego with both passengers and freight. Thereafter she maintained what some like to think was the first coastwise service.[4]

As adventurers, fortune seekers, Yankees, Chinese, and others began to people the Far West in the years following the gold rush of 1849, the steamship business increased, for a north-south rail line was not completed until 1887. With that increase came a confusing crop of companies. Ben Holladay, soon to become famous as the operator of stage lines in the West, furnished a regular steamer service between San Francisco and San Diego with a company named the California Steam Navigation Company. There was a California, Oregon, and Mexico Steam-

4 John Haskell Kemble, *The Panama Route 1848-1869* (Berkeley, Calif., 1943), pp. 8-30; Eliot Grinnell Mears, *Maritime Trade of Western United States* (Stanford University, Calif., 1935), p. 395; E. W. Wright (ed.), *Lewis and Dryden's Marine History of the Pacific Northwest* (Portland, Ore., 1895). See also John Haskell Kemble, "Pacific Mail Service between Panama and San Francisco, 1949-1851," *Pacific Historical Review*, II (Dec. 1933), 405-17.

ship Company, an Anchor Line, a North Pacific Transportation Company, an Oregon Steamship Company, several so-called Independent steamship companies and, of course, the enduring Pacific Mail Steamship Company.[5]

The company which was to become the dominant one for over forty years grew out of a most humble beginning. In 1860 two men named Charles Goodall and Chris Nelson formed a partnership to bring fresh water from springs near Sausalito in Marin County on the north side of the Golden Gate and to sell it to ships anchored in San Francisco Bay. The fresh drinking water was brought by barge alongside the potential customers. From this lowly beginning developed the Pacific Coast Steamship Company, which for a period dominated the sea lanes in the same manner that the Southern Pacific Railroad Company controlled the rail lines of the West. At first the two men used their profits from the water-boat business to purchase a 100-ton steamer, the *Salinas,* which had been operated on the San Francisco to Monterey route. The service was continued. By 1872, one of the United States senators from California joined the firm and the name was changed to Goodall, Nelson and Perkins Steamship Company. With a capital stock of $2,000,000 and eighteen vessels, fifteen of which were steamers, the new company attracted passengers. When Chris Nelson retired in 1876 from the business, the name was changed to Pacific Coast Steamship Company by which it was to be known for the next forty years.[6]

[5] Henry G. Langley (comp.), *San Francisco Directory* . . . (San Francisco, 1856, 1858, 1861 and 1867); title varies. See also Hubert Howe Bancroft, *Chronicles of the Builders of the Commonwealth* (8 vols.; San Francisco, 1891), V, 123-48; 359-458; Will Lawson, *Pacific Steamers* (Glasgow, 1927), pp. 198-99. Erle Heath, *Seventy-Five Years of Progress: Historical Sketch of the Southern Pacific* (San Francisco, privately printed, 1945), p. 17.

[6] *Pacific Marine Review,* XIII (Nov. 1916), 28; XXXII (April 1935), 110. For good, though unfortunately undocumented, accounts of the early his-

The service developed by this company was soon noted throughout the West. Even Easterners and Europeans were quick to observe that although the West might be uncouth in many other aspects, its merchant marine was distinguished. On September 15, 1883, a ship modestly called the *Queen of the Pacific* pulled away from a Seattle dock in the early morning and headed for the open sea and San Francisco. On the evening of the second day, the *Queen* steamed through the Golden Gate to her destination. She had made this trip before and would make it many times more. What was unique was a name which appeared on her passenger list, that of Sir Charles Russell, later Lord Chief Justice of England. In his diary, Sir Russell wrote: "The *Queen* is a very fine and a very fast ship; and it is no exaggeration to say that expense and ingenuity have not been spared in making her the most luxurious boat I ever saw. My apartment is splendid. I should be content to go in the *Queen* round even by Cape Horn and so home to England."[7] The wild and woolly West had passed one of the stiffest tests, the judgment of a son of the "mistress of the seas."

The Pacific Coast Steamship Company continued to improve its service with the object of providing the best coastwise service in the world. A crowning achievement of this program was the arrival in San Francisco harbor on October 6, 1913, of the *Congress* on her maiden voyage from Philadelphia. Built at a cost of over a million dollars by the New York Shipbuilding Company, the *Congress* was the largest coastwise passenger carrier under the American flag. Her arrival at the city by the Golden Gate was marked by a civic celebration and hailed by the press

---

tory of the Pacific Coast Steamship Company see *Railway and Marine News*, X (Oct. 1, 1912), 12-14, X (Oct. 15, 1912), 16-18, XIII (Jan. 1915), 27-28; Bancroft, *Chronicles of the Builders*, II, 144.

  [7] Sir Charles Russell, *Diary of a Visit to the United States of America in the Year 1883* (New York, 1910), p. 108.

as the beginning of an "epoch."[8] In addition to the *Congress* and *Queen,* the Pacific Coast Steamship Company owned the *President* and *Governor,* each of which could carry over five hundred passengers. Other units of the fleet included, the *Curacao, City of Seattle, City of Topeka, Senator, Spokane,* and *Umatilla.* The fleet of the Pacific Coast Steamship Company was by far the largest and finest on the Pacific Coast.

THE CHALLENGERS FROM PORTLAND

Despite the energy which the Pacific Coast Steamship Company employed to maintain its imposing fleet of steamers, the company was not able to prevent competitors from making substantial inroads upon the potentially lucrative trade it wished to dominate.[9] The resulting rate wars forced fares to absurdly low levels. At one time first-class passage between Los Angeles and San Francisco, which included both meals and berth, could be purchased for as little as three dollars. Second-class tickets sold for two dollars. In 1912, five other lines were actively challenging the supremacy of the Pacific Coast Steamship Company. By 1914 the number had risen to eleven.[10]

Of these the oldest was the San Francisco and Portland

[8] Los Angeles *Times,* Oct. 7, 1913; San Francisco *Chronicle,* Oct. 7, 1913.

[9] U. S., Congress, House, *Report of the Committee on the Merchant Marine and Fisheries on Steamship Agreements and Affiliations in the American Foreign and Domestic Trade,* 63d Cong., 2d sess., H. Doc. 805, 1914, pp. 350, 384. Hereafter cited as *Steamship Agreements and Affiliations.*

[10] "Advertising Dodger" in Pacific Coast Steamship Company Mss in the Honnold Library; U. S., Bureau of Corporations, *Report of the Commissioner of Corporations on Transportation by Water in the United States.* Part IV: *Control of Water Carriers by Railroads and by Shipping Consolidations* (Washington, D. C., 1913), pp. 7-9. Hereafter cited as *Control of Water Carriers.*

Steamship Company which liked to be known as the "Big 3" in reference to its fleet of three vessels. It gave the Harriman rail interests of mid-America an access to California. With its antecedent companies, the "Big 3" could claim a long, though not continuous, existence from about 1882 when a steamship line was first inaugurated between San Francisco and Portland by the Oregon Packet Company. The service was later taken over by the Oregon Steam Navigation Company and still later by the Oregon Railroad and Navigation Company which created an Ocean Division to operate the water route.[11] In 1904 the line was incorporated as the San Francisco and Portland Steamship Company of California and later was reincorporated in 1912 under the laws of Utah. Its entire capital stock of $500,000 was owned by the Oregon-Washington Railroad and Navigation Company, which in turn was controlled by the Union Pacific Railroad through the Oregon Short Line Railroad Company.[12] Though the operations of the company were kept separate from those of the rail lines, it had no executive officers of its own except a general manager who directed its affairs from Portland. The "Big 3" served as an extension of the transcontinental rail line of the Union Pacific and gave the Harriman interests direct access to San Francisco and later to southern California when it extended its shipping service to Los Angeles in 1910. By 1915, it was carrying about fifty-five thousand passengers annually on its three steamers, which provided sailings every fifth day from Portland, San Francisco, and San Pedro. The fare was

[11] *Pacific Marine Review*, XII (Nov. 1915), 66.

[12] "Annual Report of the San Francisco and Portland Steamship Company to the Railroad Commission of California for the Year Ending December 31, 1916," p. 2 in Archives of Public Utilities Commission of California at San Francisco. These archives hereafter referred to as ASF. U. S., Bureau of Corporations, *Control of Water Carriers*, p. 49.

about four dollars less than direct rail service.[13]   It was only on the San Francisco to Los Angeles portion of its route that the "Big 3" came into active competition with the Pacific Coast Steamship Company, as the latter company by-passed Portland on its run to Seattle. Two of the ships owned by the "Big 3," the *Bear* and the *Beaver,* were named in honor of California and Oregon, the states served by the line. The other was called the *Rose City* in recognition of the city of Portland.[14]

But the San Francisco and Portland Steamship Company was faced with formidable competition on the Portland to San Francisco run when James J. Hill announced, in November 1913, that his railroad companies would start a steamer service between those two ports early in 1915 using two ships which were being built especially for this purpose. Hill planned to have the ships connect with his trains at the mouth of the Columbia River, thus eliminating the slow, tortuous journey up the river to Portland which the ships of the "Big 3" negotiated each sailing. Rumors of this invasion of California by the Hill interests had been current for some time. To counteract the Hill offensive, the "Big 3" in 1913 was reported to be building two palatial, twenty-two knot vessels to compete with the Hill liners. Information which was claimed to be authentic gave the vessels the somewhat inappropriate names of *Narragansett* and *Manhattan* and claimed that each would cost $750,000. The plans miscarried and the two ships never appeared on the coastwise sea lanes. The significance of this move by the Hill

[13] "Annual Report of the San Francisco and Portland Steamship Company to the Railroad Commission of California for the Year Ending December 31, 1923," p. 502 in ASF; U. S., Interstate Commerce Commission, *Decisions of the Interstate Commerce Commission of the United States,* XXXIV (Washington, 1915), 156-57. Hereafter cited as *Decisions.*
[14] Portland *Oregonian,* Feb. 22, 1913.

interests against the virtual rail monopoly that the Southern Pacific enjoyed between Los Angeles and Portland was not lost on interested observers. The Los Angeles *Times* noted that such action would afford real competition to the crack *Shasta Limited* of the Southern Pacific.[15]

To operate the new Hill ships, the Great Northern and Northern Pacific railroads created in 1913 the Great Northern Pacific Steamship Company with a capitalization of $5,000,000. This company is easily confused with the Great Northern Steamship Company, which had been organized in 1900 to operate the *Dakota* and *Minnesota* between Seattle and the Orient. At the time, these were the largest vessels of their type afloat. The *Dakota* ended a fairly short life when she struck a rock in Japanese waters on March 3, 1907, and became a total loss. The *Minnesota* enjoyed a longer career. When she was sold for junk in 1923, she still could lay claim to the title of being the largest freight carrier under the United States flag.[16]

In explaining why he dropped the original project of building a rail line into California and established a steamship service instead, Hill declared that the "right of way is cheaper and the operating expenses are not so high."[17] He was to find that the first part of his statement was more accurate than the second. The two ships were named, appropriately enough, the *Great Northern* and *Northern Pacific*.

The arrival of the *Great Northern*, the first of the vessels to be completed, from her East Coast shipyards was an

15 Los Angeles *Times*, Sept. 4, Nov. 10, 11, 1913.

16 San Francisco *Chronicle*, Jan. 19, 1923. For the story of this part of the career of Hill, see W. Kaye Lamb, "The Trans-Pacific Venture of James J. Hill: A History of the Great Northern Steamship Company," *American Neptune*, III (July 1943), 185-204.

17 Portland *Oregonian*, March 17, 1915.

event. Up to that time she was the largest ship of her type
to sail through the Panama Canal. Her arrival in San
Diego was hailed with a six-column spread on the front
page of the local paper. The almost six hundred passengers, whose total wealth was estimated "to aggregate
$50,000,000," were taken as guests of the city to the
Panama-California Exposition. The women passengers
each received some California oranges and a bouquet of
violets. During the few hours the ship was in port, it was
estimated that over ten thousand San Diegans visited her.
At Los Angeles the next day the passengers were given a
civic welcome and luncheon.[18] The ship made the run
between San Francisco and Flavel, the Hill docks west of
Astoria, in less than twenty-four hours and was greeted
by the "greatest crowd that ever assembled at the mouth
of the Columbia River." More than two thousand citizens
of Portland descended upon the little town from special
trains which were used to convey this "largest excursion
ever sent" from Portland. Astoria businessmen donated
money to buy a chronometer for the new vessel. As the
Great Northern approached the dock, the ceremony of
the "Wedding of the Rails" was celebrated in which
"Sails" and "Rails" were joined by George L. Baker, the
president of the Portland Advertising Club.

The two sister ships were reported to have cost approximately twelve million dollars; it was revealed later that
five million was a nearer estimate. Because of the luxury
of their passenger accommodations, the operators gave
them the name of "Twin Palaces of the Pacific." Among
other attractions, the ships provided the passengers with
palm garden verandas, sun parlors, and glass-enclosed
promenades. With such equipment, the Hill lines were
in a position not only to compete with the "Big 3" but

[18] San Diego *Union*, Feb. 10, 11, 1915; Los Angeles *Times*, Feb. 12, 1915.

with the fastest trains of the Southern Pacific between San Francisco and Portland.[19]

Hill had always wanted to invade California. The Panama-Pacific Exposition in San Francisco in 1915 provided the needed impetus to establish the new steamship line as it was anticipated that such an event would swell the number of tourists coming to California. By establishing a through service from Chicago to Flavel in Oregon by rail and thence to San Francisco by water, the various Hill companies placed themselves in a favorable position to obtain a major share of this business. Another struggle between the Hill and Harriman interests, similar to the one over the control of the Northern Pacific Railroad, seemed imminent. During the first summer the "Twin Palaces" carried approximately thirty-five hundred persons weekly, but after the summer season, one of the "Palaces" was placed on the Honolulu run. The temporary withdrawal of the Pacific Mail Steamship Company from this trade in November 1915, ostensibly because of the passage of the La Follette Seamen's Act, was given as the reason for the move. It was known, however, that passenger revenue on the Flavel to San Francisco route during the winter months was not up to expectations.[20]

In addition to the "Big 3" and the Hill line, there was

19 Portland *Oregon Journal*, March 21, 1915. San Francisco *Chronicle*, March 27, 1917. *Railway and Marine News*, XV (June 1917), 19. For a technical article with excellent charts, diagrams and pictures concerning the building of these two ships, which were the largest turbine-driven passenger ships constructed in the United States up to that time, see "S. S. Great Northern and Northern Pacific—New 23-Knot Turbine Passenger Ships Built at Cramp's for the Spokane, Portland & Seattle Railway Company" in *International Marine Engineering*, XIX (Dec. 1914), 535-45. An informal and highly readable biography of one of the twin ships, the *Great Northern*, was written by John Carroll Carrothers, " 'Hot Foot'—The Story of a Ship" in *United States Naval Institute Proceedings*, LXXXII, Number 2 (Feb. 1956), 170-79.
20 Los Angeles *Times*, April 14, 1916, May 25, 1916. *Pacific Marine Review*, XII (Nov. 1915), 65.

another company which furnished service out of Portland. This was the independent North Pacific Steamship Company which had, in 1915, a fleet of eight vessels. Its ships, however, were small and slow. Its largest steamer carried only 234 passengers in contrast to the 800 passengers that each of the "Twin Palaces" could carry. The company offered service, not only from Portland and San Francisco, but also from Santa Barbara, Los Angeles, San Diego, and the smaller ports along the coast which were by-passed by the larger lines.[21]

[21] *North Pacific Ports* (2nd ed.; San Francisco, 1915), p. 343. San Diego *Union,* Dec. 31, 1916. *Pacific Marine Review,* XII (Jan. 1915), 35.

The Admiral Line
Becomes Supreme

THE RISE OF H. F. ALEXANDER

ON THE ROUTE from California to Seattle, the
Pacific Coast Steamship Company was faced with
opposition furnished by a man who was later hailed
as the "monarch of Pacific shipping." This was Hubbard
Foster Alexander, who liked to be known as simply H. F.
Alexander. Born in Colorado Springs, Colorado, in 1879,
young Alexander was brought to the coast by his parents
who settled at Tacoma, Washington. The panic of 1893
swept away the family fortune and, as his father had
become an invalid, H. F. Alexander at the age of fourteen
obtained a job on the docks of Tacoma at twenty cents an
hour in order to help support the family. His career from
this humble beginning to the presidency of several steamship companies within a span of a few years was looked
upon as "one of the classics of American shipping" and
was in the best tradition of a generation imbued with the
success stories of Horatio Alger.[1]

At the age of twenty, H. F. Alexander acquired control
of the Commercial Dock Company of Tacoma. In 1907,
he became president of the Alaska Pacific Steamship
Company, which had recently established a weekly passenger and freight service between Puget Sound and San
Francisco. In the same year, control of the Alaska Coast

Company was acquired by Alexander. Using three small ships, this company maintained a service from Seattle to various Alaskan ports. In order to coordinate the activities of the two companies, the Pacific Alaska Navigation Company was formed in 1911 as a holding company. Two years later, on January 1, 1914, the holding company took over the operation of all vessels owned by the two earlier companies, which continued their corporate existences but ceased to be operating organizations. Fortunately for the public, who might otherwise have been confused by the similarity of names and profusion of companies, H. F. Alexander decided to call his various steamship enterprises the Admiral Line. With the slogan "Safety, Courtesy and Food," the Admiral Line began to win favor with the public and to challenge the dominance of the Pacific Coast Steamship Company.[2]

In its struggle for a share in the coastwise trade, the Admiral Line in 1910 found a welcome ally when the Metropolitan Steamship Company decided to bring to the Pacific Coast its two speedy turbine-propelled vessels, the *Harvard* and *Yale*. These two vessels had been oper-

[1] *Marine Digest,* I (Sept. 2, 1922), 5; *Daily Journal of Commerce* (Seattle), Oct. 18, 1922; "Corporation Papers," Alaska Pacific Steamship Company Mss, Honnold Library.

[2] Information concerning the life of Alexander and his early companies can be found in a variety of places, although few of them are adequately documented. The best is probably a "Confidential Report to the United States Shipping Board" submitted by Frank Woolsey, secretary of the Admiral Line, dated July 28, 1921, in Pacific Coast Steamship Company Mss, Honnold Library. Other helpful references are letters from H. F. Alexander dated Feb. 17, March 16, 1948, in possession of the author; "Corporation Records" in Alaska Coast Company Mss and "Corporation Papers" in Pacific Alaska Navigation Company Mss, Honnold Library; "Growth of the Admiral Line in Ten Years," *Railway and Marine News,* XIV (Sept. 1916), 26; Magner White, "Alexander, Once a Dock Hand, Now Owns a Fleet," *American Magazine,* CI (April 1926), 16-17 ff.; *Marine Digest,* I (Sept. 2, 1922), 5-6; *Pacific Marine Review,* XIII (Nov. 1916), 29-30. For a report in his own words see: H. F. Alexander, "Why We Made Money When Nearly Everybody Said We'd Fail," in *System,* XLVII (April 1925), 449-55.

ating on the New York to Boston route in competition
with the steamships of the New York, New Haven and
Hartford Railroad Company. Their arrival brought to
the West two of the most famous American coastwise
steamers of the twentieth century. Planned by Charles
Wyman Morse for express service between New York
and Boston as a challenge to the venerable Fall River
Line, they were designed by William Denny and Brothers
of Dumbarton, Scotland, and built in the United States.
Their triple screws, driven by Parsons steam turbine
engines, provided enough power to make them the fastest
merchant ships under the American flag at the time they
were completed in 1907. The two provided sharp competition to the Fall River Line of the New York, New
Haven and Hartford Railroad Company. In 1910 their
engines were converted from coal to oil burners which
made them pioneers in the use of oil fuel on the high seas.
Following the collapse of his financial empire, Morse was
sent to a federal penitentiary and the control of the ships
passed to other hands. The exact reason and method by
which the operators of the *Harvard* and *Yale* were forced
to withdraw from the East Coast have been lost in the
maze of high corporate finance. The Interstate Commerce
Commission, after an investigation, concluded that the
"devious methods used indicated that the purpose of these
circuitous methods was to conceal the hand of the New
Haven" in eliminating the two ships as competitors.
Nine companies, most of them with dummy officers, were
used in the process which was termed "a remarkable
exhibition of corporate legerdemain." At one time the
general counsel for the New Haven became the trustee
in bankruptcy for one of the companies. Out of the
baffling network of financial dealings, there emerged the
Pacific Navigation Company, organized under the laws of
New Jersey, with a capitalization of $750,000. The exact

ownership of the *Harvard* and *Yale* was carefully concealed; even before the Interstate Commerce Commission, the officials of the company refused to disclose who actually owned them on the ground that their competitors should not know the private affairs of the Pacific Navigation Company. The two ships were brought around South America through the Straits of Magellan in the fall of 1910 and began to operate between Los Angeles and San Francisco in December of the same year. The next year, the service was extended to San Diego.[3]

H. F. Alexander was quick to appreciate the advantage that the new service could be to his Admiral Line in its struggle against the Pacific Coast Steamship Company. The result was that on November 12, 1910, before the two ships had even arrived on the West Coast, an understanding was reached between the Pacific Navigation Company and the Alexander organization whereby it was mutually agreed to route passengers and freight over each other's lines with through tickets and bills of lading. The Admiral Line was to operate between Puget Sound ports and San Francisco with three of its ships, and leave the San Francisco–Los Angeles route open to the *Harvard* and *Yale*. Sailings were to be arranged so that "as far as possible" passengers would not have to remain overnight at San Francisco. Each company promised to "use its best efforts" to direct passengers and freight to the other and both agreed not to enter into any contravening agreements with other steamship companies.[4]

When the *Yale* sailed from Los Angeles on December 20, 1910, she inaugurated the new service and thereby created for the first time in many years a rival combination which could challenge the venerable Pacific Coast

---

[3] *Decisions,* XXXI, 45-47 ff.

[4] Copy of the agreement dated Nov. 12, 1910, in Alaska Pacific Steamship Company Mss, Honnold Library.

Steamship Company all the way from Southern California to Puget Sound. Since the *Harvard* and *Yale,* in addition to being among the first ships to use turbine propulsion, were among the fastest merchant vessels flying the American flag, their presence on a Pacific coastwise route was a definite asset to the development of the marine transportation of the West. They were able to make the voyage between San Francisco and San Pedro, the port of Los Angeles, in nineteen hours, whereas the ships of the Pacific Coast Steamship Company and the "Big 3" required between twenty-three to twenty-five hours.

By 1914, the Pacific Navigation Company was maintaining four weekly sailings each way between San Francisco and the south while its two rivals together were furnishing but three. That the public was favorably inclined to the service is evident from the fact that about 120,000 passengers were carried annually. The reception given the new company by other transportation companies was not, however, as cordial. In 1914, it was necessary for the Pacific Navigation Company to appeal to the Interstate Commerce Commission to compel the Southern Pacific, Santa Fe, Western Pacific, and Salt Lake railroads to establish through routes and joint fares with it as they had done with the Pacific Coast Steamship Company and the "Big 3." At the time, the rail officials confirmed the success of the *Harvard* and *Yale* in attracting passengers from their lines.[5]

Two conditions made the joint service with the Admiral Line somewhat unsatisfactory. The first was the obvious disadvantage which required passengers to change ships at San Francisco. Freight too had to be transshipped, which increased costs and delayed shipments. The obvious solution to this problem would have been a pooling of the

[5] *Decisions,* XXXI, 474-76.

two fleets to provide through service, but the difficulties
of coordinating sailings of vessels which differed greatly
in speed and the possibility that the two companies would
lose their identities in the process tended to postpone
action. A second problem arose from the different methods
of establishing fares employed by the two concerns. The
Pacific Navigation Company issued tickets which were
good for transportation only. Berths and meals were
extra. The Admiral Line, on the other hand, followed
the more traditional pattern of marine transportation
and included both meals and berth in its fares. A
through ticket, therefore, might entitle a person to free
meals and berth for part of his journey but on the
remainder the confused passenger found that he would
have to pay if he wanted to eat or sleep comfortably.

The fare charged by both the Pacific Coast Steamship
Company and the "Big 3" between San Francisco and
Los Angeles was $10.35 including meals and berth. The
Pacific Navigation Company charged $8.35 for transporta-
tion only. Berths were 50¢ and up while the meals were a
la carte. The average expense per passenger was estimated
at $10.92, which was slightly higher than the rate charged
by its two rivals, but the faster time made by the *Harvard*
and *Yale* offset this financial disparity. Another advantage
these two ships enjoyed was a passenger capacity of 896.
The largest vessels of the Pacific Coast Steamship Company
and the "Big 3" accommodated 651 and 583 respectively.[6]

Although the Admiral Line was the best known, there
were other lines functioning along the coast (see Table 1).
The McCormick Steamship Company, operated by the
lumber company of the same name, provided a somewhat
infrequent service between San Diego and Portland with
stops at San Pedro, San Francisco, Coos Bay, and other
points along the route. The Independent Steamship
Company maintained a five-day service between San Fran-

6 *Ibid.*, 475; "Advertising folders" in Admiral Mss, Honnold Library.

cisco and southern California with its single steamer.
Several lumber concerns furnished northbound service of
a limited nature and one of these, the Charles Nelson
Company, was to find the trade lucrative enough eventually to build one of the largest coastwise fleets.[7]

Table 1. Coastwise Steamship Lines Serving
Principal Cities, January 1916

City	Company
Seattle	Pacific Coast Steamship Company
	Admiral Line
Portland	"Big 3" (Harriman line)
	Hill line
	North Pacific Steamship Company
	McCormick Steamship Company
San Francisco	Pacific Coast Steamship Company
	Admiral Line
	Pacific Navigation Company
	North Pacific Steamship Company
	"Big 3"
	Independent Steamship Company
	McCormick Steamship Company
	Hill line
Los Angeles	Pacific Coast Steamship Company
	Pacific Navigation Company
	North Pacific Steamship Company
	"Big 3"
	Independent Steamship Company
	McCormick Steamship Company
San Diego	Pacific Coast Steamship Company
	Pacific Navigation Company
	North Pacific Steamship Company
	Independent Steamship Company
	McCormick Steamship Company

[7] San Diego *Union*, Feb. 5, 1916; Los Angeles *Times*, March 7, 1916;
Steamship Agreements and Affiliations, p. 350; *Decisions*, XXXIV, 165-68.

Since the movement of lumber from the Pacific Northwest by water was the cheapest method of transporting that bulky commodity, most of the major lumber corporations maintained their own fleets of steam schooners. These slow vessels, which had become characteristic of Pacific coastwise shipping, were a constant threat to the regularly established steamship lines. The movement of lumber was always southbound which meant that cargo space was available on the northbound trips. The slowness of these schooners prevented them from competing for passenger traffic but did not hinder them from becoming serious rivals for the available freight business in which speed was not essential. As a result, the "Big 3" carried only about half as much freight-tonnage northward as it did on its southward sailings. Since most of the established lines depended more on their cargo than on their passenger revenues, the activities of these lumber schooners always played a significant role in the struggle for existence. The keen competition had a depressing effect upon freight rates, which tended to continue to go lower as the result of frequent rate wars. By 1916, the seriousness of the situation was noted by a prominent maritime journal when it declared that for years "water rates have been anywhere from $1 to $3 per ton less than that [i.e. coastwise] trade should bear."[8]

CONSOLIDATION BEGINS

Fortunately for the coastwise steamship lines world conditions came to their assistance. Though the outbreak of war in 1914 brought misery and despair to many people, it brought help to the shipowners on the Pacific Coast.

[8] *Railway and Marine News*, XIV (March 1916), 9.

Soon after the war began ship values rose sharply. In one year, the insured valuations on British steamers increased 50 to 100 percent. American valuations were quick to follow. Lucrative offers were received by shipowners, and consequently many coastwise vessels were transferred to foreign runs through sale or charter. The reduction in the tonnage available for coastwise service meant less competition and a gradual increase in rates. This trend was accelerated by the rising cost of operations. For example, over a period of five years, the price of fuel oil doubled.[9]

The year 1916 began with many companies fighting for the coastwise trade; it closed with one dominating the field. For several months, there had been rumors that H. F. Alexander desired to expand his control but few thought that the dominance of the powerful Pacific Coast Steamship Company could be seriously challenged. The first move made by Alexander was the purchase, in February, of the *Aroline,* the only vessel of the Independent Steamship Company. The name was changed to *Admiral Goodrich* in keeping with Alexander's policy of naming ships after admirals. The annals of coastwise shipping are full of independent steamship companies. This particular one was at times called the Aroline Steamship Company. An immediate result of the withdrawal of the Independent Steamship Company was the announcement by the North Pacific Steamship Company that it would add a third vessel to its fleet, which had dwindled to two by 1916. The new schedule provided a sailing every five days instead of once a week and also direct service from Southern California to Eureka and Coos Bay for the first time. Although admitting that it had received favorable offers for its ships, the company

9 *Pacific Marine Review,* XIV (Feb. 1917), 74; "Freight Advance Seems Assured," *Railway and Marine News,* XIV (March 1916), 25.

declared that it did not contemplate abandoning its coastwise service.[10]

With the coming of spring, the major lines put forth their best efforts to capture as much of the lucrative summer season business as possible. Approximately one hundred thousand dollars was expended by the Harriman line in installing new boilers and making other repairs on the *Rose City,* with the hope that an improvement in speed and fuel economy would be shown. The Admiral Line and the Pacific Navigation Company, which had already appointed a single person to serve as general passenger agent for the two systems, held a joint banquet in April for the members of the San Francisco traffic departments of both concerns in order to promote closer relationships.[11]

On May 31, 1916, the body of James J. Hill was buried on the shore of Pleasant Lake, Minnesota; in respect for his memory, the *Great Northern* was brought to a five-minute stop off the coast of Oregon while en route to Portland. But the death of Hill did not deter the drive by his company to increase its business. The next day, the scheduled sailings between San Francisco and Portland were increased to three a week and a through sleeping car to Seattle, which made a dockside connection with the ships at Flavel, was provided. In May, the Pacific Navigation Company applied to the Railroad Commission of California for permission to reduce its one-way rate between San Francisco and Los Angeles to $6.00. Shipping circles expected that the other lines would also reduce

10 "Annual Report of the Pacific Alaska Navigation Company to the Interstate Commerce Commission for the Year Ended December 31, 1916," p. 226, in Pacific Alaska Navigation Company Mss, Honnold Library; letter from Charles P. Spicer, vice president of the Detroit Trust Company to A. B. Thacher, dated Oct. 11, 1918, in Admiral Line Mss, Honnold Library; Los Angeles *Times,* March 7, 1916.

11 *Pacific Marine Review,* XIII (June 1916), 41; *Railway and Marine News,* XIV (May 1916), 20.

fares. For some time, the daily papers had carried reports that the Pacific Navigation Company was planning to institute daily service between San Diego, San Pedro, and San Francisco by bringing to the coast a third vessel, the *Old Colony,* to operate in conjunction with the *Harvard* and *Yale.*[12]

Along the entire sweep of rocky coast, the supremacy of the venerable Pacific Coast Steamship Company was being challenged. Rumors persisted that the Admiral Line was seeking control of its more powerful rival. Early in 1916, the report gained credence that H. F. Alexander had tried to purchase the *Congress, Governor,* and *President,* the three largest ships of the Pacific Coast Steamship Company, and was told that while individual ships were not for sale, an offer for the whole fleet might be considered. In the spring, a group of eastern financial and industrial men, who had come west ostensibly for an Alaskan bear hunt, was entertained by H. F. Alexander who afterwards accompanied the men on their way east.[13]

The rumor that Alexander was negotiating with the Pacific Coast Steamship Company proved so irritating that it was termed a "malicious falsehood" in a circular sent by the operating officials of that company to its employees. The circular further stated: "We are advised by Mr. William H. Barnum, president of the Pacific Coast Company, New York [the parent company], and also by the president of the Pacific Coast Steamship Company, Mr. J. C. Ford, and its vice-president, Mr. E. C. Ward, that there are no negotiations now pending with the Pacific-Alaska Navigation Company [the Admiral Line], nor have there been either with that or with any other company, looking toward the sale of the 'President,' the

12 San Francisco *Chronicle,* June 1, 1916; Los Angeles *Times,* May 4, 25, 1916; San Diego *Union,* March 20, May 30, 1916.
13 San Francisco *Examiner,* June 1, 1916; *Pacific Marine Review,* XIII (July 1916), 58.

'Governor' or the 'Congress' or contemplating any change whatever in the ownership, operation or control of the Pacific Coast Steamship Company."[14]

On June 13, 1916, speculation on the fate of the Pacific Coast Steamship Company was temporarily eclipsed by a marine disaster when the *Bear,* flying the flag of the "Big 3," grounded less than a mile south of the Bear River, Mendocino County, California. Five persons lost their lives when one of the lifeboats overturned in the surf. The survivors were taken from Eureka to San Francisco by a special train. The public reaction was immediate and unfavorable. Criticism was leveled against all steamship lines as well as the "Big 3." The Portland *Oregonian,* in an editorial entitled "Why a Wreck?" belligerently demanded: "It may be there are good reasons, reasons other than saving of time and economy of operations, why coastwise liners should not stand out farther to sea. But . . . it would be interesting to be told what they are." The loss of the *Bear* was a severe blow to the Harriman line, not from a financial standpoint as the ship was adequately insured and the company made a profit of $89,779 "due to adjustment of the accounts incidental to writing off on the books the value of S.S. 'Bear' wrecked June 14, 1916," but because it was impossible to obtain a suitable replacement under the war conditions. The result was that sailing schedules had to be reduced just at the time when passenger travel was on the increase due to the summer tourist season.[15]

14 Los Angeles *Times,* June 12, 1916.
15 Portland *Oregonian,* June 16, 17, 1916; San Diego *Union,* June 17, 1916; Portland *Oregon Journal,* June 15, 1916; U. S., Department of Commerce, Steamboat Inspection Service, *Annual Report of the Supervising Inspector General Steamboat Inspection Service to the Secretary of Commerce for the Fiscal Year Ended June 30, 1916* (Washington, 1916), p. 22. Hereafter cited as *Annual Report.* "Annual Report of the San Francisco and Portland Steamship Company to the Railroad Commission of California for the Year Ending December 31, 1916," pp. 17 and 19 in ASF.

The next month, H. F. Alexander made a further advance in his bid to dominate the coastwise field. On July 31, 1916, in San Francisco, he announced that his company had leased the *Harvard* and *Yale* from the Metropolitan Steamship Company, which was revealed for the first time publicly as the real owner of the two ships. The Pacific Navigation Company was dissolved and effective September 1, 1916, the flag of the Admiral Line was hoisted above the two ships. Under the terms of the lease, the Admiral Line guaranteed a minimum income to the Metropolitan Steamship Company of $30,000 a month provided both ships were operating. In addition, any profits resulting from the operation of the vessels above this amount were to be divided equally between the two parties. The agreement was to run until December 31, 1921, with the privilege of an extension for an additional five years. A complicated system was adopted to determine how the operating costs were to be apportioned.

At the same time, rumors were current concerning the next plans of Alexander. The *Railway and Marine News* predicted that the "acquisition of the Yale and Harvard, while the last and most important move made by Mr. Alexander, is probably not the final act in his career of development, as he has various other plans in view and other additions to the fleet would not be surprising."[16]

Under the new operators, the *Harvard* and *Yale* were kept on the same schedule and most of the former employees were retained. The only physical change made in the appearance of the vessels was that their smoke stacks were painted buff in place of black and were provided with the insignia of the Admiral Line. To conform to

16 Copy of the agreement in Pacific Alaska Navigation Company Mss, Honnold Library; San Francisco *Chronicle,* Aug. 1, 1916; "Growth of the Admiral Line in Ten Years," *Railway and Marine News,* XIV (Sept. 1916), 27.

the policy of the Alexander organization, the price of the tickets included both meals and berth. During the summer of 1916 the two ships continued to attract passengers in large numbers. In the first twenty-four days of August, nearly four thousand people arrived at San Diego on them. The *Harvard* carried 802 persons on a single trip.[17]

Coastwise shipping was recovering to some extent the public confidence lost as a result of the wreck of the *Bear* when a new blow came. On September 14, 1916, the *Congress,* the pride of the fleet of the Pacific Coast Steamship Company, caught fire off Coos Bay. For a time the passengers were not informed of the fire, which had started in one of the holds, while attempts were made to smother the flames with steam. But such efforts soon proved futile and the captain ran for shore, anchored, and prepared to abandon ship. Owing to the density of the smoke and the growing heat, it proved impossible to use any lifeboats except on the windward side. The stiffness of the *Congress* fortunately allowed all the lifeboats on the one side to be lowered without heeling the ship. The 253 passengers and 175 crew members were safely transferred to a seagoing dredge which happened to be nearby. The fire left the *Congress* a smoldering skeleton and further increased the shortage of coastwise ships. How war conditions had raised the value of marine equipment is illustrated by the fact that the Pacific Coast Steamship Company had been offered a few months before the fire over two million dollars for the *Congress,* a sum almost twice the original cost of the vessel three years before. The offer had been refused. The engines and boilers of the *Congress,* which survived the fire, were sold for $850,000 although they had only cost $675,000 when new.

A few days previous to the burning of the *Congress,* a fire had broken out on the *Beaver*, the sister ship of the

[17] Los Angeles *Times,* Aug. 30, 1916; San Diego *Union,* Aug. 25, 1916.

ill-fated *Bear* of the "Big 3" line, while the ship was en route from Portland to San Francisco. It was discovered in a cargo hold shortly after midnight while the ship was off the Mendocino Coast and was smothered under battened hatches while the ship raced for port. When smoke began to seep through the staterooms, the passengers were aroused and the lifeboats made ready. Thirteen hours later the *Beaver* reached San Francisco where the flames were brought under control. The two fires, either of which could have developed into major disasters and taken a large number of lives, startled maritime circles and disturbed the always easily disturbed public.[18]

THE ADMIRAL LINE VICTORIOUS

When the new sailing schedule necessitated by the loss of the *Congress* was announced, E. C. Ward, vice president of the Pacific Coast Steamship Company, again formally denied that the Admiral Line was about to absorb his company.[19] Actually twelve days before, on September 9, 1916, an agreement had been signed between the two companies by which a new concern was organized to be known as the Pacific Steamship Company "for the purpose of chartering and operating the combined fleets." Not until September 27, 1916, however, was this agreement publicly announced.[20] In a prepared statement, H. F. Alexander called attention to the scarcity of vessels because of recent losses and the inability to obtain additional ones

18 *Pacific Marine Review*, XIII (Oct. 1916), 40, XIV (March 1917), 79-82; San Diego *Union*, Sept. 15, 16, 17, 1916; Los Angeles *Times*, Nov. 14, 1916; Portland *Telegram*, Sept. 11, 1916; Portland *Oregonian*, Sept. 12, 1916.

19 San Diego *Union*, Sept. 22, 1916.

20 "Annual Report of the Pacific Alaska Navigation Company to the Interstate Commerce Commission for the Year Ended December 31, 1916," p. 104, in Pacific Alaska Navigation Company Mss, Honnold Library.

and declared that the two companies " have decided that
they can best serve the interests of the public with more
efficient service and more frequent sailings by operating
the two fleets under a management that will eliminate
the disadvantages to the traveling and shipping public
which necessarily attend the operation of the two fleets
separately."[21] If H. F. Alexander had not now become
the "steamship king of the Pacific," he was well on his way
to the royal throne.

The new Pacific Steamship Company controlled the
largest fleet under the American flag on the Pacific Ocean
(Table 2). Alexander now operated three-fourths of the

Table 2. THE GROWTH OF THE ADMIRAL LINE, 1916

Companies Entering Merger	January	December
Pacific Coast Steamship	18	
Pacific Alaska Navigation	5	20
Pacific Navigation	2	
Independent Steamship	1	
Companies Outside Merger*		
"Big 3"	3	2
Hill line	2	2
North Pacific Steamship	2	3
Total	33 vessels	27 vessels

* Lumber companies maintaining irregular sailings for a limited number
of passengers and amount of cargo have been omitted.

ships and over two-thirds of the tonnage in the coastwise
passenger-freight trade. Under the terms of the agreement,
the new company was to be known as the Admiral Line
but its blue flag diplomatically included the white stars
of the original Admiral Line and the red Maltese cross

[21] Los Angeles *Times*, Sept. 28, 1916; "Great Merger of Coast Steamship
Lines under the Corporate Name of Pacific Steamship Company," *Railway
and Marine News*, XIV (Nov. 1916), 36-37.

The *Yale*, West Santa Fe Wharf, San Diego, 1910. Possibly the Arrival of the *Yale* on the West Coast. *Courtesy of the Historical Collection, Title Insurance and Trust Company, San Diego*

H. F. Alexander

of the pioneer Pacific Coast Steamship Company. At midnight, October 31, 1916, the flag of the Pacific Coast Steamship Company, which had waved for forty years along the coast, disappeared and the new company officially began its life. Proudly the Tacoma *New Herald* declared: "The Pacific Steamship Company is not the ordinary outgrowth, wherein the big octupus [sic] reaches out and absorbs its smaller rivals. . . . In this case the small concern has grown out of obscurity, and taken over the whole works. The Pacific Coast Steamship Company has dominated coastwise shipping since the time of man runneth not to the contrary, while the company formerly headed by Mr. Alexander was started as a 'doubtful venture' but a few years ago, and builded up to proportions that, in order to secure the services of a man who could successfully combat its supremacy . . . , the established line concedes the point of submerging its own identity in the big merger. The transaction is a high tribute to the executive capacity and fighting spirit of a 'Tacoma boy,' who has grown to be a mighty big man right in his own home town."[22] That there was some truth in this laudatory account is indicated by the fact that eight out of the thirteen major officers of the new line were former members of the Alexander company and that of the five top offices, all but one, that of Vice President E. C. Ward, were filled by men from the original Admiral Line.

The personal story of the rise of H. F. Alexander from dock hand to president of the Pacific Steamship Company fitted the temper of a generation that admired material

[22] Tacoma *New Herald*, Sept. 30, 1916. Of the twenty-one ships in the new combined fleet, eight were from the old Admiral Line (*Yale, Harvard, Admiral Schley, Admiral Evans, Admiral Farragut, Admiral Goodrich, Admiral Dewey,* and *Admiral Watson*) and thirteen from the Pacific Coast Steamship Company (*Queen, Senator, Ravalli, Congress, Governor, Spokane, Umatilla, Homer, Aurelia, City of Seattle, Curacao, City of Topeka,* and *President*). "Organization Papers" in Admiral Mss, Honnold Library; *Pacific Marine Review,* XIII (Nov. 1916), 31-34.

gain. In a magazine of national circulation, it was stated that success came to him "because Mr. Alexander doesn't admit failure as possible."[23] Mr. Alexander, along with thousands of other Americans, was to discover later that failure was possible.

The willingness of the Pacific Coast Steamship Company to submerge its identity puzzled the shipping circles of the day but the explanation was not hard to find. For a number of years the line had been controlled by the Pacific Coast Company, an eastern concern. Of its board of directors, none lived farther west than New York. Consequently its interest in the West was purely one of financial return on its investments which included, in addition to the steamship line, the Pacific Coast Railroad Company of Washington, the Pacific Coast Railway in California which ran between Port San Luis, San Luis Obispo, and Los Olivos, and several coal mines.[24]

The steamship line had usually shown a profit but at times it was a small one. In 1913 a dividend of less than 2.5 percent was earned. Since 1915 its property was under mortgage to the Bankers Trust Company and although dividends at the rate of over 17 percent were declared for the years 1915 and 1916, the line had a net operating loss for the later year. The surplus of the company had shrunk in a twelve-month period from over $414,000 to $138,000. The burning of the *Congress* had deprived the company of its largest vessel, which meant that sailings had to be cut and service curtailed. In view of the aggressiveness of the Alexander interests, the future apparently held nothing but the strong probability that competition would become keener and rate wars more frequent. Under the circumstances, the opportunity to pool the two

[23] A. Mobley Sutton, "H. F. Alexander," in *System*, XXXIX (Feb. 1921), 209. See also "Achievement" (editorial), Seattle *Times*, Feb. 18, 1925.

[24] *Moodys Manual of Railroads and Corporation Securities, Industrial Section* (New York, 1919), pp. 564-67.

fleets under joint operation in which each company enjoyed a half interest seemed financially wise. There were some along the coast, men who had been brought up during its heyday, who looked upon the passing of the Pacific Coast Steamship Company as a tragic event; but to its owners the merger, whereby the pioneer company lost its corporate existence, was merely a means of protecting their investments. In the steamship business as in other types of endeavors, profits and nostalgia rarely mix.[25]

The consolidation made the Pacific Steamship Company virtually supreme in the coastwise service. The two steamship lines maintained by the Hill and Harriman railroads continued to furnish service from Portland south but since the new company had not as yet entered that route, these two lines challenged its supremacy very little. The full impact of the various moves by Alexander upon the trade of the West can be readily appreciated by comparing the scheduled departures of ships from the port of Los Angeles:

BEFORE CONSOLIDATIONS (February)

Date	Ship	Company	Destination
18	*Harvard*	Pacific Navigation	San Diego
	Yale	" "	San Francisco
19	*Harvard*	" "	San Diego
	Beaver	"Big 3"	Portland
20	*Queen*	Pacific Coast Steamship	San Diego
	Harvard	Pacific Navigation	San Diego
	Yale	" "	San Francisco
21	*Harvard*	" "	San Diego
	Queen	Pacific Coast Steamship	Seattle
	Aroline	Independent Steamship	San Francisco
22	*Yale*	Pacific Navigation	San Francisco

[25] "Annual Report of the Pacific Coast Steamship Company to the Railroad Commission of California" for the years 1912 through 1916 in ASF.

BEFORE CONSOLIDATIONS—*Continued*

Date	Ship	Company	Destination
22	*Harvard*	Pacific Navigation	San Diego
	Roanoke	North Pacific Steamship	Portland
23	*Governor*	Pacific Coast Steamship	San Diego
	Harvard	Pacific Navigation	San Diego
24	*Governor*	Pacific Coast Steamship	Seattle
	Harvard	Pacific Navigation	San Diego
	Yale	" "	San Francisco

AFTER CONSOLIDATIONS (November)

Date	Ship	Company	Destination
18	*Rose City*	"Big 3"	Portland
	Harvard	Admiral Line	San Francisco
19	*Yale*	" "	San Diego
	Admiral Dewey	" "	Seattle
20	*Yale*	" "	San Francisco
22	*President*	" "	San Diego
23	*President*	" "	Seattle
24	*Yale*	" "	San Francisco[26]

At the time of its formation, the Pacific Steamship Company promised to provide daily service between San Francisco and Los Angeles. By December, it was offering six sailings weekly. The following month the number was raised to seven each week.[27]

The only serious rival the new company faced was in the Alaskan trade where the Alaska Steamship Company, controlled by the Morgan-Guggenheim Alaska syndicate, had a favored position. In November, the Pacific Steamship Company was advertising that it operated "Fast Commodious Steamers along 7000 Miles of Coast" from San Diego to Nome on "Six Great Routes Under One

[26] Los Angeles *Times*, Feb. 18, Nov. 18, 1916.
[27] San Francisco *Examiner*, Dec. 30, 1916; San Francisco *Chronicle*, Jan. 17, 1917.

Flag." Though R. B. Wilcox, a leading stockholder in the Alexander company, had claimed that "talk of any further consolidations is wrong as we have not considered anything further," rumors arose that the "Big 3" and possibly the Hill line were to be next on the list of companies to be absorbed.[28] Fears of an outright monopoly were not allayed when H. F. Alexander told a newspaper reporter in October 1916 that there were plans for an agreement with the Atlantic Gulf and West Indies Line which controlled the well-known Mallory, Ward, and Clyde lines. Alexander declared that a "merger between the Pacific and Atlantic lines is not beyond the range of possibility when normal shipping conditions are restored after the war."[29]

But there were cross currents on what might have been a calm sea for the new concern. In December a report began to circulate that the Hill and Guggenheim interests were considering a merger whereby the *Great Northern* and the *Northern Pacific*, the "Twin Palaces of the Pacific," would be chartered to the Alaska Steamship Company and placed on the Puget Sound to San Diego run. In the fall of 1916, the *Great Northern* had set a new Honolulu to San Francisco record and was acclaimed the fastest passenger carrying craft "whose prow has ever cut the waters of the Pacific."[30] Since these vessels were both fast and luxurious, they would be able to furnish keen competition to the *Harvard* and *Yale*. In the same month the "Big 3" announced that the *Northwestern,* a sister ship of the *Nome City,* had been obtained to replace the lost *Bear,* enabling the Harriman company to resume its regular service as far south as Los Angeles. The two ships had been built side by side at Chester, Pennsylvania,

28 *Railway and Marine News,* XIV (Nov. 1916), 48; Portland *Oregon Journal,* Sept. 28, 1916; Los Angeles *Times,* Sept. 28, Oct. 1, 1916.
29 Los Angeles *Times,* Oct. 9, 1916.
30 *Pacific Marine Review,* XIII (Dec. 1916), 66.

although they had never been operated before on the same trade lane. But misfortune continued to harass the "Big 3" for on its first trip under the Harriman flag, the *Northwestern* collided with another vessel and was damaged. Owing to the time which was necessary to make the repairs, the charter was cancelled and the fleet of the "Big 3" was reduced again to two.[31]

A few months later Frank Waterhouse, head of a successful trans-Pacific line, announced that he was considering establishing a coastwise service in competition to the Admiral Line.[32] While these threats of potential competitors were current, the Admiral Line found itself charged with being a monopoly. The Commercial Club of Everett, Washington, petitioned the United States Shipping Board to cancel the increases in freight rates which had taken place since the consolidations and to order a refund of the additional charges. It expressed the belief that the Admiral Line had been instrumental in forcing the Charles Nelson Steamship line to discontinue its services to Everett. Though nothing resulted from these charges, it was evident that the course of the Admiral Line was not to be free from difficulties. Along with its predecessor, the Admiral Line would have to fight to maintain its dominance.[33]

[31] San Diego *Union*, Dec. 6, 1916; San Francisco *Chronicle*, Dec. 30, 1916; *Railway and Marine News*, XV (Jan. 1917), 22; *Pacific Marine Review*, XIV (March 1917), 83.
[32] San Diego *Union*, Sept. 27, 1917. For other activities of Rank Waterhouse see Seattle *Times*, Jan. 15, 1922, March 20, 1930.
[33] San Diego *Union*, Sept. 12, 1917.

THREE

World War I and Coastwise Shipping, 1917-1920

ARMAGEDDON DEMANDS ITS PRICE

THE ENTRY of the United States into World War I brought serious difficulties to the shipping industry. Speculation was rife concerning the fate of the larger coastwise vessels, most of which, particularly the *Great Northern, Northern Pacific, Yale,* and *Harvard,* were suitable for governmental requirements. One trade journal pessimistically estimated that about thirty thousand tons might be withdrawn for use on the Atlantic routes. As early as March 1914 the Department of the Navy had requested permission of the "Big 3" to examine the *Beaver, Bear,* and *Rose City* in order to determine their adaptability for military service. Though by 1917 the *Bear* lay a broken hulk on the coast of northern California, the other ships were still performing their regular runs. What made the possible commandeering of their ships so critical to the operators was the fact that there was little they could do either to anticipate or to ease the blow.[1]

Under war conditions, slight hope existed for obtaining replacements. Each operator realized that the loss of a ship for governmental purposes would simply mean the loss of that portion of his business to rivals in the transportation field, whether those rivals were steamship lines or railroads. In view of the circumstances, the problem became one of attempting to hold the vessels as long as possible without appearing to be unpatriotic. Special efforts were therefore made to impress the public with the loyalty of the lines. The news that the Admiral Line had purchased $200,000 worth of Liberty Bonds was circulated by a trade magazine. That the amount of this purchase might have been in the realm of wishful thinking is indicated by the records of the company, which reveal only $20,000 subscribed for that particular loan. An additional zero added by a zealous publicity agent could account for the difference.[2]

On May 8, 1917, the North Pacific Steamship Company was sold to Thomas Crowley and Andrew Mahony of San Francisco. For years, Charles P. Doe had operated the fleet between San Diego and Portland. In 1915, he had controlled eight vessels, but by 1917 three of these had been lost and two sold. Of the remaining ships, the *George W. Elder* was under charter in the offshore trade and only the *F. A. Kilburn* and the *Breakwater* were maintaining coastwise sailings between San Francisco and Portland on a five day schedule. The new owners changed the name to the Independent Steamship Company, or the Emerald Line. Explanations varied as to why the fleet was sold, but it was generally held that the new owners had purchased the vessels merely for speculation.[3]

The days of the once-popular coasting fleet of the North

[1] *Railway and Marine News*, XV (July 1917), 34; *Pacific Marine Review*, XIV (Aug. 1917), 93; Los Angeles *Times*, March 3, 1914.

[2] *Pacific Marine Review*, XIV (Dec. 1917), 92; "Annual Report to the Interstate Commerce Commission" (1917), p. 213, in Admiral Mss, Honnold Library.

[3] *North Pacific Ports*, p. 343; *Pacific Marine Review*, XIV (Feb. 1917), 25; San Francisco *Chronicle*, May 9, 1917; U. S., Bureau of Navigation, *Annual List of Merchant Vessels of the United States* (Washington, 1916), p. 420, (1915), p. 423; *Annual Report* (1916), p. 21; Los Angeles *Times*, May 9, 1917; San Francisco *Chronicle*, May 9, 1917; *Pacific Marine Review*, XV (Jan. 1918), 145.

Pacific Steamship Company appeared to be numbered. Although the new company announced that more tonnage was being sought, there were signs that no permanent improvement would or could be made. A straw in the wind was the prompt return to the Hill company of its general freight and passenger agent who had resigned his post just the month before to join the Emerald Line. When the sale of the fleet of three vessels to the Mexican Fruit and Steamship Company was announced in the early part of 1918, the shipping fraternity expressed little surprise.[4]

In order to take advantage of the increased business brought about by the war, the "Big 3" early in 1917 altered its schedule to provide a sailing every six days instead of every seven. In July a consolidation of all the floating property of the Oregon-Washington Railroad and Navigation Company under the management of the "Big 3" was made in the interest of economy. This move placed seven steamers plying the waters of the Columbia River, Snake River, and Lake Coeur d'Alene under its control.[5]

The Admiral Line continued its expansion. On August 21, 1917, it organized a subsidiary, the Pacific Lighterage Company, which purchased a tug and two barges. By using this equipment in the Puget Sound area, the Admiral Line was able to put its ships on a closer schedule. Time was saved which had formerly been consumed in moving ships from dock to dock to pick up or deliver small quantities of cargo. In September the company entered the transpacific trade when it dispatched the *Senator* from Seattle to Singapore. From this beginning, there developed the American Mail Steamship Company.

4 *Railway and Marine News*, XV (June 1917), 20, XV (July 1917), 35, XVI (April 1918), 33-34; *Pacific Marine Review*, XIV (Aug. 1917), 81.
5 *Pacific Marine Review*, XIV (Feb. 1917), 87, XIV (Aug. 1917), 81.

To anticipate the criticism that the Admiral Line was neglecting its domestic routes, A. F. Haines, its general manager, declared, "Our offshore activities will not decrease our attention to the coastwise service," and he promised that improvements were being planned for "the largest fleet flying the American flag on the Pacific."[6]

At the end of January 1917 the logs of the Hill liners revealed that the "Twin Palaces" had traveled almost three hundred thousand miles in making 198 trips along the coast and 13 journeys to the Hawaiian Islands. Such a prodigious record was in the Hill tradition. That the company appeared satisfied seemed evident. When the rumor again appeared that the Great Northern Railway was planning to build into California, President Louis W. Hill flatly declared: "The Great Northern will never build into California. We have seen too much of the expenses of the other railroads in this state to make such an investment attractive. We have reached California by water and we prefer to confine our connections . . . to the high seas."[7]

But a story continued to circulate that all was not well with the financial earnings of the two lines and both the Alaska Steamship Company and the Admiral Line were known to be attempting to purchase the ships.[8] On March 28, 1917, the San Francisco *Chronicle* published the story that the two "Palaces" had been sold to the Admiral Line for about six and a half million dollars.[9] Two days later, the San Diego *Union* asserted that the

[6] "Corporation Papers" in Pacific Lighterage Company Mss, Honnold Library; *Railway and Marine News*, XV (Aug. 1917), 25, XV (Oct. 1917), 34; *Pacific Marine Review*, XIV (Oct. 1917), 77, XV (Oct. 1918), 103; letter from H. F. Alexander dated Feb. 17, 1948, in possession of the author.

[7] Quoted in *Railway and Marine News*, XIV (March 1916), 23.
[8] Portland *Telegram*, March 21, 1917.
[9] San Francisco *Chronicle*, March 28, 1917.

Admiral Line would place the ships on a direct San Diego to Portland run. The promised completion of the San Diego and Arizona Railway, which would increase the tonnage moving through San Diego, was supposed to be responsible for the decision. Unfortunately for the immediate plans of San Diego, the railway was not completed until almost three years later.[10]

In May, the Admiral Line startled the shipping world by proposing to purchase not only the Hill line but the Harriman company as well. This move would have given Alexander an unchallenged access to Portland. The Hill line asked the civic groups of Portland to endorse the plan whereby the *Great Northern* and *Northern Pacific* would operate between Seattle and California. The *Governor* and *President* were to replace them on the Columbia River route. The reaction in Portland was prompt and violent. The Portland *Telegram* maintained that the proposal "is a move to the final strangulation of Portland's commerce." It chided the civic bodies for taking the matter under advisement by asking, "Why should there be even the implication of chance or doubt concerning the action of the Chamber of Commerce?" After a lengthy investigation, the Chamber of Commerce voted to oppose the merger and intimated that legal action might be taken to prevent the consolidation. In view of the public reaction, the proposal was dropped.[11]

Portland had saved the "Twin Palaces" for her trade but it was a temporary salvation. On September 17, 1917, the Hill company took the initiative and notified the United States government that the big ships were available

---

10 San Diego *Union*, March 30, 1917; *Railway and Marine News*, XVIII (Jan. 1920), 13.

11 Portland *Oregonian*, May 27, 1917; "Can Such Things Be?" (editorial), Portland *Telegram*, June 4, 1917; Portland *Oregonian*, June 7, 8, 9, 1917.

for war service whenever they were needed. The Shipping Board telegraphed immediately that the *Northern Pacific* should report to the nearest Navy yard on September 19 and her sister ship two days later. The *Northern Pacific* was unloading at Flavel in Oregon at the time and left immediately. The *Great Northern* sailed from San Francisco on her last voyage under the Hill flag on September 20, 1917. At the Bremerton Navy Yard, the "Palaces" were stripped of their beautiful woodwork and costly decorations. Their holds were converted into oil tanks to provide sufficient fuel for a round trip across the Atlantic Ocean. The price paid by the government was $4,244,618. At first it was thought that the "Palaces" would be used as hospital ships, but they were assigned to troop service.[12] The loss of the two great liners was regretted by shipping circles. The *Railway and Marine News* summed up a general reaction: "It will be years before any corporation . . . will be in a financial standing such as is essential in the successful operation of vessels equal to the Great Northern and her twin sister."[13]

The voluntary withdrawal of the Hill company was commonly attributed to the fact that railroad men were placed in charge of the ships with the result that they were operated on "train orders."[14] A more prosaic, and probably a more accurate explanation, was advanced by Captain Robert Dollar who said of the Hill endeavor, "This was spectacular and exciting, but the cost of maintaining the service after the Panama-Pacific Exposition closed was found to be too expensive."[15]

[12] *Railway and Marine News*, XV (Oct. 1917), 23; *Pacific Marine Review*, XIV (Nov. 1917), 90; Portland *Oregonian*, Jan. 15, 1918; San Diego *Union*, Dec. 18, 1917.

[13] *Railway and Marine News*, XV (Oct. 1917), 23. See also Portland *Oregonian*, Sept. 19, 1917.

[14] *Railway and Marine News*, XVII (Sept. 1919), 19.

[15] Robert Dollar, *One Hundred Thirty Years of Steam Navigation* (San Francisco, privately printed, 1931), pp. 121-22.

The loss of the Hill liners proved to be merely the first setback sustained by the shipping industry on the West Coast. On October 15, 1917, the *Governor* and *President,* the two largest ships in the Admiral fleet, were commandeered and turned over to the Matson Navigation Company for operation on the Honolulu run. This was a particularly hard blow as the *Harvard,* at the time, was laid up because of turbine trouble. The requisition of the two ships proved temporary, however, for the Shipping Board returned them in March 1918 to the coastwise run. With the return of these two ships and the anticipated completion of the repairs on the *Harvard,* the Admiral Line planned to resume its old schedule of six weekly sailings between San Francisco and Los Angeles. But a new blow fell the same month when, on March 10, 1918, the Department of the Navy decided to take both the *Harvard* and *Yale.* The ships were purchased outright. The *Yale* made her final trip from Los Angeles to San Francisco on March 11, 1918, and was delivered to the government two days later. The *Harvard* followed on March 21.[16]

The departure of the *Great Northern, Northern Pacific, Harvard,* and *Yale* marked the exit from the coast of the high speed, turbine ships. On April 13, 1918, a presidential order placed most of the remaining passenger vessels under the supervision of the Railroad Administration, although the actual management of the ships was left to the operators. The purpose of this action was to provide an authority for excluding unnecessary traffic should conditions warrant it. The only coastwise steamship line to be actually operated by the Railroad Administration was the "Big 3," which was taken over in May 1918. The government also forbade the publication of

16 San Diego *Union,* Feb. 3, 1918; *Railway and Marine News,* XVI (March 1918), 43, XV (Dec. 1917), 54.

sailing times, which caused some confusion since the regular schedules were being constantly altered because of the requisitioning of ships. The public received information concerning arrivals and departures by calling at or telephoning the offices of the companies. Just how this arrangement prevented the leak of information to the enemy is difficult to understand. In at least one case, a line ignored the rule and published the date and time of departure.[17]

In April 1918, Portland learned that the Navy planned to take over the *Beaver*. Businessmen were quick to point out to government officials that the Admiral Line still had five steamers on the Puget Sound–California route whereas the projected move would leave Portland with only the *Rose City*. The Chamber of Commerce of Portland summarized this sentiment when it objected to the action "unless similar steps should be taken to commandeer the large coastwise steamers plying out of Puget Sound to San Francisco and Los Angeles." Because of these objections the order was cancelled. A few weeks later a second order for the *Beaver* was received and later cancelled. On June 19, 1918, a third and final order turned the *Beaver* over to the Navy and the once-proud fleet of the "Big 3" was reduced to a single vessel. The Navy purchased the *Beaver* and converted her into a mother ship for a flotilla of submarines. Apparently the argument which saved the Admiral ships was the one advanced by the managing editor of the San Francisco *Call*, who succeeded in convincing the Secretary of the Navy that the Admiral ships were needed to prevent further reduction in the already tight supply of newsprint from the Puget Sound region.[18]

[17] Los Angeles *Times*, April 12, 14, 1918; San Diego *Union*, Oct. 12, 1918; letter from Admiral Line to the Railroad Commission of California dated March 31, 1919 in ASF Letter Files.

During 1918, H. F. Alexander began to tighten his control over the Admiral Line. Under the terms of the original merger in 1916, the Alexander company and the Pacific Coast Company each shared equally in the ownership of the new line. The first two months of its operations had produced a net loss of $72,000, but the year 1917 resulted in a modest profit of about $230,000. In 1918, there were indications that a loss would be suffered.

On September 30, 1918, an agreement was signed by which H. F. Alexander, through the Pacific Steamship Company, purchased for $5,000,000 the interest of the Pacific Coast Company. Under the terms, the Pacific Coast Company sold 5,000 shares of Admiral stock, ten vessels, its good will, and the terminal properties at San Diego, Moss Landing, and Eureka. The money was to be paid in quarterly installments of $125,000 with an interest rate of 6 percent on the unpaid balance. A mortgage on sixteen vessels of the Admiral fleet was given as security. Succinctly the *Pacific Marine Review* observed, "In a nutshell, the old Pacific Coast crowd, which until the advent of Alexander a few years ago, was the dominant factor in coastwise and Alaska freight and passenger traffic, is to retire."[19]

The expansion of the Admiral Line continued at a rapid rate. It opened a New York office in the summer of 1918, established more agencies in the Orient, and operated a dozen vessels for the Shipping Board in addition to its own fleet of twenty-five ships. In December

---

[18] Portland *Telegram*, May 27, 30, 1918; Portland *Oregonian*, June 20, 1918; Los Angles *Times*, June 4, 20, 1918, Jan. 27, 1919; letter from E. H. Hall, official of the Admiral Line, dated June 7, 1948, in possession of the author; "Annual Report of the San Francisco and Portland Steamship Company for the Year Ending December 31, 1921," p. 15 in ASF.

[19] "Financial Statement" and "Purchase Papers" in Admiral Mss, Honnold Library; *Pacific Marine Review*, XV (Oct. 1918), 102; certified copy of the approval of the Shipping Board in Admiral Mss, Honnold Library.

1918 the Admiral Line entered the Columbia River trade when it placed the *City of Topeka* on a run from California to Portland.[20]

During the war, the Shipping Board drew heavily on private owners for officers, engineers, and seamen to man the many vessels which were being built. A scarcity of trained men soon developed, with a consequent rise in wages. At a conference called by Secretary of Labor William B. Wilson in Washington, D. C., in August of 1917, Andrew Furuseth of the Seamen's Union proposed to ease the shortage of coastwise sailors by using the estimated five thousand German nationals then sailing under the American flag on other trade routes. Furuseth argued that a seaman had a prime loyalty to his ship rather than to his country and little danger existed in employing enemy aliens in the purely coastwise trade. Secretary of Labor Wilson disagreed and President Woodrow Wilson is reported to have said that such a scheme would create a "furore . . . so great no administration could stand up against it." Despite the pleadings of Furuseth, the unusual plan was dropped.[21]

Operating costs continued to rise. The price of fuel oil nearly doubled in one year. Repair costs and food prices increased. The effects of the inflation were soon reflected in the rates for water transportation. Effective May 5, 1917, the Admiral Line raised its charges about 25 percent. The next month it discontinued round trip fares and advanced all ticket prices one-third. In 1918, the Railroad Commission of California authorized the steamship lines in intrastate traffic to raise rates approximately

[20] *Pacific Marine Review,* XV (Dec. 1918), 125-26, XVI (Jan. 1919), 144; *Railway and Marine News,* XVI (Dec. 1918), 43; "Historical Data" in Admiral Mss, Honnold Library.

[21] Wilson was quoted in *Pacific Marine Review,* XIV (Sept. 1917), 55-56; *ibid.,* XV (April 1918), 86; Los Angeles *Times,* May 4, 1917; San Francisco *Examiner,* Aug. 1, 1918.

The *Harvard*, San Pedro, 1912. *Courtesy of the William T. Miller Collection, San Francisco Maritime Museum*

The *Admiral Farragut*, A Typical Admiral Line Vessel, San Francisco, 1913. *Courtesy of the William T. Miller Collection, San Francisco Maritime Museum*

25 percent. This action was taken not only at the request of the shipping companies but at the suggestion of the Railroad Administration. Rail rates had recently been raised. To prevent a rush of traffic to the water routes, the Railroad Administration desired a comparable increase in marine transportation.[22]

During the first few months of active participation by the United States in the war, some concern existed that passenger travel would be adversely affected. To allay fears, one magazine optimistically claimed that the Pacific Ocean was freed of enemy raiders early in the war "and it would be a physical impossibility for a submarine to get around Cape Horn and into the great western ocean." It concluded, "There is not a remote possibility of any Western traveler by land or water, being molested or inconvenienced to the slightest degree." Any depressing effect on passenger travel was of a temporary nature. Before the end of the war, the vessels which remained were carrying large numbers of travelers.[23]

Another marked influence of the war was the activity it produced in salvage operations. The six boilers of the *Bear,* wrecked in 1916, were sold one year later for twice their original cost. Ships were scarce; wrecks which had been abandoned were salvaged. An example was the *Northland,* which had capsized and sunk in the harbor of Kate Kupreanoff Island, Alaska, on June 25, 1916. During the initial salvage operations, the ship slid into deeper water. A year later she was eventually raised, sold to the Pacific Steamship Company in 1918, and renamed the *Admiral Nicholson.* The company which salvaged the

22 Los Angeles *Times,* April 27, May 1, 1917; San Diego *Union,* June 10, 12, 1918; California, Railroad Commission, *Report of the Railroad Commission of California, From July 1, 1918 to June 30, 1919* (Sacramento, 1919), p. 55. Hereafter cited as *Report.*
23 "No Need for Alarm," *Railway and Marine News,* XV (June 1917), 10; San Diego *Union,* Aug. 26, 1918.

freighter *Bandon,* after she had been given up as a total loss, realized $65,000 on the ship in 1917. The machinery of the *Coos Bay,* after being buried in the sand of Ventura beach for three years, was dug up and sold. Some whiskey was also recovered which was "still capable of doing business."[24]

The general effect of the war was to bring a temporary prosperity to those companies which survived. As to its lasting effects, there were divergent views. A. F. Haines, the general manager of the Admiral Line, told the international convention of Rotary Clubs in 1918, "Transportation by water is receiving an impetus from this world war that will carry it through generations as one of the most important fields of human endeavor." A dimmer view was held by Captain Robert Dollar who bluntly stated, "Anybody can run a ship today and make lots of money, but [there will come a] time when we will have to get down to the keenest competition the world has ever seen." Somewhere, between the extremes, lay the future.[25]

THE QUEST FOR NORMALCY

The shipping industry had its full quota of adjustments that needed to be made as the result of the war. One of the most pressing was the problem of rates. In the delicate balance which kept the flow of goods equalized between the rail and water lines, any fluctuation in the rate structure of one carrier started a chain reaction which

[24] *Railway and Marine News,* XV (Nov. 1917), 18, XVI (Feb. 1918), 37, XV (Feb. 1917), 28; *Pacific Marine Review,* XV (Oct. 1918), 91, XV (Feb. 1918), 80, 98; Los Angeles *Times,* Dec. 29, 1917, Feb. 4, 1918.

[25] Haines' speech was printed in *Pacific Marine Review,* XV (Aug. 1918), 118; Robert Dollar, *Memoirs* (2nd ed.; San Francisco, 1922), II, 2.

affected all. The hurried rate adjustments which had been made during the war created, or at times perpetuated, inequalities. For example, in 1919 a ship built in Long Beach was sent empty to San Francisco to pick up her first cargo, which consisted of agricultural products grown in southern California. To assure profitable operations, adjustments between rail and water rates needed to be made. In this area, the shipping lines made very little progress.[26]

A more immediate problem developed when the postwar inflation began to create large deficits. The "Big 3" lost over seventy-three thousand dollars during 1919. The Admiral Line found that for the first seven months in 1919, the operating ratio on the Puget Sound–California route was 116.43, which meant that for every dollar received as revenue, the company had expended $1.16. In the same period, the average loss per month on all routes was $70,718. The principal reason for these deficits was the operating costs, which reached higher levels than those of war time. In August 1919 the Admiral Line had increased wages of its employees about 23 percent. The increase added almost one million dollars a year to the payroll. A comparison of costs in the summer of 1919 with the same period for the year before showed the following increases: fuel oil, 21 percent (at San Francisco), 149 percent (at Los Angeles); wages of longshoremen, 25 percent; wages of crews, 13-27 percent; office expenses, 20-44 percent; provisions, 3-27 percent.

After investigating the request of the Admiral Line for an increase in rates, the Railroad Commission of California concluded pointedly that the company "must have additional revenue to enable it to continue." The Admiral Line was consequently authorized in October 1919 to

26 *Pacific Marine Review*, XVI (Feb. 1919), 134.

raise rates on its California routes.[27] In general the coastwise companies would have preferred to absorb the extra expenses, because their charges for transportation were about on a parity with the railroads and any further increases would tend to divert business to the rail lines.

The condition of the Admiral Line was fast becoming critical, for despite the October increase, the company in 1919 showed a loss of $1,025,000. To obtain ready cash, it sold $241,900 of its Liberty Bonds at a loss of $8,905. The Alexander company had companionship in its misery. In August 1920 the Railroad Commission granted to it and fifty-four other transportation companies authority for a further 25 percent freight rate increase and a 20 percent raise in passenger fares. Since these increases applied to rail as well as water carriers, the steamship companies were able to take advantage of them without fear of diverting business to their rivals.[28]

In spite of financial difficulties, the Admiral Line continued its expansion. By the end of 1919, it had sixty salaried employees in the Orient and had opened offices at Manila, Yokahama, Kobe, Vladivostok, and Shanghai. In December a new line between California and Mexico was inaugurated in which the venerable steamers, *Senator* and *Curacao,* were used. The Shipping Board continued

[27] *Report* (1920), p. 807; "Annual Report" (1919, 1920) in Admiral Mss, Honnold Library; *Pacific Marine Review,* XVI (Sept. 1919), 90; California, Railroad Commission, *Decisions of the Railroad Commission of the State of California* (Sacramento, 1919), XVII, 405-17. The average cost of fuel oil per barrel rose from 72 cents in 1917 to $2.31 in 1921. *Pacific Marine Review,* XVIII (April 1921), 208. San Francisco *Examiner,* Oct. 29, 1919.

[28] "Anuual Report to the Interstate Commerce Commission" (1919), pp. 301, 507 in Admiral Mss, Honnold Library; California, Railroad Commission, *Decisions* (Sacramento, 1920), XVIII, 646-54; *Pacific Marine Review,* XVII (Oct. 1920), 117. See also petition of Pacific Steamship Company and San Francisco and Portland Steamship Company, *Before the Interstate Commerce Commission Ex Parte 74 In the Matter of Application of Carriers in Official Southern and Western Classification Territories for Authority to Increase Rates* (Washington, [1920]) in Library Association of Portland.

to assign more vessels to the Alexander company. At the beginning of 1920, the Admiral Line claimed that it was operating tonnage which almost equaled the entire off-shore tonnage of the United States before World War I. With understandable pride, the Pacific Steamship Company boasted, "For the first time in the history of the United States a company on the Pacific seaboard operated the largest fleet under the American flag."

To carry on the work which had been brought about through this business growth, the stockholders on November 29, 1919, authorized the issuance of $25,000,000 of preferred stock. At Tacoma, A. F. Haines, the general manager, commented that there was no other special significance to the move. But it was widely reported that plans included the purchase of new fast passenger steamers for the coast service.

In 1920 the Admiral Line advertised that it was operating ninety-seven steamers on eight routes. The sailings between San Francisco and Los Angeles had been increased in March 1920 to four weekly. A new service between Portland and San Diego with calls at San Francisco and Los Angeles was inaugurated on May 2, 1921. For the first time since the days of the old North Pacific Steamship Company, a through service from the Columbia River to San Diego was provided. The surface prosperity of the Admiral Line and its officials was accentuated when its president, H. F. Alexander, and one of its leading stockholders, D. C. Jackling, became joint owners of the *Acquilla,* the second largest steam yacht on the Pacific Coast.[29]

In large measure because of the various rate increases

29 "Historical Data 1919" in Admiral Mss. Honnold Library; Tacoma *Ledger,* Nov. 30, 1919; Portland *Oregonian,* April 17, 1921; San Francisco *Chronicle,* April 17, 1921; *Pacific Marine Review,* XVI (July 1919), 136.

which had been made, the Admiral Line was able to make in 1920 a slight profit of $47,000. Compared with the $1,025,066 loss in 1919, the improvement was remarkable. Normalcy had almost been attained. As this prosperity was shared by the shipping industry generally, one magazine confidently predicted that the year 1920 would "mark a very permanent milestone in the history of American maritime progress" and rhetorically concluded, "Nineteen twenty! Even the figures as written have a 'forward' look. For the first time, the year has gone ahead of the century." Twelve months later, however, the same magazine was trying to buoy up the spirits of the industry by arguing that the bottom had not dropped out. "The fact is that in marine and shore business we have for the last three or four years been floating around on foamy bubbles, and the bubble, not the bottom, is dropping out."[30]

The editorial had the ring of truth in it. The aftermath of the war had brought a false prosperity to the shipping world. Goods and services were being sold for prices far above their real value. The Admiral Line in 1920 received $120,000 for the *City of Topeka,* for which it had paid $75,000 two years before. The bubble, however, soon broke. By February 1921, Page Brothers, who for years had been prominent ship brokers, reported, "In all our experience, we have never had such a bad condition of affairs in the way of transacting business in ships and shipping as exists today."[31]

To add to the gloom, the Admiral Line lost its largest steamer on April 1, 1921. En route from California to

[30] "Financial Statement" in Admiral Mss, Honnold Library; "A Forward Look" (editorial), *Pacific Marine Review,* XVII (Jan. 1920), 64; "The Good Ship Pacific Marine" (editorial), *Pacific Marine Review,* XVIII (Jan. 1921), p. II.
[31] Page Brothers, "Freight Report" in *Pacific Marine Review,* XVIII (March 1921), 184; "Annual Report to Interstate Commerce Commission" (1920), p. 507 in Admiral Mss, Honnold Library.

Seattle, the *Governor* was rammed shortly after midnight by the *West Hartland* off Point Wilson in the Puget Sound. The *Governor* sank in about thirty minutes. Of the 309 on board, 9 were lost, most of whom were pinned in the wreckage. Since the *Governor* was the burdened vessel, the local board of the United States Steamboat Inspection charged Captain H. H. Marden, the pilot, with inattention to duty and suspended his license for one year. The sentence proved to be too long, for Captain Marden died within two months.[32]

The *Governor* had been something of a black sheep along the western sea lanes. In 1916, she ran ashore off Point Grey but floated free at high tide. In 1917, she rammed and sank the Coast Guard cutter *McCulloch* off Point Conception. Although the federal inspectors exonerated the captain of the *Governor,* a naval board of inquiry placed the blame for the collision on the *Governor.* In the same year she sank the *McCulloch,* the *Governor* hit the San Pedro breakwater with such force that her prow cut through the twenty-five-foot mass of granite rocks and showed on the opposite side. No one was injured but the passengers had to be taken off and placed on another ship. The next year she struck the outer breakwater of Victoria harbor and ripped a large gash in her bow. Prompt action, in which a sail was placed over the hole, prevented the ship from sinking.[33] Though her record had been spotty, the Admiral Line needed the *Governor.* Her ability to carry more passengers

32 For details of the wreck see: Los Angeles *Times,* April 3, 1921; Seattle *Times,* June 1, 25, July 23, 1921; *Railway and Marine News,* XIX (May 1921), 32; *Pacific Marine Review,* XVIII (Sept. 1921), 545, 568; *ibid.,* XVIII (Oct. 1921), 615; *ibid.,* XIX (March 1922), 30-31, 193-95; San Francisco *Journal,* Sept. 12, 1921; *Annual Report* (1921), p. 17.

33 San Diego *Union,* Oct. 26, 1916, Nov. 2, 3, 1917, May 14, 1918; Los Angeles *Times,* June 14, 15, Aug. 7, 1917, March 3, 1918; *Pacific Marine Review,* XIV (July 1917), 97; "Equipment Record" in Admiral Mss. Honnold Library.

than any other Admiral vessel was certain to be missed, for new companies were challenging the supremacy of H. F. Alexander.

RIVALS OF ALEXANDER

By the end of the war, the dream of Alexander to control the coastwise trade had been almost realized. Of the seven companies which had existed at the opening of 1916, only two remained and the single vessel of one of them, the "Big 3," was hardly a serious rival. There was, however, room for improvement. The Admiral Line could boast of no express ships in its fleet. Its fastest ship could average only sixteen knots, which was not sufficient to provide running times equal to those of the prewar period. Though rates were still going up, the service offered the public had tended to decline.

The first company to begin rival operations held little promise of becoming a serious contender. Under the trade name White Flyer Line, a group of San Francisco men purchased, in 1919, the veteran steamer *Humboldt* with which they established service between San Francisco and Los Angeles. The new owners purchased the ship for $125,000. They spent about twenty thousand dollars and used fifty tons of white paint to recondition the 685-ton vessel. Looking "like a private yacht," the *Humboldt* steamed out of San Francisco Bay on April 10, 1919, to begin her new career.

The *Humboldt*, in a way, was an appropriate choice. Its immediate predecessor had been built by the people of Eureka, California, to combat the hold of the old Pacific Coast Steamship Company on the commerce of that city. The original *Humboldt* went on the rocks in 1895, but a new *Humboldt* was built. When launched in

November of 1896, it was hailed as "The People's Favorite
Boat Born Again." "For the old boat gone to its rest,
there will always be a kindly feeling, for she freed our
commerce from monopoly and gave us competition rates;
and in the new boat there will be a feeling of satisfied
pride, a feeling of ownership, for they know she is wedded
to Humboldt county, to her development, upbuilding
and growth. . . ."[34] After operating out of Eureka for a
short time, the new ship was placed in the Alaskan service.
In the Klondike gold rush of 1898, she was reputed to
have carried out five times her weight in gold.[35]

The initial fares charged confirmed the suspicions of
the shipping fraternity that the line was hoping to attract
"that portion of the traveling public which is especially
partial to cheap fares." Originally the *Humboldt* was to
make a round trip every four days but her fourteen knot
speed was not sufficient and the schedule had to be reduced
to a trip every five days. During 1919, she made thirty-
eight voyages and carried almost sixty-seven hundred
passengers. The next year, seventy trips were completed
and over ten thousand passengers carried. Since it operated entirely within the state of California, the White
Flyer Line had to report to the Railroad Commission of
that state. It stated that the *Humboldt* had a passenger
capacity of 140 and yet during 1919 the average number
of passengers carried per trip was 176. No satisfactory
explanation for this discrepancy is apparent.[36]

Although its entry was modest, the White Flyer Line
had big plans. In July, W. S. Scammell, its general man-

34 *Western Watchman* (Eureka, California), Nov. 28, 1896; San Francisco
Chronicle, March 8, 1919, April 17, 1921.
35 *Railway and Marine News*, XXIII (April 1926), 17.
36 Letter from White Flyer Line to California Railroad Commission
dated June 30, 1924 in ASF, Letter Files; San Francisco *Chronicle*, March
11, April 9, 11, 1919; Los Angeles *Times*, April 12, 1919; "Annual Report
of the White Flyer Line to the Railroad Commission of California for the
Year Ending December 31, 1919" in ASF.

ager, announced that the line planned to build a twenty-four-knot, 15,000-ton passenger vessel at an estimated cost of $1,500,000. "We are preparing to go ahead and build the first unit of our future modern fleet at this time for two reasons. First, because we believe that the costs are now about as near normal as they will be for another decade and also it is imperative that something be done to provide modern and up-to-date facilities for the coast-line business. . . . The vessels we propose will be luxurious and just a bit faster than the fastest craft ever used commercially on the Pacific. . . . The satisfactory liner of the future will have to negotiate the passage between this port [San Francisco] and San Pedro in sixteen hours. We hope to do even better."[37]

This announcement, while producing nothing tangible, directed attention to the lack of high-speed equipment on the coast. The four fast liners—*Harvard, Yale, Northern Pacific* and *Great Northern*—were being missed. Though each had been sold outright at the time of her withdrawal from the Pacific, shipping circles hoped that some, if not all, of them could be brought back. Early in 1920, these hopes were strengthened when the Navy announced that the *Harvard* and *Yale* were to be sold on February 20 to the highest bidder.

During the war, the two sisters had ferried thousands of troops across the English Channel between Southhampton and Le Havre. Following the armistice, they had carried French troops, released from German prison camps, from Dutch ports to Le Havre. Bidding for the ships was brisk. To the surprise of the Admiral Line, a group of Southern California capitalists submitted the highest bid. But the first bids were rejected by the Department of the Navy as being too low. In the second bidding, the Los Angeles group was again high with a bid

37 Los Angeles *Times*, Aug. 1, 1919.

of $1,755,000, which was $55,000 above the appraised value of the ships. The new rival of the Admiral Line was a "community enterprise" according to a telegram which the mayor of Los Angeles sent to the Secretary of the Navy. In this message the mayor asked for "all proper concessions and favors in connection with the completion of arrangements."[38]

This newest competitor was a more serious threat to Alexander than the White Flyer Line. The *Yale* and *Harvard* were six to eight knots faster than the fastest ship in the Admiral fleet. The new owners were closely connected with the Los Angeles Pacific Navigation Company, which had been formed in February of 1919 to operate a route from Los Angeles to the Orient. On May 27, 1920, these men organized the Los Angeles Steamship Company, which became known as LASSCO. Directors included Harry Chandler, E. L. Doheny, and Ralph J. Chandler. The Chandlers were also prominent in the control of the Los Angeles *Times* and that paper reflected the close relationship between the two enterprises. LASSCO was authorized by the Railroad Commission of California to issue $3,500,000 of common stock to the individuals who had purchased the vessels in exchange for the title to the property. In this way, the men who bought the ships for $1,755,000 received $3,500,000 worth of stock. The clear profit was reduced somewhat by expenses incidental to bringing the ships to the Pacific Coast.[39]

The progress of the two sisters from the Philadelphia

38 San Diego *Union*, Jan. 2, 1919; Los Angeles *Times*, Feb. 21, 22, March 31, May 14, 1920; San Francisco *Chronicle*, April 22, 1920.

39 *Pacific Marine Review*, XVI (March 1919), 134; *Railway and Marine News*, XVIII (July 1920), 30; Los Angeles *Times*, May 28, 1920; "Annual Report of the Los Angeles Steamship Company to the Railroad Commission of California for the Year Ending December 31, 1921" in ASF; California, Railroad Commission, *Decisions*, XIX, 789-90. For a perceptive study of the Los Angeles Steamship Company see James A. Merrill "A History of the Los Angeles Steamship Co." (unpub. M.A. thesis, Honnold Library).

Navy Yard, where they were at the time of their sale, to the West Coast was followed with interest by the people of Los Angeles. At dawn on July 10, 1920, the *Harvard*, which during the war had been called the *Charles*, arrived at the outer Los Angeles harbor and docked a little before noon. She was hailed as the forerunner of a mighty fleet of passenger steamships flying the flag of Los Angeles. Two days later, the *Yale* was welcomed back to her home port by a serenade of whistles from numerous harbor craft. The *Yale* had been delayed because of a temporary shortage of fuel at Panama.

On August 23, 1920, the Los Angeles Pacific Navigation Company and Los Angeles Steamship Company were combined under one management "for the purpose of bringing about greater efficiency in operation." Fred L. Baker, who was president of the Los Angeles Steamship Company and the Los Angeles Shipbuilding and Drydock Company, was elected president of the Los Angeles Pacific Navigation Company. A. J. Frey, formerly associated with the old Pacific Mail Steamship Company, was appointed general manager for both companies. To accommodate the new service, the Board of Harbor Commissioners of Los Angeles Harbor announced plans for a new terminal and arrangements were made to have Pacific Electric cars arrive directly at the pier.[40]

The two ships were given a thorough reconditioning. In order to eliminate vibration which had been an objectionable feature before, 275 tons of structural steel were used in extending the original partial steel deck the entire length of the ship. Steel channel frames were also carried up through the superstructure. The twelve Scotch marine boilers, which supplied steam to the three Parsons turbines, were left unchanged, but the installation of the

[40] Los Angeles *Times*, July 4, 11, 13, Aug. 24, 1920, Jan. 6, 1921; *Pacific Marine Review*, XVII (Oct. 1920), 119, XVIII (Feb. 1921), 124.

Coen oil-burning system resulted in increasing the speed of the *Yale* to 24.6 knots. This speed made her by far the fastest vessel on the coast. In recognition of their war service, in which they had transported thousands of troops between England and France, both vessels were decorated with two gold chevrons painted on their forward stacks.[41]

Although there had been some uncertainty at first as to which trade lanes they would be assigned, it soon became known that they would be placed on their former Los Angeles to San Francisco run about March 1, 1921. Delays were encountered. Not until May 2, 1921, did the *Yale,* escorted by a destroyer, two submarine chasers, and a "fleet of small boats and tugs," leave Los Angeles Harbor to inaugurate the new eighteen hour service. Upon the orders of the Commander in Chief of the Pacific Fleet, the *Yale* passed through a double line of battleships anchored in the outer harbor and received a salute from the Navy for her part in the war. In August, the *Harvard* joined her sister in providing five sailings weekly from each port. The fares ranged from $18 to $50, depending upon the type of accommodations. The Admiral Line charged a dollar less for ships which were slower. Because of the addition of de luxe suites, the passenger capacities of the *Harvard* and *Yale* were reduced from 896 under the old Pacific Navigation Company to 466 under the new flag.[42]

In losing the *Harvard* and *Yale* to LASSCO, the Pacific Steamship Company also lost its dominant position in the California trade. Along with other factors, the competition of LASSCO reduced sharply the patronage on Admiral ships between Los Angeles and San Francisco. The follow-

41 San Francisco *Chronicle,* April 17, 1921; *Pacific Marine Review,* XVIII (June 1921), 329-30; Los Angeles *Times,* April 16, 1921.

42 San Francisco *Chronicle,* May 1, 1920; *Pacific Marine Review,* XVIII (Jan. 1921), 59; Los Angeles *Times,* May 3, 1921; *Railway and Marine News,* XIX (June 1921), 11; *Decisions,* XXXI (1915), 475.

ing figures indicate the number of persons carried by the Alexander company between the two ports:[43]

Year	Passengers	Year	Passengers
1919	45,725	1923	19,569
1920	40,000	1924	22,635
1921	18,185	1925	19,509
1922	15,226	1926	19,060

The Admiral Line had tried unsuccessfully to obtain the *Great Northern* and *Northern Pacific*. To bolster its lagging leadership, it announced plans for building new equipment. In the same papers which carried the story of the sale of the *Harvard* and *Yale*, the details of the new Admiral liners were revealed. The ships were to have gyroscope stabilizers, moving pictures, glass enclosed concert halls, elevator service, a telephone in every stateroom, and sea garages for sixty cars. These "floating hotels" were to accommodate 572 passengers, cost $4,000,000 each, and have a speed of twenty-five knots. To emphasize the superiority of the new ships, the following comparison was given:

	Dimensions (in feet)		
Ship	Length	Beam	Depth
Governor	416¾	48	37⅓
Great Northern	500	63	50
New vessels	587½	72	53

By every test—speed, size, luxury of accommodations, and provisions for passenger comfort—the new Admiral ships would surpass the *Harvard* and *Yale*. Plans were even made to release the *President* and *Governor* for the Columbia River trade when the new ships were finished.

[43] "Statistics" in Admiral Mss, Honnold Library.

But this paper offensive against the new Los Angeles line produced nothing but news releases. The ships were never built.[44]

With two new competitors in the California trade firmly established, the Admiral Line was also faced with renewed activity by the Harriman line. The "Big 3" had suffered severely from the war. Its fleet had been reduced to a single vessel and attempts to charter or purchase other equipment had failed. In December of 1918, its only vessel, the *Rose City,* was laid up in San Francisco for repairs. The next month, the general manager of the "Big 3" died in Berkeley. A report circulated that the line had decided to go out of business. To provide the *coup de grâce* for the Harriman company, the Admiral Line offered to purchase the *Rose City* and backed up this move by increasing its service between Portland and San Francisco on February 10, 1919.[45]

Portland was in danger of losing its last steamship line to the Seattle-controlled Pacific Steamship Company, which a few years before had tried to "throttle her commerce." Business interests in Portland did not conceal their joy when the "Big 3" decided to continue. The *Rose City* arrived in Portland on May 3 to begin a new nine-day schedule between the Columbia River and San Francisco. A Portland paper fondly remarked that the thirty-year old steamer looked like "a new ship both inside and out" and reported that she brought a capacity passenger list and a full cargo of freight. In January 1920 the officials of the line announced that three new steel ships would be built to provide sailings comparable to pre-war schedules.

44 Los Angeles *Times,* May 14, 1920; *Railway and Marine News,* XVIII (June 1920), 30; *Pacific Marine Review,* XVII (June 1920), 122; Portland *Oregonian,* May 9, 1920.
45 Los Angeles *Times,* Jan. 28, 1919; Portland *Telegram,* Feb. 7, 1919. Previously Alexander had announced plans for building new ships. See San Francisco *Chronicle,* Nov. 23, 1919.

The first increase in service did not occur until September when the *Alaska* was chartered from the Guggenheim interests to run opposite the *Rose City*. A five-day schedule was established between the two ports. For the *Alaska*, this move was something of a return to home port since she had operated under the Harriman flag as the *Kansas City* prior to 1910. In 1921, the "Big 3" and LASSCO arranged an interchange service in which the *Harvard* and *Yale* made connections with the *Rose City* and *Alaska* at San Francisco. Through tickets were sold and baggage checked under conditions reminiscent of the day prior to 1916 when a similar arrangement provided connection between the *Harvard* and *Yale* and the Alexander ships. This time the plan was a direct challenge rather than an asset to Alexander.[46]

In addition to the White Flyer Line, LASSCO, and the "Big 3," the Admiral Line was concerned over the possible invasion of the coastwise trade by the Guggenheim company in the north. Each winter when the Alaskan trade slumped the danger of competition from the Alaska Steamship Company became real. In the winter of 1920-1921, five of its vessels were placed in the coastwise trade carrying passengers, lumber, and merchandise from the Pacific Northwest as far south as San Pedro.[47]

The war and its aftermath had brought to the Admiral Line the loss of its two fastest ships, the addition of two new competitors, and the revival of a third. The spring of 1921 brought a catastrophe which affected all lines alike. This was the maritime strike.

[46] Portland *Oregon Journal*, April 18, May 4, 1919, Sept. 17, 1920 Los Angeles *Times*, Jan. 16, 1920; San Francisco *Journal*, June 27, 1921.
[47] *Railway and Marine News*, XVIII (Dec. 1920), 27.

FOUR

The Strike and After, 1921-1924

THE STRIKE OF 1921

THE EVENTS which led to the bitter strike in the spring of 1921 had cast their shadows before them. For years the struggle between capital and labor had been a source of unrest along the waterfronts of the West Coast. Strikes, although of short duration, were frequent. In 1920 the agreement between the unions and the operators, which expired on January 1, 1921, was not renewed and by mutual consent its provisions were temporarily continued until either party gave notice of abrogation.

By April 1921 all steamship companies had served such notice and requested a conference for the purpose of discussing wage reductions. Falling revenues and high operating costs were given by the owners as reasons for the action. Wages were at war-time levels whereas the amount of commerce had declined because of the depression. The Shipping Board, which was sustaining great losses, lent its prestige and support to the drive. At a New York conference, held in April 1921, the operators presented a tentative 25 percent wage cut to the unions. Two days later, the union refused the proposed reduction and demanded the maintenance of the old scale. As a result, the operators announced that effective May 1, 1921, the cut would be made. The unions countered with their own demands. William S. Brown, president of the Marine Engineers' Beneficial Association, declared that wages were not at war-time levels, that reduction of the cost of living had not reached the small purchaser, and that if shipping conditions were not so depressed, the union would be requesting a raise. Andrew Furuseth, president of the Sailors' Union of the Pacific, gave a six-point program which included the enforcement of all sections of the La Follette Seamen's Act, preference for union men in hiring, and the right of unions to give rating examinations.[1]

Compromise appeared impossible. At a meeting on April 27, 1921, in Washington, D. C., Admiral W. S. Benson, chairman of the Shipping Board, declared, "I am convinced that the economic conditions at the present time fully warrant a reduction in marine wages. I am convinced that the amount of this reduction must be not less than fifteen per cent of the present wage scales."[2] The operators agreed to the Benson scale. The unions did not. The engineers pointed out that the inclusion of a new class F would cause some men to receive cuts as high as 33 percent, and Furuseth noted that the practical elimination of overtime would mean a 40 to 60 percent reduction for most men. To which a spokesman for the owners replied that "a wee bit of algebra discloses" that a seaman, whose stipulated pay was eighty-five dollars per month, would have to earn ninety-five dollars in overtime to make a 60 percent cut possible. He concluded that any man who accumulated that much overtime was either

[1] Seattle *Times,* June 5, 1921; Seattle *Union Record,* May 1, 1921; *Pacific Marine Review,* XVIII (May 1921), 267, XVIII (June 1921), 338-39, 373. A revealing biography of the president of the Seamen's Union is: Hyman Weintraub, *Andrew Furuseth: Emancipator of the Seamen* (Berkeley, 1959).

[2] Admiral W. S. Benson, "The Marine Wage Situation," *Pacific Marine Review,* XVIII (June 1921), 337.

working at a killing pace or robbing his employer.[3] The
operators and the Shipping Board announced on April 28,
1921, that the 15 percent cut and modified working rules
would go into effect May 1. On that date the unions
struck.[4]

The Admiral Line led the campaign to break the strike
along the West Coast. It centered its efforts on an attempt
to dispatch the *City of Seattle* to Alaska, for it was in the
Alaskan trade that the shipowners could count on the
fullest amount of support from the public. The long
Alaskan winter had just ended. Many laboring men were
anxious to obtain passage in order to seek employment in
the fish canneries which were scheduled to open. Each
spring the people of Alaska depended on the steamers to
bring supplies to replenish the depleted stocks of food,
clothing, and other essentials. The stopping of shipments
to Alaska could be referred to as an inhuman act of
irresponsible labor organizations.

Though its rival, the Alaska Steamship Company, canceled all sailings, the Admiral Line proceeded to sign on
a non-union crew and announced a sailing date. Of this
activity, a union official said, "We do not regard the
possible departure of the City of Seattle seriously. The
Admiral line is concentrating all its efforts on getting
that boat out. It is costing them lots of money and will
cost ship operators more yet to clear their boats with scab
crews. The Seamen are just beginning their fight. We
intend to stand solidly in every port of America for our

[3] *Ibid.*, 373. For the Benson scale see *ibid.*, XIX (March 1922), 187.
[4] The six West Coast unions which participated in the strike were:
Marine Engineers' Beneficial Association; Masters, Mates and Pilots of
the Pacific; Marine Firemen, Oilers and Watertenders of the Pacific; Marine Cooks and Stewards; Wireless Operators; and Sailors' Union of the
Pacific. For accounts of events leading up to the strike see: Seattle *Union
Record*, May 1-4, 1921; *Pacific Marine Review*, XVIII (May 1921), 267;
ibid., XVIII (June 1921), 337-39, 373; Seattle *Times*, June 5, 1921; San
Francisco *Chronicle*, May 1, 1921; *Seaman's Journal*, Feb.-May, 1921.

present standards.”[5] His assessment of the situation was at first correct. Unable to obtain sufficient men, the Admiral Line on May 3 canceled the departure of the *City of Seattle.* But the victory of labor was temporary. Within a month the Admiral Line had provided thirty-two sailings using non-union crews.[6]

To bolster their sagging morale, the six unions in June adopted resolutions which appealed for public cooperation in their “lawful efforts to protect against starvation wages and destructive hours . . . the men who man our ships. . . .” The strike was characterized as being solely in “self defense” because the shipowners had arbitrarily put into effect a wage cut and changes in working rules which were “onerous and unjust.” “Nothing was left the men of the union but to accept the lockout thus effected and to decline to work further on the terms proposed.”[7]

Attempts to settle the strike met with little success. The operators soon took the position that since the strike was not interfering seriously with shipping, further negotiations were needless. The president of the American Steamship Owners’ Association frankly stated that the companies were entirely satisfied with the progress of the strike, that sailings of the larger concerns were practically normal, and that the smaller companies were being helped by older ones to obtain adequate crews. The American Steamship Owners’ Association was composed of eastern men. On the West Coast there were two employer groups, the Shipowners Association of the Pacific Coast for operators of lumber schooners and the Pacific American Steamship Association to which the Admiral Line and other common carriers belonged. The employers told John J.

---

[5] Quoted in Seattle *Union Record,* May 3, 1921.

[6] Seattle *Times,* June 2, 1921; Seattle *Post-Intelligencer,* June 3, 1921; Seattle *Union Record,* May 4, 1921; *Astorian* (Astoria, Oregon), June 10, 1921.

[7] Copies of the resolutions appeared in the Seattle *Times,* June 2, 1921.

Davis, the Secretary of Labor, that his efforts to bring about a settlement through the unions had done more to prolong the strike than to get the men back aboard the vessels and they embarked on an active campaign to destroy the unions.[8] An appeal, sent to all members of the Marine Engineers' Beneficial Association, started: "Loyalty is a commendable sentiment provided it expresses itself in a common sense manner. Loyalty to a labor union has kept you out of your job and cut off your wages. Another man is taking your place and so long as he can do his work efficiently he will continue to occupy it. You will find it easier to quit your job than to get another one. What has become of your loyalty to your employer—to the source of your living—to your ship—to your family? Is your union going to support you when this strike is over and you are without a job?"[9]

In line with their campaign to crush unionism, the owners pledged to protect all who continued working during the strike. To spread defeatism, they declared, "We know plenty of marine engineers who will break away from their organization just as soon as Secretary of Labor Davis declares that he is through. . . . These men wisely do not care to break away from their union while there are possibilities of adjustment. For that reason they have been patiently marking time pending promises of settlement. Consequently, a declaration of a deadlock from Washington will mean just as much, if not more, to ship owners generally than word of a satisfactory compromise."[10]

Outside of labor papers, the strikers received little

8 The *Pacific Marine Review* served as the official organ for both employer groups on the West Coast. *Pacific Marine Review*, XIX (Jan. 1922), 31-32; San Francisco *Journal*, May 27, 1921.

9 Quoted in San Francisco *Journal*, May 28, 1921. See also *Astorian*, June 10, 1921.

10 Quoted in San Francisco *Journal*, June 2, 1921.

support from the public press or maritime journals. The attitude of shipping circles generally was reflected by the *Shipping Register*: "At the keelson of this strike there lies the Marine Engineers' Beneficial Association. The *Shipping Register* has a very deep sympathy and affiliation with all black squads. But we feel very deeply that the engineers are wrong in this instance." Injunctions against the strikers were sought and only in one case did a court refuse to issue a restraining order.[11]

But injunctions did not prevent violence and sabotage. On May 27, 1921, a few minutes before the *Admiral Sebree* was scheduled to leave San Francisco with a non-union crew, it was discovered that the steering gear had been spiked, the signal whistles plugged, and the electric light switches put out of commission. Two union members were arrested as they left the ship shortly after the plot was discovered. The Pacific American Steamship Association declared, "We believe that such acts of sabotage as attempted today [May 27, 1921] on the Admiral Sebree while leaving her dock will meet with the strongest disapproval of the conservative members of the Marine Engineers' Beneficial Association and that the radical members of that association could take no surer course toward speedily losing their arbitrary strike."[12] Other cases of purported sabotage followed. On June 8, 1921, the *Admiral Evans* became helpless off Blunt's Reef as a result of engine trouble and was rescued from her somewhat dangerous position by a Standard Oil tanker. On June 19, the venerable *Queen* sent out an S.O.S. when her main feed pipe broke at midnight and efforts to repair the break proved futile. At the time, she was off the

[11] *Shipping Register*, III (May 21, 1921), 10; Seattle *Union Record*, July 27, 1921; "Another Sane Decision" (editorial), *ibid.*, July 28, 1921; "Lockout of Seamen" (editorial), *ibid.*, May 2, 1921.

[12] Statement printed in San Francisco *Journal*, May 28, 1921. See also San Francisco *Chronicle*, May 28, 1921.

Oregon coast with 140 passengers aboard. Five hours later she was taken in tow.[13]

No positive evidence of sabotage was uncovered but on July 20, 1921, the *Queen* experienced another breakdown while off Point Sur. When the vessel arrived in San Francisco, all members of the engine-room force were removed because the Admiral officials were convinced they were guilty of sabotage. A new "black gang" was recruited. The passengers on board the *Queen* were not so convinced that the breakdown could be traced to the strike. A petition, signed by about a hundred of the 160 passengers on board, asked the Shipping Board to declare the vessel unseaworthy. The fact that six months before the strike her steering gear had broken when the *Queen* was off Point Arena lent credence to the charge that the vessel was the victim of old age rather than sabotage. Before her S.O.S. was answered, waves had broken over the decks, flooded staterooms, and torn off the guard rail along one side of the ship. During the strike, other cases occurred in which sabotage was suspected.[14]

As weeks went by, the owners became more confident of victory. Following the lead of the Admiral Line, which was maintaining 90 percent of its sailings, the "Big 3" announced that by June 9, its two ships would be running on their regular five-day schedule between Portland and San Francisco. In justifying the position of the operators, A. F. Haines, who was vice president of the Pacific American Steamship Association as well as general manager of the Admiral Line, claimed that the steamship lines were merely backing up the government: "Admiral Benson

13 San Francisco *Chronicle*, June 10, 1921. Three days later, the *Admiral Evans* was again in trouble and had to be towed to Astoria. *Astoria Evening Budget*, June 13, 1921; Seattle *Times*, June 20, 1921.

14 San Francisco *Chronicle*, July 21, 1921; Seattle *Times*, July 24, 1921; Seattle *Post-Intelligencer*, July 22, 1921; San Francisco *Chronicle*, Jan. 10, 11, 1921; San Francisco *Examiner*, July 8, 1921.

led the movement to save the merchant marine by a
fifteen per cent reduction in wages and the revision of
the much-abused overtime payment pay. The strike was
not against the steamship companies but against the government. Naturally the steamship companies are backing
up the Shipping Board. . . . We have no quarrel with
the unions, but we are prepared to back up the United
States Shipping Board to the last extremity in its refusal
to submit to a union dication [sic] which gives no heed to
economic laws and demands."[15]

The cloak of legalism thrown over the strikebreaking
activities was soon discarded by the operators. When news
arrived on June 14 that an agreement had been reached
between the Shipping Board and the Marine Engineers'
Beneficial Association, Haines pointedly declared, "The
agreement reached at Washington will not in the least
affect our attitude as far as our own ships are concerned,
and we will continue operating our coastwise . . . fleet
with independent crews."[16] The determination of the
operators "to back up the United States Shipping Board
to the last extremity" had vanished. Instead, they reaf-
firmed a previous declaration that they would "not confer
or negotiate, now or at any time, with the Marine Engineers' Beneficial Association as at present constituted and
organized."[17] That the owners had been the stumbling
block to an earlier settlement became common knowledge
when Admiral Benson revealed that the engineers had
agreed to the original proposition of the Shipping Board
and in some respects had gone further in their efforts to

[15] Haines prepared this statement at the request of a newspaper.
Astorian, June 10, 1921; Seattle *Post-Intelligencer*, June 3, 1921.
[16] Seattle *Post-Intelligencer*, June 14, 1921. In the agreement, the engineers accepted the 15 percent cut and the elimination of most overtime.
Ibid., June 17, 1921.
[17] *Pacific Marine Review*, XVIII (July 1921), 429; San Francisco *Journal*,
June 10, 1921. For an able statement on why the engineers had organized,
see *American Marine Engineer*, XIII (Oct. 1918), 35.

reach a settlement, but that the board did not act at the time because the private owners refused to agree.[18]

On the West Coast there was union dissatisfaction with the agreement. The San Francisco local of the Marine Engineers' Beneficial Association decided to defy its national officers and continue the struggle. Ernest F. Pegg, its business agent, went to Seattle where he urged the Seattle local to take a similar stand. Despite the pleadings of Pegg, the Seattle members voted, on June 22, 1921, to accept the wage cut. Whereupon Pegg belatedly ordered the end of the strike in San Francisco on Shipping Board vessels.[19]

Officially the strike continued against the private lines. But the owners knew their strength. Their strikebreaking activities had produced results. Men were returning to their former jobs in spite of the unions. By the first of July, the operators claimed that no craft was tied up in the San Francisco region. By the middle of the month, both the Admiral Line and the "Big 3" were offering normal service. Before the end of the month, the White Flyer Line had resumed operations. The strikers had been defeated. By a 480 to 50 vote, the engineers in San Francisco abandoned the hopeless struggle on July 19, 1921. Other locals followed. Pegg urged the men to forget their grievances and seek work with the private operators on the basis of the 15 percent cut. "We have simply done the only thing there was to do under the circumstances," he said. "The men are . . . prepared to show the shipowners that the members of this organization are the most efficient operators in their line obtainable." The other unions took similar action. Making the best of the defeat, the Seattle *Union Record* observed that the

18 New York *Journal of Commerce*, June 3, 1921; Seattle *Times*, June 2, 1921.

19 Seattle *Post-Intelligencer*, June 23, 1921; Seattle *Times*, June 21, 23, 1921.

strikers were going back to work with little difficulty and that the shipowners seemed to be glad to employ union men whenever possible in place of their "scab crews."[20]

The reasons for this disastrous rout of trade unionism were several. The nation-wide depression had created a pool of men who were willing to become strikebreakers in order to obtain a job. It was estimated that in twenty-two leading industries, one out of every four workers was unemployed. The Seattle *Times* stated that the "strike was foredoomed to defeat . . . [because] operators . . . simply could not run their craft under the wages and working conditions previously prevailing."[21] The historian of the Sailors' Union of the Pacific listed as important factors "slack shipping conditions, the hostility of the government, and the existence of a large surplus of war-trained sailors willing to fill the places of the striking seamen."[22]

The fact that the employers were well organized while the unions were torn by dissensions played a significant role. After William S. Brown, the national president of the Marine Engineers' Beneficial Association, had signed the agreement with the Shipping Board, several locals demanded his resignation. The operators claimed that the "fallacy of the doctrine of collective bargaining" was proved when Brown issued a twenty-seven page statement which revealed that local districts refused to follow the lead of the national officers and even hampered negotiations by "going so far as to falsify the reports." When the

[20] San Francisco *Chronicle*, July 1, 28, 31, 1921; Portland *Oregonian*, July 9, 1921; Pegg was quoted in San Francisco *Journal*, July 20, 1921; Seattle *Times*, July 31, 1921; Seattle *Union Record*, Aug. 5, 1921.

[21] Seattle *Times*, June 24, 1921; Seattle *Star*, June 22, 1921.

[22] Paul S. Taylor, *The Sailors' Union of the Pacific* (New York, 1923), p. 140. Taylor was an instructor in economics, University of California, Berkeley. The *Pacific Marine Review* refused to publish this book because it claimed it was a "biased, one-sided account of the story." *Pacific Marine Review*, XXI (Aug. 1924), 406.

engineers returned to work on the Shipping Board vessels, the other unions felt that they had been betrayed. This break between the engineers and the other unions was significant, for it ended the tradition that "the licensed men and the men before the mast were standing shoulder to shoulder." In 1923, the engineers withdrew from the American Federation of Labor as the result of the sentiment that they had no place in the ranks of organized labor.[23]

During the strike, the San Francisco local of the Marine Engineers' Beneficial Association was torn by factions; a suit, charging illegal diversion of funds, was filed against Ernest Pegg and eight other officers. The alleged sabotage by strikers tended to weaken the allegiance of the more conservative members. Despite the claim of the union leaders that the various accidents experienced by coast-wise ships were due to the incompetence of the non-union workers, there was some evidence to support the opposing view. The influence of the I.W.W. was not entirely absent. In the fall of 1921, Andrew Furuseth expelled the editor of the *Seamen's Journal* for his alleged bolshevist leanings.[24]

THE AFTERMATH OF THE STRIKE

Perhaps the most important effect of the strike was the establishment of the open shop along the Pacific Coast. When the strike collapsed, A. F. Haines announced that the strikers "will be given jobs as vacancies occur. None of the engineers who kept the ships running during the

23 New York *Journal of Commerce*, June 16, 1921; Seattle *Post-Intelligencer*, June 14, 1921.

24 San Francisco *Chronicle*, July 31, 1921; San Francisco *Journal*, May 28, 1921; Taylor, *Sailors' Union of the Pacific*, p. 144; *Pacific Marine Review*, XVIII (Dec. 1921), 758; Weintraub, *Andrew Furuseth*, pp. 160-61.

strike, however, will be displaced. They stuck by us and we'll stick by them."[25] This attitude was generally accepted by maritime circles. One trade magazine declared, "As there was no reason for the strike and the men should have stood by their companies which for years had provided for them on a permanent all the year round basis, those who remained away cannot in justice look for re-instatement."[26] But the motive in back of the open-shop policy was fully revealed when the operators laid down the condition that all members of the Marine Engineers' Beneficial Association "must resign" from that organization before positions would be offered to them.[27]

The anti-union campaign, which had begun during the strike, was continued. In an open letter addressed to their employees the operators observed: "Anybody knows that nothing will ruin discipline as quickly or as completely as having too many bosses. Your very life then depends on this discipline which is made impossible by the divided allegiance demanded by maritime unions and so-called beneficial associations."[28]

Another result was the establishment of employment bureaus by the Pacific American Steamship Association and the Shipowners' Association of the Pacific Coast. These company hiring halls registered the men desiring marine work, issued numbered identification cards, and assigned personnel to jobs. Theoretically the man with the lowest number received the appointment. After discharge or quitting such employment, the man had to re-register and "go to the bottom of the list." The system was supposed to cause the "men to be more careful in the discharge of their duties because they know when

---

[25] Quoted in Seattle *Times*, July 24, 1921.
[26] *Railway and Marine News*, XIX (July 1921), 17.
[27] *Pacific Marine Review*, XVIII (Aug. 1921), 501. For a rival organization for marine engineers see *ibid.*, XIX (April 1922), 216.
[28] Printed in *ibid.*, XVIII (Oct. 1921), 579.

they are discharged or quit their positions they must be re-registered and await their turn for employment." On September 1, 1921, the first of these bureaus opened simultaneously in San Francisco and San Pedro. They also served as clearing houses where disputes concerning unfair treatment, overtime, or other abuses could be aired. The employers claimed, "By these means we shall cause marine employees to realize that shipowners and operators will give more prompt, adequate and fair consideration to any claims justly made than could delegates of any unions, and this without cost to the men."[29]

That the bureaus did not provide full employment is evident from the figures issued by the operators. Of the 6,000 men who registered for work, only about 1,600 were placed during the first three months of operations.[30] These employment bureaus were constantly attacked by the unions, but with little effect. When in 1925, W. J. Petersen, the general manager, boasted that because of the company hiring halls coastwise vessels were comparatively free of radicals, the Seamen's Journal exclaimed, "This information will be surprising to the members of the International Seamen's Union of America who are constantly compelled to work, eat and sleep with traveling agents of the I.W.W. because Mr. Petersen insists upon supplying such men with employment."[31]

A third important result of the strike was a reduction in freight rates, the first since the close of the war. Both the "Big 3" and the Admiral Line filed new tariff sheets with the Interstate Commerce Commission calling for reductions of about 10 percent effective July 10, 1921. The reduction in certain class rates went as high as 40

---

[29] Quoted from a circular dated Sept. 1, 1922, which was reprinted in ibid., XIX (Jan. 1922), 30.

[30] Ibid., 31.

[31] Seamen's Journal, March 1, 1925.

percent; wharfage and handling charges, which had hither-
to been paid by the shipper, were included in the freight
rates.[32]

LOS ANGELES BUILDS A NAUTICAL EMPIRE

On May 2, 1921, the day after the strike began, the *Yale*
sailed out of Los Angeles Harbor on her maiden voyage
under the flag of the Los Angeles Steamship Company.
When she arrived the following day at San Francisco,
the unions requested that the company sign a one-year
contract. LASSCO refused. Since the wages of the crew on
the *Yale* were at the old rate and did not include the 15
percent cut, the unions allowed their members to operate
the ship for two more round trips. On May 7, the officers
and crew were called off the ship at Wilmington by
union officials to enforce their demands for a contract.
After a nine-day layup, the *Yale* resumed operations when
the men decided to return to work without a contract.
On May 15, 1921, Admiral Benson sent a telegram to
LASSCO requesting that a wage reduction be made to
conform with the action taken by both the Shipping
Board and the other private operators. In reply, the
company asserted that a cut was not practicable for two
reasons: first, the men who were needed to run the de
luxe service had to be of a more skilled type, and second,
the crew had been assembled from other jobs on the
promise that the pay level would be maintained.[33]

   This partial break in the otherwise solid front which
the operators presented to the strikers gave the unions

---

[32] San Francisco *Examiner,* June 24, 1921; Portland *Oregonian,* June
17, 1921; San Francisco *Journal,* June 21, 1921; Seattle*Times,* June 26, 1921.
   [33] Los Angeles *Times,* May 19, 1921. Copies of the telegrams appeared
in the same issue.

only a slight advantage and influenced the final results of the strike very little. LASSCO was soon ready to place the *Harvard* in service opposite the *Yale*. With a passenger list of notables including Andrew Furuseth of the Seamen's Union, the *Harvard* sailed from her southern California slip at Wilmington on August 5, 1921. Her arrival at San Francisco the next morning was accompanied by a "steady staccato of fog signals, steamer whistles and other noise." A newspaper man who made the trip described the *Harvard* as "floating serenely across the Golden Gate like a great white swan" and added: "Moonlight and the sea. Maidens will do well to travel on the Harvard with their hearts kept under lock and key. And wise husbands will not send pretty wives on too many of these excursions alone. For the great white swan never goes sailing without a Lohengrin on board."[34]

The same newspaper which described the arrival of the *Harvard* also announced the news of a major disaster to coastwise shipping. To save mileage and display their skill as mariners, captains of coasting vessels were tempted to hug the coast instead of standing farther out to sea. About nine o'clock on the evening of August 6, 1921, the *Alaska* of the "Big 3" line struck the half-hidden rocks of Blunts Reef off Cape Mendocino while steaming full speed in a dense fog. Confusion reigned. In the emergency the union and non-union men tended to hold aloof from each other. Lifeboats did not have sufficient equipment. Passengers later testified that it was only their own

---

34 The reporter was S. Fred Hogue. Los Angeles *Times*, Aug. 7, 1921. The eighteen-hour schedule provided a sailing from Los Angeles Harbor on every day except Saturday and Sunday. The departure time was 3 P.M. The arrival at San Francisco was made the following morning at 9 A.M. Return trips left San Francisco at 4 P.M. on every day except Sunday and Monday. The arrival in Los Angeles Harbor was at 10 A.M. on the following day. LASSCO Sailing Schedule," LASSCO Mss, Honnold Library; San Francisco *Chronicle*, Aug. 7, 1921.

concerted action and coolness which lessened the loss of life. Of the 220 persons on board, 42 lost their lives.[35]

The public was shocked by the tragedy not only because of the high percentage of life lost but because it was obvious that the accident could have been avoided. The *Oregonian* suggested that cutting corners to save time was the cause and noted that the "Big 3" had run on a five-day schedule until the competition of the Admiral Line forced it to dispatch a steamer every four days. The paper demanded a full inquiry. A few days later, the influential San Francisco *Chronicle* stated that the public wanted to know whether the lifeboats were out of condition, whether the crew was trained and assigned lifeboat stations, and whether the crew could launch the boats without dumping the passengers into the sea. The public "wants a satisfactory answer to the whole question. And it will not be satisfied with one that merely makes officers the goat for owners' policies."[36]

The decision rendered by the Steamboat Inspection Service was clear and direct. "After careful consideration of the evidence adduced at the trial, it is positively shown that Captain Hobey was responsible for the loss of the steamer *Alaska* through his negligence in navigating his vessel full speed in a dense fog without taking soundings." The investigation left little room for the contention that owners' policies were at fault. Captain Harry Hobey was saved the disgrace of hearing the decision. He had gone down with his ship.[37]

As the result of the sinking, the coastwise passenger

[35] Seattle *Post-Intelligencer,* Aug. 9, 18, 1921; Los Angeles *Times,* Aug. 7, 1921; Portland *Oregonian,* Aug. 8, 1921; *Pacific Marine Review,* XVIII (Sept. 1921), 544; U. S., Bureau of Navigation, *List of Merchant Vessels* (1922), p. 450.

[36] Portland *Oregonian,* Aug. 8, 1921; "The Public Wants to Know" (editorial), San Francisco *Chronicle,* Aug. 12, 1921.

[37] Excerpts of the decision were printed in *Pacific Marine Review,* XVIII (Nov. 1921), 682.

business slumped. That the vessels plying between the Northwest and California were apt to hug the coast could not be contradicted. At the instigation of the Neptune Association, the supervising inspectors of the Steamboat Inspection Service held a hearing to investigate the advisability of requiring all ships to be equipped with submarine bell receiving apparatus. The government had already installed submarine bells in various places along the coast which could be heard, with the proper receiving equipment, for a distance of fifteen or twenty miles. But the inspectors found that the captain of the *Alaska* had been so negligent that the presence of this apparatus would not have prevented the wreck.[38]

The fleet of the Harriman company was again reduced to a single vessel. In spite of its past misfortunes, the company announced tentative plans for building three new passenger steamers which were to cost $1,750,000 each. The new ships were to be fast enough so that service could be extended from Portland as far south as San Diego. In November 1921 the number of steamships to be built was reduced to two. Actually none was built, but the "Big 3," with its one ship, continued to operate out of Portland in competition to the Admiral Line.[39]

In the same year as the strike and the loss of the *Alaska,* the steamship lines faced another problem. Since the early days of the republic, the coastwise trade had been reserved for American vessels. There was nothing to prevent foreign ships, however, from competing for the passenger and freight business between one American port and a foreign port. Shipping circles were somewhat alarmed, therefore, when a report began to circulate that

38 The Neptune Association was an organization of marine officers. *Pacific Marine Review,* XVIII (Sept. 1921), 544, XVIII (March 1922), 195, XIX (April 1922), 254.

39 Portland *Oregon Journal,* Oct. 25, 1921; Portland *Telegram,* Nov. 28, 1921.

the Canadian government steamers, *Prince Rupert* and *Prince George,* were to operate between British Columbia and San Francisco in competition with the Admiral Line. Old salts thought that the ships ought to be prevented from rounding Cape Flattery, at the entrance of Puget Sound, because their amount of "top hamper" caused them to be top heavy.[40]

While this rumored move was not made, the threat of foreign opposition became real in July 1921 when the Canadian Government Merchant Marine, Ltd., established a ten-day schedule between British Columbia and San Francisco with three of its ships. The Canadian line had been able to obtain the lucrative contract for carrying paper from Ocean Falls, B. C., to California which had formerly been held by the Admiral Line. To counteract this intruder, the Admiral Line announced resumption of direct passenger and freight service on a weekly basis between Vancouver and San Francisco. The fact that the new line was both foreign and governmentally controlled caused its activities to be denounced as unfair to the American private lines. Although the foreign ships could not compete for domestic trade, they proved to be a constant source of irritation.[41]

The year 1921 had been an unhappy one for the merchant marine. The strike, the wreck of the *Alaska,* the loss of the *Governor,* the advent of foreign competition, and a depression caused one trade publication to observe, "It is futile to review railway and shipping activities of 1921, as the record has few bright spots. . . ." The need for new equipment to bring the coastwise service up to the standard maintained before World War I was critical, yet shipping circles were clearly in a weak position. The

40 *Railway and Marine News,* XIX (March 1921), 26.
41 *Pacific Marine Review,* XVIII (May 1921), 319, XX (March 1923), 32 in advertising section; *Railway and Marine News,* XIX (June 1921), 30, XIX (July 1921), 26.

same publication stated that with tonnage as low as $25 to $45 per ton, investing in a company which owned ships bought at $210 per ton "is not good business." "Some prominent people have sunk fortunes in ships in recent years so how can the landlubber expect to make his stock pay." The investing public was advised to "look before you leap."[42]

Frank Waterhouse, a well-known northwestern shipper, declared, "There can be no questioning the utter inadequacy of the present services operating between Los Angeles, San Francisco and British Columbia and Puget Sound Ports. . . . That a new line of first-class combined passenger and freight vessels rendering fast and efficient service on the coastwise route would be well patronized by passengers and shippers is a virtual certainty."[43] His claim that the coastwise service was in need of a renaissance was patent. While the return of the *Harvard* and *Yale* had raised the quality of the California service, no adequate replacements had been found for the "Twin Palaces," the *Congress,* or the *Governor.* The loss of the *Bear, Beaver,* and *Alaska* had further depleted the number of passenger ships.

THE FOUR "ALEXANDER" SHIPS

There were signs that the Admiral Line was losing its dominant position. By the end of 1921, it had abandoned the so-called "narrow gauge" route between San Francisco and Santa Barbara, which included stops at the smaller ports. In the fall of 1922, the Shipping Board announced that it was not entirely satisfied with the way the Admiral

42 "The Outlook 1922" (editorial), *Railway and Marine News,* XX (Jan. 1922), 16; "A Warning" (editorial), *ibid.,* 17.
43 *Pacific Ports,* IV (Dec. 1921), 50.

Line was operating the government ships to the Orient. As a result, the government requested Robert Dollar, one of the largest stockholders in the Admiral Line, to form a new company to take over the Oriental route. The loss of the Oriental trade was a blow to the prestige of the Alexander company.

The rise of the Dollars in the Admiral Line had begun in 1919 when they had acquired a substantial amount of stock. As a result, Stanley and Melville, sons of Robert Dollar, were elected to the board of directors. In addition, Stanley became one of the vice presidents. In 1921, the Dollars controlled 3,767 out of 15,000 shares outstanding as compared with 2,974 owned by Alexander. That there was rivalry between the Dollars of San Francisco and the Alexander interests of Seattle was known in shipping circles. In 1921, the rumor had circulated that H. F. Alexander would resign and that the Dollars would reorganize the line.[44]

The rise of the Dollars did not improve relations between the Admiral Line and the people of Portland. When Captain Robert Dollar suggested in 1922 that the Admiral Line and the Pacific Mail Steamship Company might form a pool to purchase the ships of the Shipping Board which operated out of Portland, the *Oregonian* objected to the proposal. It observed that since Captain Dollar had lost a ship off the mouth of the Columbia River about forty years before, "he has not known it was possible for a ship to enter the river. Portland does not wish to cause risk that another ship in which Captain

[44] Santa Barbara *News*, Dec. 29, 1921; "Annual Report to Interstate Commerce Commission" (1921), p. 506 in Admiral Mss, Honnold Library; Robert Dollar, *Memoirs*, IV (San Francisco, 1925), 61-63; Seattle *Times*, Oct. 15, 1922; *Pacific Marine Review*, XIX (Dec. 1922), 663; Portland *Oregonian*, Jan. 9, 1920; "Annual Statement" in Admiral Mss, Honnold Library; "Confidential Report to the United States Shipping Board" dated July 28, 1921 in Pacific Coast Steamship Company Mss, Honnold Library; New York *Tribune*, Feb. 25, 1922; Tacoma *Ledger*, June 9, 1921.

Dollar is interested should be lost. It is in every respect safer to have a Portland line that knows the way in and out and that will keep a regular schedule."[45] In 1925, the Dollar influence was further increased when Herbert and Mortimer Fleishhacker, San Francisco bankers, were elected to the Admiral board of directors. The Fleishhackers were close business associates of the Dollars. The next year, the friction between Alexander and the Dollars came into the open when H. F. Alexander attempted unsuccessfully to have the Admiral Line named as operator of the Oriental service in place of the Dollar company.[46]

Since the loss of the *Governor* in April 1921, the Admiral Line had needed a ship to alternate with the *President,* but the strike and the lack of a suitable vessel had resulted in delay. In December 1921 the Robert Dollar Company purchased the *Callao* from the Shipping Board. This ship had been built as the *Sierra Cordoba* by a German concern in 1913 for the South American trade. At the outbreak of war in 1914, she was seized by Chile, was given later to the United States as part of the reparation plan, and was offered for sale by the government to private capital. Her twin-screw, triple-expansion reciprocating engines could send the *Callao* through the water at speeds up to fifteen knots. The passenger accommodations were of a high grade and included hot and cold running water in staterooms, a gymnasium, and various social rooms. Under an agreement by which it was to pay all expenses and receive all earnings, the Admiral Line chartered the *Callao* at a monthly rental of $10,000. The ship, renamed the *Ruth Alexander* in honor of the wife of H. F. Alexander, arrived on the West Coast

45 "He Might Lose Another" (editorial), Portland *Oregonian,* March 11, 1922.
46 "Corporation Papers" in Admiral Mss, Honnold Library; *Railway and Marine News,* XXIII (April 1925), 11, XXIII (Feb. 5, 1926), 7, 10, XXIII (March 15, 1926), 8.

in March 1922 and was placed in service opposite the *President* between Seattle and California.[47] She made her maiden trip from Puget Sound to San Francisco in a little more than fifty-three hours, which lowered no speed records, but the luxury of the ship pleased the passengers. While one hundred miles out of San Francisco, they sent the following wireless message to the marine editor of the San Francisco *Chronicle*: "We, the passengers on the steamer Ruth Alexander on her maiden voyage, desire to express our enthusiasm and delight in being afforded the travel luxuries of this wonderful ship. Her remarkable steadiness, spacious decks, elaborate furnishings and public rooms, conveniences, including telephones in every room, together with the well-known Admiral cuisine, brought to a state of perfection, have all convinced us that the Pacific Coast and San Francisco in particular, is fortunate indeed in having the addition of a vessel of the type of the Ruth Alexander added to your port."[48]

In 1920, the Admiral Line had lost in its attempt to obtain the *Harvard* and *Yale* to a group of Los Angeles businessmen who were neophytes in the coastwise industry. When the government, in 1921, decided to sell the *Northern Pacific*, the two groups were again rivals. This time the Admiral Line made the higher offer, and in February 1922 the former Hill liner was purchased by the Pacific Steamship Company for one million dollars. With her speed, the *Northern Pacific* could cut the time between Seattle and San Francisco from about fifty-five hours to under forty. Had LASSCO been successful in obtaining the *Northern Pacific*, the Alexander company would have lost its leadership in the coastwise trade lanes.

---

[47] "Annual Report to Interstate Commerce Commission" (1922), p. 314 in Admiral Mss, Honnold Library; Seattle *Post-Intelligencer*, Dec. 4, 1921; San Francisco *Chronicle*, Dec. 11, 1921; *Pacific Marine Review*, XIX (Jan. 1922), 78; Los Angeles *Times*, March 12, 1922.

[48] San Francisco *Chronicle*, April 4, 1922.

None of the Admiral ships could exceed sixteen knots, and the possession of three vessels in the twenty to twenty-four knot category by a rival company would have been disastrous. Before the sale had been completed, it was known that the bid of LASSCO was only $15,000 under that of the Admiral Line. The margin of victory was too close for security. Both H. F. Alexander and Stanley Dollar went to Los Angeles to attempt to persuade the rival company to concentrate on its projected Hawaiian route and to allow the Admiral Line to purchase or charter the *Harvard* and *Yale*. The merger plan developed far enough for Robert Dollar to announce that the discussions were under way. But no basis for agreement was reached and the plans were dropped.[49]

The triumph of the Admiral Line in its campaign to bring the speedy *Northern Pacific* to the West Coast was short-lived. On February 8, 1922, two days after the sale, the ship caught fire off Cape May, New Jersey. Attempts to control the flames proved futile, and the crew abandoned her, a blazing wreck. At the time, the ship was en route from New York to Chester, Pennsylvania, where she was to be reconditioned. Though the captain refused to discuss the tragedy, it was reported by the newspapers that the fire which had started shortly after midnight from leaky oil tanks could not be brought under control by the skeleton crew on board.[50]

This blow stimulated efforts on the part of the Admiral Line to obtain the *Great Northern*, which the Navy was using as the flagship of the Atlantic fleet, the first time in modern naval history that a merchant vessel had been assigned this type of duty. The Navy was well pleased

49 San Francisco *Examiner*, Dec. 17, 1921; Victoria *Times*, Dec. 24, 1921; "Financial Statement" in Admiral Mss, Honnold Library; San Francisco *Examiner*, Jan. 27, 1922.
50 New York *Times*, Feb. 9, 10, 11, 1922.

with its acquisition, had renamed her the *Columbia,* and had declared that the ship was necessary for the efficiency of the service. When the efforts of the Admiral Line to acquire the vessel became known, the Los Angeles *Times,* with some satisfaction, observed, "Unless Congress passes a law directing the Secretary of the Navy to sell the Great Northern, sister ship of the Northern Pacific, which was burned last week, it is unlikely that the great passenger and cargo carrier will go to the Pacific Coast."[51] The men who controlled both the paper and LASSCO did not want a speedy rival to their ships.

But Alexander was not the type of man to let problems stand in his way. While in Washington, D. C., attending a conference of shipping men, he figured up the cost of fuel that the *Columbia* would consume each year and found the amount to be around one million dollars. He personally took these figures to the Secretary of the Navy, Director of the Budget, Senate Naval Affairs Committee, and finally to President Harding. To an economy-minded administration, the plan to sell the big ship seemed logical. Accordingly the Secretary of the Navy reversed his previous position and, on February 23, 1922, requested the President to transfer the *Columbia* to the Shipping Board in line with the policy of reducing expenditures of the Navy. The President, in turn, praised his Secretary of the Navy for the suggestion and issued the executive order for the transfer. On the first of March it was rumored that the Shipping Board, after opening competitive bids, had sold the ship to Alexander. Two days later the official announcement of the sale was made. Somewhat caustically, the Los Angeles *Times* observed that the argument "which apparently was successful was, that the company had to have the Great Northern by next

[51] Los Angeles *Times,* Feb. 14, 1922; Portland *Oregonian,* July 30, 1921; San Francisco *Examiner,* July 29, 1921.

June to carry the Shriners' excursion from San Francisco to the Hawaiian Islands and return."[52]

When the Shipping Board received custody of the *Columbia* on February 24, 1922, she was at Guantanamo Bay, Cuba. It immediately ordered the ship to proceed at full speed to New York. She arrived February 28, 1922, and tied up alongside the battleship *Maryland* which was to become the new flagship of the Atlantic fleet. The personal effects of the admiral, officers, and crew were transferred in a hurry. Messboys reportedly toiled up the gangways with "one arm filled with dress uniforms on hangers and the other arm filled with vegetable, dressed fowls and other stores from the galley and wardroom. . . . There was no salute and no forming of the lines or ceremonies that befitted the disembarkation of the highest Navy officer afloat. All was confusion and speed." The next day, the *Columbia* left for Chester, Pennsylvania, "and in its wake were some sore and disgruntled veterans of the Navy. The transfer had been brutal and not nice."[53] This newspaper account may be distorted but that the transfer caused injured feelings is clear.

Within a short time, an unnamed naval officer aboard the *Columbia* sent a letter to a congressman in which H. F. Alexander was quoted as saying that he had forced the sale and that he was a bigger man than the Secretary of the Navy. In March, Representative James V. McClintic of Oklahoma requested the House Naval Affairs Committee to investigate. Since the sale took place five days before the date set for the opening of the bids, McClintic

---

52 Los Angeles *Times,* Feb. 22, 1922; New York *Times,* Feb. 28, March 4, 1922; Robert Dollar, *Memoirs,* IV, 18-21; Magner White, "Alexander, Once a Dock Hand, Now Owns a Fleet," *American Magazine,* CI (April 1926, 16-17; Board minutes of the Admiral Line for March 3 and April 28, 1922 in Robert Dollar Company Archives, San Francisco; San Francisco *Examiner,* March 2, 1922; "Annual Report to Interstate Commerce Commission" (1922), p. 504 in Admiral Mss, Honnold Library.

53 Los Angeles *Times,* March 6, 1922.

declared that the proceedings were "calculated to arouse suspicion." That the Navy had spent more than half a million dollars in refitting the ship was duly noted by the congressman. At the inquiry held by the House Naval Affairs Committee in March as the result of these disclosures, the Secretary of the Navy, Edwin Denby, admitted that the ship was sold prior to the date set for opening the bids but with the understanding that any bidder offering more than the sale price would get the ship. Telegraphic notices had been sent to every shipping man who was likely to bid but only H. F. Alexander had submitted a bid. Denby acknowledged to the committee that he had at first opposed the transfer of the ship from the Navy. Remembering the public praise Denby had received from the President for "suggesting" the transfer, one of the committee members asked, "Was the order issued over your protest?" Evasively he replied, "I don't want to bring in my commander-in-chief." That the circumstances surrounding the transaction were "peculiar" was evident.[54]

After being reconditioned at a cost of more than half a million dollars and being renamed the *H. F. Alexander,* the former *Great Northern* arrived on the West Coast in June 1922. She made the trip from New York to San Francisco via the Panama Canal in thirteen steaming days, breaking all records. Before entering the coastwise trade, the *H. F. Alexander* in June took about six hundred Shriners to and from the Hawaiian Islands as surmised by the Los Angeles *Times.*[55]

On July 9, 1922, she arrived in the Puget Sound on her maiden coastwise voyage under the Admiral flag. Head winds had delayed her between San Francisco and Seattle but the forty-two and a half hours between the two ports

54 *Ibid.,* March 10, 1922; New York *Times,* March 16, 1922.
55 Los Angeles *Times,* June 5, 15, July 5, 1922; San Francisco *Chronicle,* June 16, 1922.

was a new steaming record. The first man to go up the gangplank when the vessel tied up at Pier D was H. F. Alexander. Later nearly ten thousand Seattle residents swarmed aboard to inspect her. The next day the ship was taken to Tacoma where, at a luncheon held on board, H. F. Alexander was given the Peace Medal sent by President Harding for his achievements in behalf of the welfare of the American merchant marine and restoration of normal conditions. Alexander was again hailed as the "monarch of shipping."[56]

The initial departure of the *H. F. Alexander* from Seattle on July 11, 1922, was the cause for a civic celebration. "Amid the applause of more than 5,000 persons who thronged the open spaces of Pier D," the mayor of Seattle cast loose the lines of the ship. Thereafter the huge ship was placed on a regular weekly run between Seattle, San Francisco, and Los Angeles. Because of her speed, an extra fare was charged.[57]

In his drive for new ships, H. F. Alexander decided to change the name of the *President,* the largest ship in the old Admiral fleet. On the same day that his daughter, Dorothy, changed her name by marrying Joseph Carman Jr., H. F. Alexander had the *President* rechristened the *Dorothy Alexander.* The name-changing proved to be good publicity. One newspaper headlined the story: "Girl Loses Name; Gives It to a Steamer."[58]

A fourth "Alexander" ship was also originally in the fleet of the old Pacific Coast Steamship Company. The *Congress,* which had been left by her owners in 1916 a smoldering wreck off Coos Bay, had been sold eventually

[56] Seattle *Times,* July 10, 11, 1922; *Marine Digest,* I (Sept. 2, 1922), 5-6.
[57] Seattle *Times,* July 12, 1922; the schedule of thirty-nine hours between Seattle and San Francisco was ten hours faster than the previous running times. San Francisco *Chronicle,* Oct. 21, 1922; *Marine Digest,* I (Sept. 16, 1922), 3.
[58] San Francisco *Chronicle,* July 15, 1922; "Annual Report to Interstate Commerce Commission" (1922), p. 402 in Admiral Mss, Honnold Library.

to the China Mail Steamship Company in 1918. A reported two million dollars was spent in rebuilding the burnt-out hull and the name was changed to *Nanking*. But the China Mail ran into serious difficulties during its brief career. Because it was partly foreign owned, it could not operate in the Hawaiian trade. Heavy fines were assessed against its fleet of three vessels for violations of the Harrison-Miller narcotic law. On one run, the government imposed a total of $450,000 in fines and penalties as the result of opium seizures. In April 1923 the company announced that the *Nanking* would be laid up indefinitely. To satisfy the claims of the bondholders, the *Nanking* was auctioned on the floor of the Merchants' Exchange of San Francisco in November 1923. The Admiral Line was the only bidder and possession of the vessel was obtained for $750,000. The ship was renamed the *Emma Alexander* in memory of H. F. Alexander's mother, who had recently died.[59]

By February 1924 the *Emma Alexander* was ready for service. At a luncheon held on board on February 6, Judge Thomas Burke of Seattle declared: "The United States constitution guarantees individual initiative. . . . To that fact we owe the career of Mr. Alexander who beginning on a small scale in 1906 has built up his Admiral Line until last year its gross revenues exceeded $19,000,000. . . . Think of more than $19,000,000 gross in one year! And the man who did it, is only at the beginning of his career! The Admiral Line is one of the modern wonders. It is one of the romances of the age. It has become one

[59] To raise the purchase money, the Admiral Line issued $750,000 in 7 percent preferred mortgage gold bonds which were to mature within four years. Board minutes of Admiral Line for December 7, 1923, in Robert Dollar Company Archives, San Francisco; "Annual Report to Interstate Commerce Commission" (1923), p. 229 in Admiral Mss, Honnold Library; *Pacific Marine Review*, XXI (Jan. 1924), 101; Los Angeles *Times*, Dec. 3, 1923; *Railway and Marine News*, XXI (Dec. 1923), 19; San Francisco *Chronicle*, April 7, 1923; Portland *Oregonian*, Nov. 18, 1923.

of our heritages of the sea."[60] The president of the Seattle
Chamber of Commerce also praised H. F. Alexander.
"He has fulfilled his vision of years ago. To fulfill that
vision required the same courage, the same patience and
the same determination required of other empire builders,
such as James J. Hill."[61]

The return of the *Congress* under the name *Emma
Alexander* was welcomed along the entire coast. She was
placed opposite the *Ruth Alexander* on the Seattle to
Southern California run. The *Dorothy Alexander* was
transferred to the Portland trade. On February 23, 1924,
the *Dorothy* started her initial trip from Portland. There
was the usual open house and complimentary luncheon
but the flowery speeches in praise of H. F. Alexander
were missing. The assignment of the ship to the Portland
route proved temporary. Later the same year she was
returned to the route between Seattle and California.[62]

COMPETITORS ALL

The Admiral Line had never been able to monopolize
the Columbia River commerce as it had that of the Puget
Sound. In January 1923 a new rival for this trade had
appeared when the New Electra Line brought the *Cuba*
to the Pacific Coast. On January 30, 1923, this seventeen-
knot vessel left San Francisco for Portland and inaugurated
the new service. The New Electra Line was owned by
Charles L. Dimon, who for many years had been active
in coastwise navigation on the Atlantic. Originally built

60 Quoted in *Marine Digest*, II (Feb. 9, 1924), 4.
61 Quoted in *ibid.*, 8.
62 San Francisco *Chronicle*, Feb. 12, 1924; Los Angeles *Times*, Feb. 13,
1924; Portland *Oregonian*, Feb. 22-24, 1924; *Pacific Marine Review*, XXI
(Feb. 1924), 128; "Annual Report to Interstate Commerce Commission"
(1924), p 403 in Admiral Mss, Honnold Library.

as a steamer, the *Cuba* has been refitted in 1920 with electric gear and was the first electrically driven vessel to be used along the Pacific Coast. Her speed allowed her to furnish a sailing every seven days as compared to the nine-day schedule maintained by the steamer *Rose City* of the "Big 3."[63]

The people of the Columbia River region welcomed the new company. The Portland *Telegram* observed, "Since the passing of the steamships Great Northern and Northern Pacific, this port has lacked express service by water to the metropolis of California" and added that the opportunity "to lay down each Monday morning on the docks of San Francisco 200 tons of butter, eggs, fruits, vegetables, meats, fish and fish packing house products, is a considerable widening of the open door for Oregon growers." With the slogan "at home at sea," the New Electra Line hoped to establish itself in the coastwise trade. By fall, the line was forced to reduce fares 20 percent and in December it suspended service. In May 1924, after an absence of five months, the *Cuba* resumed regular service at the reduced rates.[64]

Not discouraged by the reception accorded the *Cuba*, Charles L. Dimon announced in May plans for bringing to the coast the *Dixie*, which could carry 500 passengers. He planned to use this second vessel on the Puget Sound to California trade lane on a weekly schedule beginning in August. But these plans of the New Electra Line never materialized. In October the *Cuba* was quietly withdrawn and Dimon left the coastwise field to the Admiral Line.[65]

The new Alexander ships were proving attractive to

[63] *Pacific Ports,* IX (March 1923), 97; San Francisco *Chronicle,* Jan. 30, 31, 1923; Portland *Oregonian,* Jan. 18, 1923.

[64] Portland *Telegram,* Feb. 3, 1923; *Pacific Marine Review,* XX (March 1923), 123-25, XX (Dec. 1923), 593, XXI (Jan. 1924), 54; Portland *Oregonian,* May 9, 23, 1924.

[65] San Francisco *Chronicle,* May 30, 1924; Los Angeles *Times,* Oct. 20, 1924.

the traveling public. In 1924, the *H. F. Alexander* received
new boiler tubes, new propellers, and a general tune-up,
which increased her speed to more than twenty-five knots.
The result was new steaming records. In March, the *H. F.
Alexander* broke her own Seattle to San Francisco record
by making the journey in thirty-seven hours and thirteen
minutes. Continuing to Los Angeles, the ship made the
1,172-mile trip in fifty-four hours and thirteen minutes,
which was more than four hours under the fastest rail
schedule.[66] Because of her speed and frequent service,
one magazine stated that the *H. F. Alexander* "probably
has logged a greater mileage . . . than any vessel during
a like period in the history of the world's commerce."
Another noted that she was the "fastest privately-owned
American-built seagoing steamer in the American Merchant Marine."[67]

Despite these transportation records, LASSCO had developed into a strong competitor to the Admiral Line in
the California trade. Born in the time of the maritime
strike of 1921, the company surmounted that difficulty
and continued to strengthen its position. In April 1922
overnight express service was inaugurated between Los
Angeles and San Francisco in connection with the newly
organized Pacific States Express. Freight leaving San
Francisco on the *Yale* or *Harvard* was delivered in the
wholesale district of Los Angeles within twenty-four hours
after it had been received at the wharf in San Francisco. A
similar northbound service was offered. In June, San
Diego was added as a port of call. On her first trip to the
border city in five years, the *Yale* was greeted on June 22,
1922, by a brass band, city officials, and a throng of persons

66 *Pacific Marine Review*, XX (Sept. 1923), 434, XXI (April 1924), 25 in
advertising section; *Marine Digest*, II (March 8, 1924), 3; Los Angeles
Times, March 7, 8, 1924.
67 *Marine Digest*, III (July 11, 1925), 4. *Pacific Marine Review*, XXI
(April 1924), 242.

who were boarding and walking about the steamer from eight in the evening until nearly midnight.[68]

The summer of 1922 proved a bonanza in passenger travel. By using cots, each of the coastwise ships of LASSCO could take an extra fifty or sixty persons. In advertising this overflow service, the company declared, "The cots used for such emergencies are most comfortable and while those who take them do not have the privacy of a state-room, they are most pleasantly located and have ample dressing-room accommodations near by." In 1923 LASSCO began operating a third ship on its coastwise route. While primarily a fast freighter, the *Waimea,* which had seen previous coastwise service as the *City of Topeka* both under the old Pacific Coast Steamship Company and the Admiral Line, had facilities for eighty first-class cabin passengers. Because of its slower schedule, the fares on the *Waimea* were lower than on the *Harvard* or *Yale.* The speed of the *Harvard* was increased by one knot in 1924 when new propellers were installed. The effect of the competition furnished by LASSCO on the fares charged by the Admiral Line was striking. Between Los Angeles and San Francisco, where LASSCO competition existed, the Admiral Line charged 6.1 cents per mile on the *H. F. Alexander.* On the San Francisco to Seattle run, where the Admiral Line was supreme, the rate was 9.6 cents per mile or more than 50 percent higher. Other factors contributed slightly to this differential. For example, fuel oil was higher in Seattle than in California, which tended to raise the operating costs; however, the difference is still significant.[69]

[68] By 1923, LASSCO was furnishing three trips each week to San Diego. San Diego *Union,* June 23, 1922; Los Angeles *Times,* April 5, May 15, June 23, Oct. 27, 1922; *Pacific Marine Review,* XVIII (June 1921), 330, XXI (May 1924), 30 in advertising section.

[69] Los Angeles *Times,* Aug. 17, 1922, Sept. 12, 16, 1924; *Pacific Marine Review,* XX (July 1923), 35 in advertising section, XX (Aug. 1923), 392.

Dining Room of the *Roanoke. Courtesy of the Historical Collection, Title Insurance and Trust Company, San Diego*

The Great Northern, Flavel, ca. 1916. Courtesy of the Angelus Collection, University of Oregon Library

Attempts by Alexander to eliminate the Harriman interests from coastwise shipping continued. In January 1923 the Admiral Line again proposed to absorb the "Big 3" by buying the *Rose City* and leasing the Ainsworth dock which the Union Pacific Railroad Company had built for its marine operations in Portland. H. F. Alexander told reporters that he expected the deal to be consummated within the next thirty to sixty days. But the Admiral Line was to fail again in its bid for the "Big 3."

Over a year later, the McCormick Steamship Company announced the purchase of the *Rose City*. Under the terms of the sale, the Harriman company agreed to reconstruct the Ainsworth dock for the use of the McCormick line and to establish joint rates with it. On her first voyage under the McCormick flag, the *Rose City* arrived at San Francisco on November 3, 1924. Three days later she appeared in Los Angeles Harbor, resuming her former route from Portland to southern California, which had been abandoned in 1918. The entrance of the *Rose City* into Los Angeles marked the fourth regular coastwise service to and from that port. The others were provided by LASSCO, the Admiral Line, and the White Flyer Line. The fourteen knot speed of the *Rose City* did not make it a formidable competitor to the *Yale, Harvard,* or the *H. F. Alexander,* which could go ten knots faster.[70]

The McCormick Steamship Company had developed

70 Portland *Oregonian,* Jan. 5, 1923; *Pacific Marine Review,* XXII (June 1925), 264, XXI (Oct. 1924), 21A; Portland *Oregon Journal,* Jan. 14, 1923, Sept. 3, 1924; "Annual Report of the San Francisco and Portland Steamship Company to the Railroad Commission of California for the Year Ending December 31, 1924," p. 203, "Annual Report of Charles R. McCormick Lumber Company to the Railroad Commission of California for the Year Ending December 31, 1924," p. 210 in ASF; *Railway and Marine News,* XXII (Nov. 1924), 21; San Francisco *Chronicle,* Oct. 29, Nov. 4, 1924. For the story of the penetration of the Union Pacific Railroad into the Columbia River see Dorothy O. Johansen, "Capitalism on the Far-Western Frontier: The Oregon Steam Navigation Company" (unpublished Ph.D. dissertation, University of Washington, 1941), pp. 1-284.

from a lumber brokerage business formed by Charles R. McCormick and Sidney H. Hauptman in 1903. Leasing a shipyard in Eureka, the two men began to build vessels, some of which they sold and others they kept for their lumber business. As the movement of lumber was southward exclusively, the company which they formed began to engage in northbound merchandise movement to insure some income on the return trip. By November 1922 the Charles R. McCormick Company had obtained control of five coastwise lumber shipping companies and merged their vessels with its fleet. The next year, the McCormick Steamship Company was organized to carry general merchandise southward as well. In January of 1924 the new line announced regular passenger and freight service between Portland and San Francisco. The steamer *Columbia* was assigned to this route on a biweekly schedule. In the later part of 1923 McCormick had filed a complaint with the Interstate Commerce Commission against certain railroads which had refused to establish through routes and joint rates with it. The Nelson Steamship Company intervened in the case, seeking the same relief. Before the hearing was held, the McCormick company had purchased the *Rose City* and had entered into a freight agreement with the Union Pacific Railroad. As a result, the McCormick line requested that the complaint be dismissed.[71]

The emergence of the McCormick Steamship Company was only one example of the rise of an Admiral competitor from the lumber business. By 1924, the Nelson Steamship Company was also becoming prominent in coastwise commerce. In January of that year it took over the "narrow gauge" line of the Admiral Line between

[71] *Pacific Marine Review,* XXIII (March 1926), 108; San Francisco *Chronicle,* Nov. 11, 1922; reports of the McCormick Company in ASF; *Railway and Marine News,* XXI (Sept. 1923), 20; Portland *Oregonian,* Jan. 25, 1924; *Decisions,* CIX, 531.

San Francisco and Portland. Its one vessel that could carry passengers, the *Nome City,* replaced the *Admiral Schley* in providing regular service to Eureka and Coos Bay points. For the past three or four years, this line had been unprofitable to the Alexander interests. The principal stockholder of the Nelson Steamship Company was James Tyson, who owned 740 out of the 1,000 shares outstanding in 1925. The name of the company had come from a Charles Nelson, who in 1858 began operating sailing vessels in connection with lumber operations.[72]

Coastwise shipping was slowly regaining the momentum it had lost through the strike, wrecks, and poor equipment. LASSCO had established a fast service along the California coast. Although the "Big 3," one of the pioneer companies, had withdrawn, its place was filled by the McCormick Steamship Company. The White Flyer Line continued to run the veteran *Humboldt* and to attract the patronage of those who desired lower rates rather than de luxe accommodations with the slogan, "family boat of the Pacific." The Admiral Line, though not without setbacks, had reestablished its leadership by introducing the "Alexander" ships, which were becoming known along the entire coast for speed, dependability, and good food. Its $900,000 deficit for 1921 was cut the next year to less than $40,000. In 1923 a profit of more than half a million dollars was earned.[73]

The optimism of the industry was tempered, however, by a new factor. The demand for lumber in California had increased the number of lumber vessels that operated along the coast. Many of these slow ships were equipped

[72] Board minutes of the Admiral Line for Jan. 23, 1924 in Robert Dollar Company Archives in San Francisco; Portland *Oregonian,* Jan. 21, 1924; *Pacific Marine Review,* XXI (Aug. 1924), 421; "Annual Report of the Nelson Steamship Company to the Railroad Commission of California for the Year Ending December 31, 1925," p. 11 in ASF; *Decisions,* CIX, 532-33.
[73] "Financial Statement" in Admiral Mss, Honnold Library.

to carry four to ten passengers. In order to attract patronage, rates were cut to low levels. Passage between San Francisco and Seattle was offered for as little as $20, which was cheaper than steerage on the Admiral ships. From the ranks of these lumber carriers, the McCormick and Nelson lines had emerged. The threat to the established lines, particularly the Alexander company, was serious. It was one of the factors which changed the half million profit of 1923 into a half million loss in 1924. Although the Admiral Line claimed 90 percent of the passenger and 60 percent of the commercial traffic moving between Pacific Coast ports, its position was far from secure.[74]

[74] *Railway and Marine News*, XXII (Jan. 1924), 17; Financial Statement" in Admiral Mss, Honnold Library; statement of H. F. Alexander in Portland *Oregonian*, Jan. 11, 1925; San Francisco *Chronicle*, Jan. 21, 1925.

FIVE

The Postwar Decade:
Three Problems

LABOR RELATIONS ON DECKS AND DOCKS

THE STRIKE of 1921 and its aftermath brought into focus three related problems which closely involved the shipping industry. The first was the field of labor relations, which had been violently shattered by the events of 1921. The second was the importance of freight revenues in the maintenance of a coastwise transportation system. The third was the realm of governmental control, which had proved somewhat ineffectual during the strike. As the steamship lines adjusted themselves to the problems of the postwar decade, each of these areas proved to be important.

Maritime labor unions had suffered a disastrous defeat in 1921. Torn by internal dissensions, they had not been able to present a united front. In the post-strike period, the unions found themselves forced to submit to the directions of the employer groups. Wages were unilaterally altered to fit the exigencies of business. From a high point in 1920, the compensation offered by the operators declined perceptibly. Following the lead of the Shipping Board, the employer organizations made a second cut in wages on February 15, 1922, which averaged about 20 percent. Although the unions had taken no part in the preparation of the new wage scale, they could offer no resistance.[1]

The meekness of labor in the months immediately following the strike could hardly be considered typical of labor relations along the waterfront. Examples of violence, intimidation, and bitterness had been frequent in previous years. During a 1916 coastwide strike of long-shoremen, the Tacoma strikers captured non-union workers who were loading the *Nome City* and took them as prisoners to a detention camp established on the tideflats.[2] The belligerent attitude of the employers during the same strike was well illustrated at a meeting of 2,000 merchants held on July 10, 1916, in San Francisco. The president of the San Francisco Chamber of Commerce declared, "We insist upon the right to employ union labor or non-union labor, in whole or in part. . . . It is time that San Francisco free its reputation, at home and abroad, as being a class-ruled city. . . . I want to stir the red blood in your veins and take this matter in hand as it should be done."[3] At the same meeting, Captain Robert Dollar was reported as saying that "the sending of several ambulances full of union men to the hospital" was the way to insure peace along the waterfront.[4] When the 1916 strike was over and the employers had won, one magazine observed, "The longshoremen have lost, and now, like whipped curs the strikers are crawling to the waterfront

---

[1] *Marine Digest*, XIV (Feb. 1, 1936), 3; copy of a letter signed by Harry Lundeberg, Executive Secretary of Sailors' Union of the Pacific, dated Aug. 17, 1936, in printed pamphlet, "Our Shippers" in Admiral Mss, Honnold Library; U. S., Bureau of Navigation, *Annual Report of the Commissioner of Navigation to the Secretary of Commerce for the Fiscal Year Ended June 30, 1918*, p. 54; *ibid.*, for 1919, p. 63; *ibid.*, 1923, p. 49; *Pacific Marine Review*, XIX (Feb. 1922), 130-31, XIX (March 1922), 186; San Francisco *Chronicle*, Feb. 9, 1922.

[2] Seattle *Star*, June 2, 1916.

[3] Quoted in *Pacific Marine Review*, XIII (Aug. 1916), 68.

[4] San Francisco *Chronicle*, July 11, 1916.

and offering to work at a tremendous decrease under what they were receiving when they struck."[5]

Most of the operators held union leaders and members in contempt. The president of the Sailors' Union was described as "Agitating Andy" or "that ubiquitous, semper virens, Andrew Furuseth." His policies were supposed to be based on the assumption that "anything which benefits the American shipowner must necessarily be wrong in principle and anti-bono publico [sic] in its application." In 1918, the president of a leading shipbuilding company declared, "The personnel of our seafaring unions is mostly alien. They are very clannish, and it has been the purpose of the union organization's management to keep the supply of men close to and even somewhat short of the demand, so as to stimulate wages and make possible arbitrary demands."[6] To unite all employers, the operators formed waterfront employer groups which included in their membership merchants as well as shipowners. Through this type of organization, the owners were able to deal with strikes more effectively.

The owners had the financial backing which the unions lacked. In 1934 LASSCO deposited $11,400 with the Marine Service Bureau of Los Angeles "for the purpose of putting the Bureau in funds to take care of extraordinary expenses due to [the] stevedore strike." In 1917, the "Big 3" wrote off to profit and loss $3,000, which represented "an amount that it was thought could be collected from the Portland Chamber of Commerce to help defray a portion of the expenses of Longshoremen's strike, in the summer of 1916. It develops that nothing can be secured

5 "Whine of the Vanquished" (editorial), *Railway and Marine News*, XIV (Sept. 1916), 9.

6 H. E. Pennel, "Rehabilitation of the American Merchant Marine Assured," *Pacific Marine Review*, XV (Feb. 1918), 67. See also *ibid.*, XXIV (May 1927), 241, XXX (May 1933), 129.

from that source." The president of the San Francisco Chamber of Commerce publicly announced in 1916 that more than $200,000 had been subscribed to a proposed strikebreaking fund of $1,000,000.[7]

The employers used a variety of methods in combating what they called the lawlessness of the waterfront. In response to a labor demand for a wage increase in 1916, the "Big 3" temporarily suspended freight shipments. The company announced, "There is not enough revenue left at present freight rates to take up the increased wages demanded by the longshoremen which with the new working conditions amounts to about fifty per cent, and the company is therefore regretfully compelled to temporarily retire from freight transportation, hereafter carrying passengers only." In 1919 the White Flyer Line tied up the *Humboldt* for a short time when the unions requested that extra personnel be employed. Such methods were extremely effective in dealing with labor demands.[8]

While the operators were prepared to meet force with force, they did not overlook the advantage of a more constructive approach. Proudly the Shipowners' Association of the Pacific Coast declared that it "is in complete control of Pacific coastal shipping and . . . its work on behalf of the merchant seamen in its employ is of more economic benefit to those seamen than the former work of the Coast Seamen's Union or the present work of the Sailors' Union of the Pacific."[9] The industry tried to show that the compensation of its employees was adequate.

[7] "Annual Report of the Los Angeles Steamship Company to the Railroad Commission of California for the Year Ending December 31, 1934," p. 208 in ASF; "Annual Report of the San Francisco and Portland Steamship Company to the Railroad Commission of California for the Year Ending December 31, 1917," p. 15 in ASF; San Francisco *Chronicle*, July 11, 1916.

[8] The "Big 3" statement was printed in Portland *Telegram*, June 2, 1916; San Francisco *Chronicle*, Oct. 16, 1919.

[9] *Pacific Marine Review*, XXI (Sept. 1924), 450.

The Admiral Line compiled a list of the wages earned by forty of its longshoremen. For the year 1926, the average amount that each man earned was about $2,190, but the list was hardly representative as the individuals were selected only from those men who "worked regularly" and the nature of longshore work creates more part-time than regular employees.[10] The superficiality of the employers' reasoning was revealed in 1927 when one employer opposed the new federal compensation law for longshoremen because "the $25 weekly maximum compensation is more than many earn."[11]

Another technique used to combat organized labor was the creation of competing organizations. In 1914, the shipowners of San Francisco had formed the Waterfront Employers' Union "to meet the ever increasing demands of the Riggers and Stevedores Union." The new group "assisted in the organization of a body now known as the Longshoremen's Association." The early days of this company union were "filled with riot and overt acts, caused by attempts of the Riggers and Stevedores Union to disrupt and disorganize the new body," but the new association "withstood attacks without a tremor" and in 1923 had nearly five thousand "conservative and efficient men." A no-strike clause was written into the agreement between the employers and this association. The usefulness of the company-sponsored union was demonstrated during the 1921 strike. Triumphantly the operators observed that the Sailors' Union was unable to persuade the members of the Longshoremen's Association to join the strike; and the *Pacific Marine Review* reported, "Not a day was lost, not a ship delayed nor an overt act committed

10 "Statistics" in Admiral Mss, Honnold Library.

11 F. P. Foisie, "The New Federal Compensation Law for Longshoremen and Harbor Workers," *Railway and Marine News,* XXIV (March 1927), 9. Foisie was the Industrial Relations Manager for the Waterfront Employers of Seattle.

during the entire period of the trouble."[12] The success of the Longshoremen's Association was short-lived. When the 1934 maritime strike occurred, the International Longshoremen's Association had become the dominant force and it readily joined with other maritime unions in aggressive action against the employers.

During the lull between the strikes of 1921 and 1934, the labor unions were weak but not dead. In 1922, the Seamen's Union accused the Admiral Line of hiring Orientals in the place of American seamen. When A. F. Haines, the general manager of the Admiral Line, announced that he would provide jobs for all American seamen out of work, about fifty men marched to his office in Seattle and demanded work. Haines interviewed a committee from the marchers and offered work to two "on the next boat that comes in." Except for the attendant publicity, this union-sponsored "march" produced few results.[13]

The first break in the downward trend of wages came on February 1, 1923, when the Shipowners' Association of the Pacific Coast granted an increase of ten dollars per month to sailors and five dollars to firemen, oilers, and galley crews. The Seamen's Union tried to assume credit for this increase. It warned its members, "If it were not self-evident that neither treachery from within nor open assault from without has prevented the unions from functioning, then indeed there would have been quite another story."[14]

The employment bureaus established by the employers after the 1921 strike proved to be a hard blow against organized labor. The seamen called these offices "slave

12 *Pacific Marine Review*, XX (Feb. 1923), 106.
13 Quoted in Seattle *Union Record*, Jan. 10, 1922.
14 "That 'Voluntary' Increase" (editorial), *Seamen's Journal*, Feb. 1, 1923; *Pacific Marine Review*, XX (Feb. 1923), 112.

markets." All maritime workers were registered and assigned work by the employers without reference to the
unions or union membership.[15] The owners were well
pleased with the system. In February 1923 their official
magazine reported, "For the first time in the history of
Pacific Coast shipping, wages and labor conditions have
been stabilized, varying but slightly from Vancouver to
San Diego."[16] In his 1926 annual report, the general
manager of the San Francisco bureau proudly asserted,
"We have maintained the public peace on the San Francisco waterfront for over five years." The total number
of men shipped through the bureaus at San Francisco and
Los Angeles between 1921 and 1926 rose from about six
thousand to over thirty-three thousand.[17] In 1929, the
operators claimed that the system "has won the admiration
and praise of all who have had occasion to observe its
work. The seamen themselves have come to look upon
the Bureau as their own institution and to trust the good
judgment and fair dealing of its management."[18]

The unions were not so convinced that the institution
could be trusted. Many attempts were made to have the
courts declare the bureaus a violation of the federal anti-
trust laws, but without success. Failing in the legal fight
against them, the seamen fell back on an old remedy, the
"Oracle." In a pamphlet published by the Sailors' Union
of the Pacific, the workings of the "Oracle" were explained:

15 Taylor, *Sailors' Union of the Pacific*, p. 142. Taylor had been an
ordinary seaman on board a coasting vessel. For a statement in defense of
the employment bureaus see Thomas G. Plant, *The Pacific Coast Longshoremen's Strike of 1934 Statement of Thomas G. Plant, President of the
Waterfront Employers Union of San Francisco, to the National Longshoremen's Board* (San Francisco, 1934), p. 26. This forty-three page
pamphlet was used at the San Francisco Public Library. Mr. Plant was
president of the Waterfront Employers Union of San Francisco.

16 *Pacific Marine Review*, XX (Feb. 1923), 106.

17 Report by Captain W. J. Petersen in *ibid.*, XXIV (Jan. 1927), 10.

18 *Ibid.*, XXVI (April 1929), 133.

To get rid of the shipowners' offices we must make the offices a failure. . . . To make the office a failure—to make it the reason for delay—to make it the cause for delay—the men must ship through it and then when the vessel is ready to cast off the lines the men walk ashore, because they were shipped in or by the office. . . .

The vessel is ready and the master orders the lines cast off. You cast your duds on the wharf and then follow your duds. The vessel is delayed. She must find another crew. . . . This crew may do the same or go up the coast and leave her there. . . . How long will the shipowner stand for that? Especially in passenger vessels? We did this years ago and abolished the offices. We did it even when we were arrested for it and were brought back to the vessel and compelled to work.

We certainly can do it now when we cannot be arrested for doing it in any safe harbor. The Seamen's law, Section 7, gives all seamen in American ports the right to quit at will.

You will lose what money you have coming to you. Yes, that is true. What are you willing to do to get rid of the shipowners' offices here and elsewhere?[19]

The struggle over the hiring halls was never settled. Between 1921 and 1934, the employers were in control. In 1934, the arbitration award created a joint authority which included representatives from both sides. Neither system met with complete approval.

There were exceptions to the usually strained relations between labor and employers. At least one strike threat occurred with which the owners were in sympathy. In August 1917 prohibition enforcement agents of the state of Oregon began to search the *Great Northern* at her Flavel dock. The crew threatened to strike if the search continued. After a gunny sack filled with whiskey bottles

[19] "How Shall We Get Rid of the Shipowners' Shipping Office? Use the Old Remedy: The Oracle," reprinted in *Pacific Marine Review*, XIX (Feb. 1922), 53, 56 in advertising section; San Francisco *Chronicle*, Feb. 15, 1929.

was discovered in the gangway of the crew's quarters, the deck and engine crews took their bags and went ashore in a body. Rather than tie up the vessel, the Oregon officers left without further action. The crew returned and the *Great Northern* departed on schedule.[20]

The most notable instance of cooperation between labor and capital was the establishment of a safety code for dock workers. On March 4, 1927, the President of the United States signed the "Longshoremen's and Harbor Workers' Compensation Act." The bill was at first opposed by the operators because it failed to limit the liability of the employers. The general manager of the San Francisco employment bureau, Captain W. C. Petersen, declared that the act was passed in an absent-minded moment during a lull in the filibuster between the members of the Reed family concerning who was the biggest crook in Pennsylvania: "The House passed it without a single member reading it or knowing what was in it. The Senate passed it the same way, and the President signed it. And now everybody will try to interpret the bill in the light of the intent Congress had when it was passed."[21]

The bill required that, when a longshoreman was disabled, the employer had to pay a certain amount in compensation to the injured man. Medical care and death benefits were also included. Because of its desire to keep the right to sue, the Sailors' Union was successful in having seamen excluded from the provisions of the bill. The law was soon accepted by longshoremen and employers and proved a step in better relations by eliminating the

20 Los Angeles *Times*, Aug. 3, 1919.
21 Petersen was in Washington, D. C., when the bill was passed. Quoted in *Pacific Marine Review*, XXIV (May 1927), 241; U. S., Congress, *Congressional Record*, 69th Cong., 2d sess., pp. 5900-5909. See also "Should Amend Federal Bill" (editorial), *Railway and Marine News*, XXIII (June 1926), 14, 7-8, 29.

"sue or settle" controversies.[22] In 1929, a federal safety engineer observed, "This law, probably more than any other one thing, brought the cost of the accidents forcibly to the attention of the industry."[23] The compensation law was a notable exception to the general hostility between the operators and the unions.

Attempts were made by the operators to improve employee relationships in a unilateral way. At the various ports, the Admiral Line made it a policy to provide a Christmas dinner each year for its employees on board one of its ships. In Seattle, it sponsored an annual picnic for members of the Admiral offices in the Puget Sound region. At one party given by Admiral Line officials, the guests danced to the "H. F. Alexander Glide," the "Ruth Alexander Wave," the "Queen Hesitation," and the "Stanley Dollar Swing." The company began publishing a monthly *Employees Magazine* in 1921. Two years later, the Board of Directors of the same company gave $25,000 to H. F. Alexander to be distributed "at his discretion among certain employees of the company by way of additional compensation."[24]

Many employees had long and faithful service with the

[22] Warren H. Pillsbury, "The Longshoremen's Compensation Law," *Pacific Marine Review*, XXIV (June 1927), 256; F. P. Foisie, "The New Federal Compensation Law for Longshoremen and Harborworkers," *Railway and Marine News*, XXIV (March 1927), 9-10; *Pacific Marine Review*, XXIV (May 1927), 241, 243; United States, *Statutes at Large*, XLIV (1917), 1424-1446. For a good discussion of the "twilight zone" between state and maritime jurisdiction which made a federal compensation law necessary see Harold M. Sawyer, "Workmen's Compensation Statutes and the Admiralty," *Pacific Marine Review*, XVII (July 1920), 101-102.

[23] Frank C. Gregory, "Recent Progress in the Safety of Stevedoring Operations," abstract of an address delivered before the Marine Section, National Safety Council at Chicago, Oct. 3, 1929, reprinted in *Pacific Marine Review*, XXVI (Nov. 1929), 44.

[24] Portland *Oregonian*, Dec. 22, 1929; Seattle *Post-Intelligencer*, Aug. 18, 1921; *Railway and Marine News*, XX (Dec. 1922), 22, XXIII (Jan. 1925), 14, XXII (March 1924), 20; San Francisco *Journal*, Sept. 7, 1921; Minutes of the Admiral Board Meeting for December 7, 1923, in Robert Dollar Company Archives in San Francisco.

company. In 1927, the records showed that two men had been with the Admiral Line and its predecessor companies for a total of 103 years. A total of 108 men had been on the payrolls for twenty years or longer. In 1935, Moubray R. Dundas with over fifty-eight years to his credit claimed to have the longest record of any individual for continuous service with a Pacific coastwise transportation company. When Captain H. H. Cousins entered the dining saloon of the *Ruth Alexander* one April morning in 1923 for breakfast, he found seated at the table H. F. Alexander and other Admiral officials. This testimonial had been arranged in recognition of his forty-five years of service. During that time, Cousins had commanded twenty different ships and had experienced no accidents due to faulty navigation. Although he had been the captain of the *Congress* when she caught fire in 1916, Cousins was commended for his coolness in getting all persons on board safely ashore. In May 1923, the *Ruth Alexander* sailed from San Francisco with the ensign of commodore flying from her foretruck. The title had been conferred upon Cousins in recognition of his seniority among the captains of the Admiral Line. In 1933, the Admiral Line had seven captains who had sixteen or more years of service in the Admiral fleet.[25]

When the agents of the Admiral Line from San Diego to Vancouver gathered in 1920 to attend the first "agents' convention" of its kind held on the West Coast, a marine publication observed, "Cooperation in every department from the innermost chambers of the executive offices in Seattle's tallest skyscraper to the desk of the humblest clerk in the company's terminals on the waterfront has been the foundation on which H. F. Alexander has

25 "Statistics" in Admiral Mss, Honnold Library; *Pacific Marine Review*, XXXII (Oct. 1935), 12 in advertising section, XX (June 1923), 303, XXX (Jan. 1933), 5; *Railway and Marine News*, XXI (May 1923), 19.

developed the Pacific Steamship Company."[26] Admiral officials gave adequate publicity to all actions which tended to demonstrate their interest in the welfare of the employees. When a seaman on board the *Emma Alexander* was stricken with appendicitis on November 5, 1930, the *H. F. Alexander* changed her course to pick up the victim. In a fog "thick enough to cut with a knife," the two ships met at sea and the man was transferred in a lifeboat from one ship to the other. The seaman arrived at a hospital twenty-four hours earlier than would have been possible had he remained on the *Emma Alexander*.[27] The unilateral policy of maintaining the good will of employees produced at least one tangible result. In 1926, Admiral employees presented H. F. Alexander with an eighty-five foot flag pole which was erected in the yard of his Seattle residence.[28]

Other steamship lines also attempted to improve employer-employee relationships. In 1927, the McCormick line presented emblems in the form of McCormick stars to its employees in recognition of length of service. Several of the companies developed teams in baseball, basketball, swimming, and bowling. In 1927, the LASSCO team was the runner-up in the basketball league championship for the Pacific Coast. The McCormick line sponsored a quartet composed of employees from its Seattle office and outfitted the singers with "nifty new caps carrying the firm's insignia and brand new uniforms." The quartet sang before various clubs and business groups in the Puget Sound region.[29]

These activities may have improved relations between labor and management but did not overcome the bitterness

---

26 *Railway and Marine News*, XVIII (Feb. 1920), 21.
27 *Pacific Marine Review*, XXVII (Dec. 1930), 517.
28 *Railway and Marine News*, XXIII (March 15, 1926), 18.
29 *Pacific Marine Review*, XXIV (May 1927), 23, 25-26 in advertising section; *Railway and Marine News*, XXIV (Feb. 1927), 24, XXIV (April 1927), 31, XXIII (Oct. 1926), 23.

The *Bear*, Aground off Mendocino County, California, 1916. *Courtesy U. S. Coast and Geodetic Survey*

The *Yale*, Municipal Wharf, San Diego. *Courtesy of the Historical Collection, Title Insurance and Trust Company, San Diego*

which developed from the strikes. The superficiality of this approach became apparent in the labor crisis of 1934. Almost nostalgically, an Admiral Line official urged organized labor in 1935 to "return to the good will, loyalty and efficient cooperation . . . in effect prior to the strike of last summer."[30] But the plea fell on barren ground.

FREIGHT ON THE SEA LANES

From the point of view of the owners, one of the crippling effects of the 1921 strike was the loss of freight revenues. Since many ships were tied up or delayed in sailing, steady customers of the steamship lines looked to the railroads and trucking companies for transportation. When normal service was resumed, many of these shippers failed to return their patronage to the water carriers.

The loss of freight business to other modes of transportation was a serious blow. In the case of the steamship lines. freight produced a far greater proportion of the operating income than passenger travel. In 1921, 67 percent of the operating income of the Admiral Line came from carrying freight, whereas only 32 percent was derived from passenger fares. The remaining 1 percent included revenues from charter hire and express. Freight traffic played an even more important part in the earnings of most other companies, since passenger service was usually offered merely in connection with their freight business. A notable exception to this dependence on freight was LASSCO, whose express service attracted a great amount of passenger trade. For ten of its sixteen years of operation, passenger revenues of LASSCO exceeded those of freight. At times, the differ-

30 H. T. Krull, "Traffic Problems of a Coastwise Steamship Service," a paper read before the annual convention of the Pacific Coast Association of Port Authorities, Aug. 16, 1935, at Vancouver, British Columbia, in Admiral Mss, Honnold Library.

ence was quite large. In 1926, passenger income totaled $2,543,675 as compared to $1,605,286 for freight. During its first three years, the White Flyer Line also derived more money from its passenger than from its freight service, but by 1925 passenger revenue had dropped to about half the amount produced by freight.[31]

In contrast to passenger travel, which declined seriously during the winter, freight traffic had no great seasonal fluctuations. Although the passenger business always attracted more attention and seemed more spectacular, the mainstay of the steamship lines was their cargo-carrying ability.[32]

Because of the fact that speed was not as critical a factor and because there were more competitors, the Admiral Line did not enjoy the same dominance as a common carrier of freight as it did in the passenger business. It was able, however, to attract the major share and easily outdistanced any other single line in the amount of tonnage carried. In 1928, the Admiral Line handled 1,070,209 of the 2,135,374 tons carried by nine of the principal coastwise carriers. The ratio varied but slightly in other years. Unlike other lines whose business was apt to be confined to certain ports, the Admiral Line served all major seacoast cities. The only exceptions to this general statement were the McCormick and Nelson lines which, after 1926, extended their service to most ports along the coast.[33]

[31] "Statistics" in Admiral Mss, Honnold Library; U. S., Bureau of Statistics, "Selected Financial and Operating Data from Annual Reports: Carriers by Water" (mimeographed) (Washington, 1924-1936); "Anuual Report of the Los Angeles Steamship Company to the Railroad Commission of California" for 1921-1936 in ASF; "Annual Report of the White Flyer Line to the Railroad Commission of California" for 1919-1925 in ASF.

[32] "Statistics" in Admiral Mss, Honnold Library.

[33] U. S., Senate, *Report of the Federal Coordinator of Transportation*, 73d Cong., 2d sess., S. Doc. 152, p. 152. "Statistics" in Admiral Mss. Honnold Library.

Because of contract and private shipping lines, the
amount carried by the Admiral Line and other common
carriers represented only a portion of the total tonnage
which was shipped by water along the coastwise trade
lanes. In 1923, the Admiral Line handled 283,000 tons
out of San Francisco. During the same year 2,072,000
tons were shipped from San Francisco to coastwise destina-
tions by all types of water carriers. Similar conditions
existed at other ports.

Accurate figures for the coastwise trade are difficult to
obtain. The lack of uniformity in the methods employed
by the various local port authorities in measuring and
recording cargo constitutes a major obstacle. Figures supplied by federal agencies are even less satisfactory. No
adequate breakdown is furnished between the common
carriers and the private or contract carriers. Since the
lumber and petroleum industry along the Pacific Coast
operated their own fleets of vessels to take care of most of
their products, a great amount of freight moved under
private auspices. Without exception, local port authorities
include this type of tonnage in their figures. Such a policy
makes the statistics of the port more impressive but
provides little help in the study of common carriers.[34]

The prosperity of the steamship lines was closely identi-
fied with the prosperity of the West. Minor economic
fluctuations were quickly registered in the tonnage figures.
For example, in May 1928 H. F. Alexander reported to
the directors of the Admiral Line that the loss of freight
tonnage was due to the lack of potato and flour cargoes:

[34] The following reports have been consulted: Port of Los Angeles,
Monthly Report of Commerce (1920-1935); Portland, *Annual Report of
the Commission of Public Docks* (1916-1936); San Diego, "Annual Report
of Harbor Department" (typed and mimeographed) (1917-1936); California (San Francisco), *Biennial Report* of Board of State Harbor Commissioners (1920-1938); Seattle *Year Book* of the Port of Seattle (1919-
1927), and *Port Warden's Annual Report* (1916-1934); California, Board
of State Harbor Commissioners, *Biennial Report* (1922-1924), pp. 63-64;
"Statistics" in Admiral Mss, Honnold Library.

"potatoes are a drug on the market and are not selling. Wheat prices have been fluctuating so much that the millers in the Northwest are not making any contracts until the wheat market is more permanent."[35]

A great variety of products and raw materials were carried by the coasting steamers. The six principal commodities handled by the Admiral Line were canned goods, flour, paper, salmon, sugar, and lumber. The relative importance of these varied from year to year. In 1923 lumber was first, but by 1926 it had dropped to sixth place. At the same time, canned goods rose from sixth to fourth place, and flour changed from third to first place. While these six were the leading commodities, they were by no means the only ones. As the ships plied between the various ports, their holds contained a cross section of the products of the Pacific region. On one voyage in June 1928 the *H. F. Alexander* carried:[36]

Cargo	Tons
Flour	266.2
Citrus fruit	69.8
Dried fruit	38.2
Packing house products	16.0
Butter	11.3
Salt	20.2
Vegetable oil	6.3
Sugar	836.5
Bar and sheet metal	16.3
Other metals	37.9
Metal castings	13.8
Automobiles	10.6
Paper	120.7
Canned goods	17.1
Merchandise	679.3
Miscellaneous	824.4

[35] Letter to directors, June 22, 1928, in Admiral Mss, Honnold Library.

A comparison of the cargo tonnage carried by other lines in 1923 shows the type of freight each company handled:[37]

Cargo	Admiral	LASSCO	"Big 3"
Manufactured products	589,610	94,409	41,377
Agricultural products	187,371	4,172	18,429
Forest products	100,054	241	1,695
Mineral products	37,051	75	8,231
Animal products	14,613	223	434
Total	928,699	99,120	70,166

There was a marked contrast between northbound and southbound cargoes. Cereals, canned goods, and lumber provided the greatest amount of freight going south. The northbound trade was composed principally of manufactured goods, fruits, vegetables, and petroleum products. The value of the goods exchanged had a wide range. During 1917, Seattle shipped $13,000,000 worth of goods to California ports but received from California $33,000,000 in various products. The reason for this discrepancy in money values lies in the types of goods offered by each section. The petroleum and manufactures of California were more expensive per unit than the lumber and grain products of the Northwest.[38]

Along the coastwise trade lanes, more tons of lumber

---

36 "Statistics" and "Recapitulations of Commodities Carried, 1928" in Admiral Mss, Honnold Library.

37 "Annual Report to Interstate Commerce Commission" (1923), p. 500 in Admiral Mss, Honnold Library; "Annual Report of the Los Angeles Steamship Company to the Railroad Commission of California for the Year Ending December 31, 1923," p. 500 in ASF; "Annual Report of the San Francisco and Portland Steamship Company to the Railroad Commission of California for the Year Ending December 31, 1923," p. 500 in ASF. LASSCO did not serve ports which shipped a great amount of products of the forests or mines.

38 Kenneth C. Kerr, "Seattle's Waterborne Commerce," Railway and Marine News, XVI (Feb. 1918), 16-17; Pacific Marine Review, XV (Oct. 1918), 68; Mears, Maritime Trade, pp. 251-52; various reports of the port authorities listed above.

were carried than of any other commodity. Each year the building industry of California consumed millions of feet of Douglas fir from the Northwest. It was estimated that during the first five months of 1922, more than a quarter of a billion feet of lumber was shipped to Los Angeles. The greatest amount of this lumber tonnage was carried by private or contract carriers. One company even transported lumber in giant log rafts which were towed in the open sea as far south as San Diego. In 1922, one of these rafts contained 5,000,000 feet of logs, 1,000,000 feet of cedar posts and telephone poles, and 300,000 feet of finished lumber. The 1,000-mile trip was made in twelve days and eleven hours. When the rafts arrived in San Diego, the owners made additional income by charging the curious public twenty-five cents to go aboard the cigar-shaped rafts. The reason why lumber did not represent a larger portion of the tonnage carried by the regular lines is to be found in the success of private carriers in transporting forest products. Private lines could send their vessels to the isolated coastal points where the lumber offerings were; public carriers could not follow the same policy because they had to maintain regular schedules.[39]

GOVERNMENTAL CONTROL

The feeling that the Secretary of Labor had prolonged the 1921 strike by his attempts to settle the problem through the unions was typical of the attitude of most operators toward the government. Along the Pacific Coast, the shipping industry pleaded to be "let alone." Regulation by government was abhorrent. In particular the operators objected to the La Follette Seamen's Act of 1915,

[39] *Railway and Marine News*, XX (June 1922), 17; *Pacific Marine Review*, XIX (Oct. 1922), 597; San Diego *Union*, Aug. 19, 1916.

which they described as an "iniquitous measure" that was "unfair, absurd and utterly inadequate" and was supposed "to throw the victim [the ship operator] into convulsions."[40] Three years later, in the midst of war, one spokesman for the operators advanced the unique thesis that Germany was the power behind the passage of "this most vicious piece of class legislation ever put through Congress."[41]

The purpose of the law was to raise the standard of living on American ships, to prevent mistreatment of sailors by owners or captains, and to provide additional life-saving equipment. The effect of the measure upon the coastwise trade was deplored: "In short, this legislation in so far as it increases operating expenses, decreases the competitive value of water carriers versus rail carriers." One source estimated that half a million dollars would be required to provide the additional equipment on the coastwise vessels.[42] It was stated that the law was not being enforced except on "the unfortunate ships operating in the U. S. coastwise trade, which were forced to go to tremendous expense to comply with the provisions," and that "beyond striking a blow at the American merchant marine, the Seamen's Bill during its first year of operation has accomplished nothing."[43] To the argument that the legislation would reduce sea tragedies, one magazine countered that the small steamer *Roanoke* had foundered

[40] *Railway and Marine News*, XIV (March 1916), 32, XIV (Dec. 1916), 8; *Pacific Marine Review*, XIII (Oct. 1916), 64.
[41] P. O. Knight, vice president of the American International Shipbuilding Company, was credited with this statement. *Railway and Marine News*, XVI (Nov. 1918), 19. For a good statement of the plea of the shipping industry to be "let alone" see "Legislation" (editorial), *Pacific Marine Review*, XIII (Oct. 1916), 64-65.
[42] *Railway and Marine News*, XIV (March 1916), 25. See also "The Seamen's Bill" (editorial), *Pacific Marine Review*, XII (April 1915), 52; *Railway and Marine News*, XIV (March 1916), 25; United States, *Statutes at Large*, XXXVIII (1915), 1164-85.
[43] *Railway and Marine News*, XV (Jan. 1917), 9.

in 1916 a short distance off the California coast, and that
all but three of her crew of fifty had perished: "Of course,
if we did not have the Seamen's Act the three survivors
would undoubtedly have been drowned also; but this, Mr.
La Follette and Mr. Furuseth, is small comfort."[44] The
Neptune Association added its voice to those opposing the
measure by claiming that captains no longer had sufficient
power to discharge their duties efficiently. That the provisions of the bill were seldom followed was generally
known. In 1931, Captain Robert Dollar wrote that President Wilson "wisely refused to enforce the law, and to this
day it has never been enforced."[45]

The reception given the measure by the seamen and
their friends was quite different. In a telegram to the
Sailors' Union of the Pacific in 1915, Robert M. La
Follette said, "As you meet to celebrate the thirtieth
anniversary of your organization I rejoice that in the
Providence of God I am permitted at last to hail you as
free men under the Constitution of our country." He
warned that except for the devotion of Andrew Furuseth
"to your cause for twenty-one years you would be bonds-
men instead of free men to-day."[46] Jubilantly the official
paper of the Sailors' Union observed, "The Seamen's Act
as such does not raise wages, but it does enable the
seamen to do so through their economic organizations."[47]
On August 2, 1917, Andrew Furuseth declared that the
seamen were loyally fighting for the American cause,
"largely because the United States passed the so-called
Seamen's Act and made the seaman a free man." After

[44] "Another Sea Tragedy" (editorial), *Pacific Marine Review*, XIII (June
1916), 56 in advertising section. A governmental investigation attributed
the loss of life to a heavy sea. A shift in the cargo had caused the ship
to founder in thirty minutes. *Annual Report* (1916), p. 21.
[45] The position of the Neptune Association was given in *Pacific Marine
Review*, XIX (March 1922), 196; Robert Dollar, *One Hundred Thirty
Years of Steam Navigation*, p. 120.
[46] Reprinted in *Pacific Marine Review*, XII (April 1915), 30.
[47] *Coast Seamen's Journal*, May 3, 1916.

quoting Furuseth, the *Pacific Marine Review* pointedly added, "We are very pleased, indeed, to learn that the seaman is so filled with patriotic fervor," but noted that no seaman had signed up in the auxiliary naval reserve though a recruitment office had been opened in San Francisco for the purpose.[48]

The Seamen's Bill was not the only governmental action to which the operators objected. In 1925, the operating manager of the Admiral Line listed some of the "foolish laws" which hampered the coastwise trade. Because Admiral ships stopped at Victoria, British Columbia, on their way from Seattle to California, one of the laws required the payment of pilotage fees. If the same ships continue southward from San Francisco, another required that all passengers and crew had to be mustered on deck for an inspection by quarantine officials. When an epidemic of infectious disease occurred in Los Angeles in 1924, all passengers on board ships had to be examined, but passengers on trains and busses were allowed to leave without an examination. The manager observed, "People leaving by train evidently could not spread the germs. . . ." A third regulation provided for an annual boiler test in which each boiler of a vessel was subjected to one and a half times the usual working pressure. Because of this rigid test, boilers were apt to develop leaks. The manager pointed out that the boilers of railroad locomotives or power houses were not subjected to a similar test. To sign on a crew for a trip from Seattle to California, a fourth law stated that a shipping commissioner had to witness the transaction. The Admiral official added, "If you employ men to run a train from San Francisco to Seattle you do not have to go through such contortions."[49] That these regulations were irritating can be appreciated

48 *Pacific Marine Review*, XIV (Sept. 1917), 55.
49 Hugh Gallagher, "Hampering Restrictions and Handicapping Laws," *Pacific Marine Review*, XXII (Jan. 1925), 32-34.

but it should be noted that, had the Admiral Line chosen to omit Victoria as a port of call, the laws requiring pilotage fees, quarantine inspection, and the use of shipping commissioners would not have applied.

In their arguments against governmental "interference," the owners pointed to the confusion which existed among the various bureaus which administered the maritime laws. Functions which the British combined in the Board of Trade were split in the American system among the Bureau of Navigation, Steamboat Inspection Service, Treasury Department, Bureau of Foreign and Domestic Commerce, Shipping Board, and other agencies. The results were not happy. One student of economics found that the reports issued by the various governmental agencies were "apparently contradictory, full of inaccuracies, and despite the excellent standing of the reporting organizations offer no sound basis of comparisons. To speak mildly, the whole situation becomes confusing."[50]

Inconsistencies within publications abound. In its *Port Series,* the Corps of Engineers of the War Department listed the Vaquero Line as offering two sailings per week between Los Angeles and San Diego but a later page claimed that the service was "irregular." In the same booklet, one page reported that the Charles R. McCormick Company carried only freight while a following page claimed that the company offered both a freight and passenger service.[51] In another issue, the number of coastwise lines operating out of Seattle varied from five to seven depending upon the page quoted.[52] In 1920, the

[50] Mears, *Maritime Trade,* p. 147; Alfred W. Dyer, "New Sea Code Wanted" in *Railway and Marine News,* XXIV (Dec. 1927), 5; *Pacific Marine Review,* XVI (Dec. 1919), 57-60.

[51] U. S., Department of War, *The Ports of Los Angeles, Long Beach, San Diego and San Luis Obispo, California,* Port Series No. 13 (1924), pp. 111, 114, 218.

[52] U. S., Department of War, *The Ports of Seattle, Tacoma, Bellingham, Everett, and Grays Harbor, Washington,* Port Series No. 7 (1932), pp. 174, 178.

Bureau of Navigation stated that the *Mary Winkelman* was owned by the Charles Nelson Company, but did not list her with the ships of that company which were given on a later page.[53]

In the case of the sinking of the *Roanoke,* one agency reported there were forty-five lost while another stated the number was forty-seven.[54] The inaccuracies contained in two pamphlets published, in 1923, by the Shipping Board made them in the judgment of one magazine, "only worthy of the waste basket." A year later, the same magazine decided, "Conflicting statements covering water-borne commerce should not be taken too seriously. It is not to be expected that the various bureaus getting out such tables will ever come together so that the net results will agree."[55]

From a political standpoint, the shipping industry was a foster child who felt at home in neither political party. One trade journal observed in 1916, "The Republican party did nothing and under that administration we were practically unknown upon the sea, but the present Democratic administration has made matters worse. . . ."[56] A year later, Captain Robert Dollar told a Pittsburgh audience, "The Republicans did their worst to hurt the American Merchant Marine, and the Democrats were only more successful because they were better at figuring." In 1920, he repeated his charges to the Seventh National Foreign Trade Convention in San Francisco by saying, "The Republicans went to work to legislate the merchant marine off the ocean and they came near doing it, but

53 U. S., Bureau of Navigation, *Annual List of Merchant Vessels* (1920), Part VI, pp. 26, 118.

54 *Annual Report* (1916), p. 21; U. S., Bureau of Navigation, *List of Merchant Vessels* (1916), p. 420. Similarly the reported number of lives lost when the *San Juan* sank in 1929, varies from seventy-one to seventy-five. Cf. *ibid.* (1930), p. 917; *Annual Report* (1930), p. 15.

55 *Railway and Marine News,* XXI (Aug. 1923), 17; "Why Worry" in *ibid.,* XXII (March 1924), 16.

56 *Pacific Marine Review,* XIII (Feb. 1916), 28.

they did not quite manage it; but the Democrats got in, and am blessed if they didn't finish the job."[57]

To improve their political power became a goal of the industry. One operator pleaded, "If there was one practical shipping man in Congress, either in the House or Senate, we might get a hearing."[58] The fact that the English Parliament had a large number of members who were engaged in shipping was held up as a major reason for British maritime success. It was urged that "shipping men should be the first consideration of Pacific ports and Pacific districts when it is a question of elections."[59] That there was some basis for the distrust of Congress is clear. In 1919, a bill was proposed in Congress which would have required passenger ships to carry a duly qualified embalmer to eliminate burials at sea. The remains of a passenger or crew member were to be embalmed provided a port could not be reached within twenty-four hours. Since the trip from Seattle to San Francisco took between thirty-eight to sixty-five hours, the companies operating between those two points would have to assume the added expense of providing an embalmer on each ship. Fortunately for the shipping industry, the bill died.[60]

In view of their hostile attitude toward most governmental action, the appeals made by the owners for governmental assistance in some areas seemed a little inconsistent. The Pacific American Steamship Association in 1920 asked President Wilson to transfer the activities of the Coast Guard to the Department of the Navy in order that the many naval vessels along the Pacific Coast could

[57] Both speeches appear in Robert Dollar, *Memoirs* (2d ed.; 1922), II, 6, 50.

[58] Hugh Gallagher, "Hampering Restrictions and Handicapping Laws," *Pacific Marine Review*, XXII (Jan. 1925), 33.

[59] "Shipping Men in Congress" (editorial), *Railway and Marine News*, XXIV (June 1927), 12.

[60] *Pacific Marine Review*, XVI (Sept. 1919), 89; U. S., Congress, *Congressional Record*, 66th Cong., 1st sess., pp. 3702, 3976.

be used as patrol craft. The telegram declared, "The
season of winter gales is rapidly approaching and only
the president can effect the transfer . . . in time to meet
the present grave emergency. . . . It is inconceivable . . .
that the government would leave its enormous merchant
marine . . . with practically no protection."[61] Pleas were
made for the government to increase the appropriations
for the Coast and Geodetic Survey, to install automatic
radio fog signals from Cape Flattery to the Mexican
border, and to render "aid for a sensible scrapping and
building program."[62] The Admiral Line in 1920 proposed
that the Shipping Board build a $6,000,000 ocean terminal
at Seattle and then sell the project to it on favorable
terms.[63] The Los Angeles *Times* with its close connection
with LASSCO joined the chorus for more governmental
control by observing in 1932, "It is the manifest duty of
the [California Railroad] Commission to employ without
hesitation their regulatory powers and especially to protect
established carriers and shippers who have suffered from
rate cutting by the free lancers of the road."[64]

The use of public funds to provide docks and other
harbor facilities was urged. Although most of this money
was provided by the various ports, the shipping industry
felt that the cost should be borne by all sections of the
country. In commenting on the statement that only six
states had issued bonds for maritime purposes, the official
organ of the Shipowners Association of the Pacific Coast
said, "Such a policy does not appear to be wise, for the
people of an entire state or of an entire section of the
country, for that matter, derive direct benefit from good

[61] Quoted in Portland *Oregonian*, Sept. 29, 1920. See also *Pacific Marine
Review*, XIII (Feb. 1916), 26.

[62] "Give the Coast Survey a Chance" (editorial), *Pacific Marine Review*,
XVI (Jan. 1919), 83-85, XIX (Jan. 1922), 68-69, XX (Oct. 1923), 482; "This
Fog Must Be Cleared" (editorial), *ibid.*, XXXII (March 1935), 65.

[63] Portland *Oregonian*, Oct. 18, 1920.

[64] "Unfair Competition" (editorial), Los Angeles *Times*, Jan. 2, 1932.

harbors, and the burden should be distributed equitably."[65] Public ownership of docks, which was opposed in 1916, was applauded in 1927. The success of public agencies in providing terminal facilities explains, in part, this changed attitude.[66] Following the opening of the Panama Canal in 1914, Portland voted a bond issue of $1,000,000 to provide bonuses for steamship lines. In 1924, Long Beach approved an expenditure of $5,000,000 for harbor improvements. In a ten year period ending in 1926, it was estimated that Los Angeles had expended more than twenty-two million dollars on its port. The shipping industry welcomed financial help from governmental divisions provided such help did not compromise its freedom of action.[67]

Under a federal law which excluded foreign vessels from the coastwise trade, companies operating domestic lines were protected from foreign competition. In 1925, H. F. Alexander admitted, "It is the one outstanding law that has been helpful and beneficial to American shipping."[68] There were attempts to change this protective measure, but any proposed modification was labeled by the shipowners as a "great injustice." The operators claimed that they had made investments "in good faith, relying upon the protection which has always been afforded them by our Government in reserving for them the exclusive enjoyment of coastwise domestic trade."[69] Be-

[65] "State Aid for Harbors" (editorial), *Pacific Marine Review*, XIX (Nov. 1922), 605.

[66] Cf. "Failure of Seattle's Public Docks Analyzed," *Railway and Marine News*, XIV (Jan. 1916), 27-28, XXIV (May 1927), 9; *Pacific Marine Review*, XXIV (Feb. 1927), 59.

[67] *Pacific Marine Review*, XVIII (Jan. 1921), 61, XXI (June 1924), 32 in advertising section; *Railway and Marine News*, XXIII (July 1926), 9.

[68] H. F. Alexander, "Shipping Development on the Pacific Coast," *Pacific Marine Review*, XXII (Jan. 1925), 32; U. S., Congress, *Annals of the Congress of the United States*, 2d Cong., pp. 1397-1411.

[69] *Pacific Marine Review*, XIII (Dec. 1916), 83. For other comments in a similar vein see: "Coastwise Shipping Attacked" (editorial), *ibid.*, XII

cause of the exigencies of the World War I, Congress in 1917 authorized the President to suspend temporarily the provisions of the law and in October of that year the coastwise trade was opened to vessels of foreign registry. The purpose of this action was to replace American tonnage which had been withdrawn for overseas service and to eliminate the necessity of foreign ships moving between United States ports empty or only partly laden.[70]

This temporary modification of the traditional coastwise law was followed in 1920 by a permanent change. Under the provisions of the Merchant Marine Act of 1920, foreign-built vessels were permitted to operate coastwise provided they were of American registry and were owned on February 1, 1920, by United States citizens. Previous to this time, only ships built in the United States could be used in the coastwise trade. For a corporation to be considered American, 75 percent of the stock had to be controlled by American citizens.[71] If for any reason the interest owned by Americans in a company should fall below 75 percent, the corporation would automatically cease to be eligible to operate in the domestic trade. Some saw a danger to property rights in this provision. Since the stock of most corporations "passes from hand to hand with almost the same freedom as money," one writer warned, "any coastwise steamship company can be wrecked, innocently by its stockholders, fraudulently by its competitors; and at a cost which may be only nominal and can rarely exceed approximately a quarter of the value of the assets." The writer decided that the provision "will apparently deprive such corporations of their property

(Jan. 1916), 52; "The Shipping Bill," *Railway and Marine News*, XIV (Sept. 1916), 10.

70 San Diego *Union*, Oct. 25, 1917; *Railway and Marine News*, XV (Nov. 1917), 27; U. S. Shipping Board, *Annual Report* (1918), p. 40.

71 *Pacific Marine Review*, XVII (July 1920), 64, XVII (Aug. 1920), 55, XVIII (Sept. 1921), 546.

without due process of law. It therefore seems clear that
the section is in conflict with the Fifth Amendment and
hence unconstitutional."[72] As far as the West Coast companies were concerned, no such dire consequences developed.

For these slight modifications of the traditional coastwise
policy, the operators blamed the influence of foreign na-
tions. When the 1917 amendment to the law was under
discussion, one magazine claimed, "Foreign interests are
not above seeking an unfair commercial advantage over
American shipowners, even in these stressful times when
the common good should be the only consideration of all
the countries opposed to German autocracy."[73] This anti-
foreign complex was an expedient rather than a funda-
mental feeling. When a Canadian shipyard offered the
lowest bid for repairing a vessel, the Admiral Line readily
awarded the contract to the foreign concern although
several American yards were anxious to do the work.[74]
The McCormick Steamship Company willingly served as
the California agent for a Canadian company, even though
that company was in competition with American lines on
the route between California and British Columbia.[75]

Between these two opposing desires—the desire for lais-
sez faire and the desire for governmental protection—lay
the true relationship of the steamship lines with the
government. The government actually exercised little
positive control over the industry. The Interstate Commerce Commission was never given the authority to
regulate water rates except on through connections between rail and water carriers.[76] Unlike the railroads,

[72] Harold M. Sawyer, "Corporation Citizenship. An Analysis of Section
38 of the Jones Bill," *Pacific Marine Review*, XVII (Oct. 1920), 60.
[73] *Ibid.*, XIV (Oct. 1917), 56 in advertising section.
[74] *Ibid.*, XIX (Feb. 1922), 138.
[75] *Ibid.*, XXII (March 1925), 27 in advertising section.
[76] U. S., Senate, *Report of the Federal Coordinator*, 73d Cong., 2d sess.,
S. Doc. 152, p. 8.

steamship companies could begin operations without obtaining a certificate of public convenience and necessity.[77] When in 1919, a bill was proposed in Congress to place coastwise shipping under the control of the Interstate Commerce Commission, the move was opposed by shipping circles. One magazine claimed that the action was "being pushed by the railroads for the purpose of eliminating water competition in the coastwise trade." It maintained that the steamship lines would be placed in "the same identical and unbearable position" which confronted the railroads. "Why utterly destroy the savior of the nation in the war emergency for the benefit of the railroads?"[78] The shipping industry was successful in preventing the proposal from becoming a law.

The lack of federal control was in contrast to the situation in the California intrastate trade. As the result of the Wilmington Case in 1915, the Railroad Commission of California had assumed jurisdiction over the water carriers serving California ports. For a number of years, the control exercised by this body was slight. But in 1932, Ralph J. Chandler, general manager of LASSCO, appeared before the Commission and urged that it prescribe minimum rates, require a certificate of public convenience and necessity, and suppress "wild cat" operators. The other major lines supported this stand.[79]

After further consideration, the commission followed these suggestions.[80] The changed attitude toward govern-

[77] Decisions, CIX (1926), 537. California and Oregon exempted the steamship lines from paying certain types of taxes. Ray Dunett, "Taxation of Vessels," Railway and Marine News, XXVII (May 1930), 12-13, 23. See also Pacific Marine Review, XXIX (April 1922), 264.
[78] "Coastwise Shipping Threatened," Railway and Marine News, XVII (Nov. 1919), 18.
[79] Wilmington Transportation Company v. California Railroad Commission, 236 U. S. 151; California, Railroad Commission, Report (1916), pp. 52-53, 279; Case Number 3154, "Reporter's Transcript" (typed), III, 333-335 in ASF.
[80] California, Railroad Commission, Decisions, XXXIX, 222-29.

mental control was further confirmed in 1933 by a poll of
Pacific coastwise lines, which showed all in favor of more
regulation. The Interstate Commerce Commission observed that the demoralization of the water carrier industry
during the depression years, 1929-1933, had "caused many
in the industry to change their former attitude of opposition to one of willingness to accept or even to seek
effective public regulation."[81]

As far as the Pacific Coast companies were concerned,
the steps taken by federal and state agencies to put into
effect these recommendations were useless. The lines were
already too deep in debt by 1933 for governmental salvation. They had asked to be "let alone" and for a while
they were amazingly successful in obtaining the freedom
they claimed to wish. The realization that this very freedom may have produced its own problems came too late
to repair the damage.

[81] U. S., Senate, *Report of the Federal Coordinator*, 73d Cong., 2d sess.,
S. Doc. 152, pp. 10-12, 169.

SIX

The Crest of Prosperity, 1925-1929

ADMIRAL REFINANCES ITSELF

To MEET the challenge of potential competitors, the Admiral Line early in 1925 took three steps to place itself in a firmer position. On the first day of January it mortgaged, for $5,000,000, its entire fleet of fourteen steamships, four motorships, one tug, and two barges. When the mortgage bonds were offered on the investment market, the prestige of the Admiral Line was sufficient to cause the amount to be over-subscribed. Under the terms of the mortgage, the bonds were to be retired in twenty sharply increasing annual payments. By 1943, the payments were to be more than three times the initial one.[1] In view of later commercial developments, the wisdom of arranging the payments in order to leave the major portion of the debt to be paid last could be seriously questioned. But in 1925, the feeling pervaded business circles that the prosperity of the country was just beginning to climb. The mortgage allowed the Admiral Line to obtain a release from the 1918 debt due the Pacific Coast Company for its fleet. The last tie between the Pacific Coast Company and Pacific coastwise shipping was thereby severed.[2]

The second step was taken on February 1, 1925, when the Admiral Line authorized the issuance of $5,000,000 in preferred stock at 7 percent interest. Only $2,250,000 was actually issued. Most of the new stock was purchased by a syndicate of bankers and corporations although a block was reserved for the employees of the company.[3]

The third major move was the dedication of the first unit of the Pacific Steamship Terminals in Seattle on April 7, 1925. Two years before, the Admiral Line had purchased twenty-five acres of terminal land to be developed along the lines of the Bush Terminal in New York. In 1924, the Admiral Line organized the Pacific Steamship Terminal Company to finance the project, which was expected to cost four or five million dollars. When completed, the terminals were to include three ocean piers, each over a thousand feet long, a five-story office building, a chapel for stevedores, and numerous warehouses. The first unit, which consisted of one pier, the chapel, and office building, was dedicated with "cheering thousands on the great pier and three bands playing America. . . . It was one of the greatest days in all the history of the waterfront. . . . As the band on the dockhouse struck up America, the vast crowd on the pier for a moment was silent and then burst into a might[y] cheer." At the same time, the *H. F. Alexander*, "a riot of color with a great maze of serpentine paper floating from her boatdeck," backed into Elliott Bay and turned her bow "toward the setting sun" to begin her regular run to California. The new office building was shared by the Admiral Line, the Dollar Steamship Company, and the Admiral Oriental Line.[4]

[1] Mortgage dated Jan. 1, 1925, in Admiral Mss, Honnold Library.

[2] Release dated Feb. 9, 1925, in Admiral Mss, Honnold Library.

[3] Portland *Oregon Journal*, March 2, 1925; "Stock Book" in Admiral Mss, Honnold Library; Minutes of Board Meeting dated Jan. 21, 1925 in Robert Dollar Company Archives.

[4] Seattle *Times*, April 8, 1925; "Statistics" in Admiral Mss, Honnold Library. For detailed plans and pictures of terminals see *Marine Digest*, III (April 4, 1925), 5; *Railway and Marine News*, XXIII (March 1925), 29, XXIII (April 1925), 10-11; *Pacific Marine Review*, XX (Oct. 1923), 489, XXII (May 1925), 13 in advertising section, XXII (June 1925), 265.

These three steps, which required the raising of a total of almost nine million dollars, were looked upon as another triumph in the career of H. F. Alexander. Shipping circles agreed that the financial moves placed the Admiral Line "in the most powerful position it had occupied since its organization."[5] In an editorial, the Seattle *Times* referred to the refinancing as the "outstanding event of the year in Puget Sound shipping circles" and predicted, "In due time . . . the fleet will have new units, even finer than the palatial vessels now operated. The possibility that the Admiral Line eventually will be extended to the East Coast of the United States cannot be ignored. Under the guidance of Mr. Alexander the Admiral Line ships will fulfill a brilliant destiny." The public was also reminded that the career of H. F. Alexander "illustrates the possibilities open to American boys."[6] In the same year, H. F. Alexander became president of the Olympic Steamship Company, which operated a tanker between California and Puget Sound. Other stockholders in this venture were R. Stanley Dollar and Herbert Fleishhacker.[7] In July 1925, H. F. Alexander reported to the directors of his company that for the "first time in ten years we have been able to issue a statement without any bank loans."[8]

Summer revenues, always larger than the other seasons, hit new highs in 1926. In January 1927 H. F. Alexander predicted that 1927 would show a half-million dollar improvement over the previous year. About a quarter of a million dollars was to be saved by a variety of measures, including the elimination of lighterage, expiration of use-

[5] Seattle *Times*, Feb. 18, 1925.

[6] "Achievement" (editorial), *ibid.*, Feb. 18, 1925.

[7] "Business Papers" in Olympic Steamship Company Mss, Honnold Library. See also: *Pacific Marine Review*, XXII (Aug. 1925), 374; *Los Angeles Times*, Oct. 11, 1925; *Railway and Marine News*, XXIII (Dec. 14, 1925), 9.

[8] Letter to directors, July 17, 1926, in Admiral Mss, Honnold Library.

less dock leases, and reduction in fuel oil costs. Alexander also anticipated substantial profits from an interchange agreement with the Southern Pacific Railroad Company, from additional passenger patronage due to reduced charges for carrying automobiles, and from fare increases for round-trip tickets and de luxe accommodations.[9] The annual report of the Admiral Line for 1926 showed that the number of passengers carried was 113,714, an increase of about four thousand. The total tonnage of the fleet had risen to 974,000 tons, which represented an increase of 28,000 tons.[10]

Expansion continued. On March 30, 1927, the Portland California Steamship Company, a wholly owned subsidiary of the Pacific Steamship Company, was incorporated for the purpose of purchasing the *Mary Weems* and the *Esther Weems,* two ships of the Baltimore and Caroline Steamship Company. The ships were brought to the West Coast and rechristened the *Admiral Peoples* and *Admiral Benson.* Each of the two ships could accommodate 200 passengers. One was named in honor of Rear Admiral Christian J. Peoples, general inspector of all Naval Supply Corps activities on the West Coast. The other honored Rear Admiral William S. Benson (retired), a commissioner and former chairman of the United States Shipping Board. The policy of renaming ships after influential men had definite advantages from the standpoint of public relations, a fact not overlooked by the marine transportation industry. With these additions, the Admiral Line had a fleet of twenty-eight vessels.[11]

In spite of the outward signs of prosperity and the

[9] Letter from H. F. Alexander to Executive Committee, Jan. 27, 1927 in Admiral Mss, Honnold Library.

[10] *Railway and Marine News,* XXIV (Jan. 1927), 15; "Annual Report" in Admiral Mss, Honnold Library.

[11] San Francisco *Chronicle,* April 1, 1927; *Railway and Marine News,* XXIV (March 1927), 19; *Pacific Marine Review* XXIV (May 1927), 238; *Marine Digest,* V (March 26, 1927) 3, V (April 30, 1927), 7.

public assumption of success, the Alexander company was not riding the crest of prosperity. The refinancing did not prevent the company from losing $230,681 in 1925, although the next year a small profit of $4,088 was realized. The net income for the first nine months of 1927 decreased $214,657 over the previous period for 1926. There were several reasons for this 1927 reversal. In 1926, both the *H. F. Alexander* and *Dorothy Alexander* had been operating on the Atlantic Coast during the winter months at a profit. Between January and March 1925 the *H. F. Alexander* earned $183,833 while plying between New York and Miami. For the same period, the *Dorothy Alexander* earned $41,083 in charter money. In the winter of 1927 both ships were laid up. The net loss in revenue was almost $225,000.[12]

Another factor was the poor Alaska season. Since its inception, the Admiral Line had continued to serve Alaskan ports; but the competition of the Alaska Steamship Company deprived the Admiral Line of the commanding position in that particular trade, despite its leadership in Puget Sound to San Diego trade. During the summer of 1927, there was an unusually small salmon catch, which drastically reduced the amount of freight offerings. In addition, the *Admiral Watson* stranded on Ivory Island in July. This mishap deprived the company of the earnings of one trip. The results were that freight revenues in August of 1927 were $138,800 less than the previous August.[13]

Even before the discouraging Alaska season was felt, the company had tried to strengthen its sagging position. In May 1927 H. F. Alexander announced that R. Stanley Dollar was "in active charge of the operations of the company with the sole object of reducing expenses both

[12] "Financial Statement" and letter to directors, July 11, 1927, in Admiral Mss, Honnold Library.
[13] Letter to directors, Oct. 12, 1927 in Admiral Mss, Honnold Library.

operating and overhead." By November reductions in the
expenses of the operating department at Seattle were made
which would save approximately seventy-five thousand dollars per year. At the same time, the overhead expenses
of the entire company were reduced in one month by
$18,227. If that rate were maintained, a saving of $218,724
could be made in a year. Giving credit where it was due,
H. F. Alexander wrote to the directors in December of
1927, "These reductions in operating expenses of the
vessels and the reduction in overhead expense can be
attributed to the close personal attention which Mr. R.
Stanley Dollar is giving the business, and we are indebted
to him for this excellent showing." The Dollar economy
drive produced results, but was not sufficient to overcome
the factors of a poor Alaska season and the loss of other
revenues. In 1927 the company suffered a deficit of
$279,213.[14]

Fortunately for the stockholders of the Admiral Line,
there were signs of a recovery. For the first half of 1928,
overhead expenses declined $71,959, while gross earnings
rose $74,187. To increase further the optimism of its
officers, the Admiral Line was awarded in 1928 the contract
to transport between 36,000 and 60,000 tons of newsprint
a year from Ocean Falls, British Columbia, to San Francisco and southern California. This contract, one of the
largest on the coast, formerly had been held by the
Canadian National Steamship, Ltd., which withdrew from
the American coastwise service when it sold its freighters,
Canadian Observer, *Canadian Coaster*, and *Canadian
Rover* to the Kingsley Navigation Company. The Admiral
Line added the freighters *Admiral Fiske* and *Admiral
Moser* to the route between Puget Sound and California
to take care of the increased business due to the contract.

[14] Letters to directors, May 14, Nov. 17, and Dec. 10, 1927, and "Financial Statement" in Admiral Mss, Honnold Library.

On July 21, 1928, H. F. Alexander reported that all the Admiral ships were in service except the *Admiral Rodman,* which was scheduled to enter the Alaskan trade within a week. Eight ships were on the route between Seattle and California, five on the one between Portland and California, and seven on the Alaskan route. H. F. Alexander concluded, "This is better service than we have given for some time and at the present time all are operating at a profit."[15]

In August 1928 the company experienced the largest net income that it had "earned in any one month since its organization." The ledger books for the first eight months of 1928 showed a net income of almost three hundred thousand dollars, as compared to a loss of over twenty thousand dollars for the similar period in 1927. As a result of these favorable developments, the Admiral Line earned about $140,000 for 1928, but it proved to be the last year that the Admiral Line made a profit.[16] In 1929, the trustees of the $5,000,000 mortgage agreed to substitute the *Admiral Chase* for the motorships *Dawnlite, Daylite,* and *Sunlite.* This concession allowed the Admiral Line to sell the motorships and "buy a second freighter, a sister ship of the *Admiral Chase,* which would give us an additional substantial earning unit in lieu of the three lite boats that have been a source of constant expense and without earning power." H. F. Alexander estimated that the new ship would carry twice the cargo of one of the "lite" ships at about the same cost.[17]

15 Letter to directors, July 21, 1928, in Admiral Mss, Honnold Library; *Railway and Marine News,* XXV (May 1928), 29, XXV (July 1928), 26; Los Angeles *Times,* Oct. 3, 1929.

16 "Financial Statement" in Admiral Mss, Honnold Library.

17 Letter to Executive Committee, Sept. 20, 1929, in Admiral Mss, Honnold Library; *Pacific Marine Review,* XIX (June 1922), 384; "Annual Reports" and letter to directors, Sept. 22, 1928, in Admiral Mss, Honnold Library.

THE *NEWPORT* RATE WAR OF 1925

Rate wars were not uncommon along the coast; that caused by the *Newport* was typical. In 1925 a veteran ship of the old Pacific Mail Steamship Company appeared on the coastwise sea lanes in the new role of a "rate cutter." The men behind this move had been associated with the ill-fated New Electra Line. The new venture, which was called the Los Angeles Dispatch Line, purchased the *Newport* from the Pacific Mail Steamship Company for $50,925. With the motto, "Steady as a Battle Ship—Punctual as the Sun," the Los Angeles Dispatch Line offered passenger and freight service between San Francisco and Los Angeles at lower charges than the regular lines. The maiden voyage of the *Newport* from San Francisco occurred on January 9, 1925, but she started one hour and ten minutes late which did little to inspire confidence that she would be "Punctual as the Sun." The running time of slightly under forty hours allowed the new line to offer a departure from each port every four days. When she arrived in Los Angeles Harbor, the *Newport* was greeted by civic officials as filling a gap in the coastwise trade. One-way fares on the *Newport* started as low as $9 whereas the cheapest ticket on the *Harvard* or *Yale* was $17. In both cases meals and berth were included in the fares. During the existence of this rival, the other companies usually omitted in their advertisements any references to fares and concentrated on extolling the quality of the service offered.[18]

The new company was less than four months old when

18 "Annual Report of the Los Angeles Dispatch Line of San Francisco to the Railroad Commission of California for the Year Ending December 31, 1925," p. 12 in ASF; Los Angeles *Times*, Jan. 11, Dec. 2, 1925; San Francisco *Chronicle*, Jan. 9, 10, Feb. 16, 1925; *Pacific Marine Review*, XXII (March 1925), 13 in advertising section; *LASSCO Sailing Schedule*, 1925, LASSCO Mss. Maritime collection of John H. Kemble, Claremont, Calif.

it caused a furore among the established steamship lines. In April 1925 it sued them for conspiring to drive it out of business by the use of unfair methods. At the trial, which was held in San Francisco, the Los Angeles Dispatch Line claimed that the other companies had combined against it, had received by stealth its lists of customers, and had carried on an illegal campaign to prevent shippers from patronizing the *Newport*. After three days of testimony, the court ruled that there was no evidence to support the charge that information had been corruptly acquired by the defendants. Damages were denied. The judge, however, held that the defendant companies had engaged in unfair practices by copying the manifests and other documents of the Los Angeles Dispatch Line. He granted an injunction to prevent, in the future, the competitors of the new firm from obtaining the records of shipments on the *Newport*.[19]

The war between the *Newport* and the established lines continued unabated into the usually profitable summer season. Whether because of this fact or of the general prosperity of the country at large, the passenger business boomed. The patronage between Portland and San Francisco was declared by the steamship lines to be the heaviest in their history. The Admiral Line reported that traffic between Los Angeles and other coastwise ports was greater than any previous summer. Almost every ship was reported sailing with full passenger lists. Within a ten-week period, the Admiral Line carried approximately thirty-five thousand travelers. When she sailed from Los Angeles on July 24, 1925, the *H. F. Alexander* carried the largest number of passengers that had left Los Angeles on any coastwise ship in regular service. Lassco estimated that during 1925 it had carried 70,900 persons in and out of San Francisco.

19 The five defendants were: Admiral, McCormick, Nelson, Lassco, and White Flyer lines. San Francisco *Chronicle*, May 1, 1925; Portland *Oregon Journal*, May 1, 1925.

To improve its service further, LASSCO inaugurated, on September 1, 1925, a twenty-four hour store-door pick-up and delivery service between Los Angeles and San Francisco, which was believed to be the fastest freight service over the same distance anywhere in the world. The McCormick line kept pace with these developments by instituting a weekly passenger service between Seattle and California in addition to its Portland route. By the summer of 1925, the McCormick Steamship Company claimed that it operated the largest fleet in the coastwise sea lanes.[20]

The lower rates of the Los Angeles Dispatch Line were felt more keenly when the boom in maritime business hit the usual autumn and winter slump. For eleven months, the other steamship lines had not cut rates to meet the competition of the *Newport,* but on November 2, 1925, the McCormick line announced a 10 to 30 percent reduction, meeting the rates offered on the *Newport.* On the same day, the White Flyer Line took similar action. Shipping circles generally felt that the water rates were as low as the companies could stand and feared the outcome of the struggle. The next week, the Admiral Line joined the rate-cutting and the Nelson Steamship Company followed on December 6, 1925. Two days later, LASSCO, the last of the major lines, announced it would meet the lower rates being offered by its rivals.[21] In the midst of the confusion which it had caused, the Los Angeles Dispatch Line intimated in December that it was considering adding another combination steamer to run opposite the *Newport.* That the new line had met with

[20] Portland *Oregonian,* July 30, 1925; Los Angeles *Times,* July 25, Sept. 1, Oct. 21, 1925; "California's De Luxe Ocean Ferry," *Pacific Marine Review,* XXII (July 1926), 308; "24-Hour Service from Store Door to Store Door," *ibid.,* XXII (Oct. 1925), 17 in advertising section, XXII (July 1925), 14 in advertising section; *Railway and Marine News,* XXIII (April 1925), 18; "Statistics Working Papers, December 1926" in Admiral Mss, Honnold Library.

[21] Los Angeles *Times,* Oct. 8, Dec. 13, 1925; California Railroad Commission, *Decisions,* XXVIII, 671-75.

some success was apparent. By the end of 1925, its single ship had carried 9,165 passengers and 30,970 tons of freight. The company had attracted from its rivals almost a quarter of a million dollars in gross revenues.[22]

But the *Newport* rate war was soon to end. Although it was taking business away from the other lines, the Los Angeles Dispatch Line was not earning money. In May 1926 the McCormick company announced that it had chartered the *Newport* and would place her on the route between Portland and California, where she would operate opposite the *Rose City*. The McCormick line could thus offer weekly in place of fortnightly sailings.[23] After the collapse of the Los Angeles Dispatch Line, the five remaining lines soon requested permission of the Railroad Commission of California to increase rates to their former levels. They frankly admitted that the lower rates had been established in the fall of 1925 to meet the competition of the Los Angeles Dispatch Line but that the expected increase in revenues and tonnage had not materialized. The petitioners claimed that for the first five months in 1926, the following losses were suffered: Admiral Line, $169,728; LASSCO, $14,708; McCormick, $17,067; White Flyer Line, $9,516. In view of the circumstances, the Railroad Commission granted their request and the lines raised their rates to levels which existed prior to the entry of the *Newport* into the coastwise trade. During its brief existence, the Los Angeles Dispatch Line sustained an operating loss of $65,000.[24]

In addition to restoring rates to previous levels, the steamship lines discontinued another technique which had

22 "Annual Report of the Los Angeles Dispatch Line of San Francisco to the Railroad Commission of California for the Year Ending December 31, 1925," p. 16 in ASF; Los Angeles *Times*, Dec. 2, 10, 1925.

23 Portland *Oregonian*, May 29, 1926; Los Angeles *Times*, May 29, June 18, 1926; *Railway and Marine News*, XXIII (June 1926), 21.

24 California Railroad Commission, *Report* (1927), pp. 78-79; Los Angeles *Times*, Aug. 10, 1926.

developed in the fight against the *Newport*. This was the so-called Red Ball freight service which provided an extra speedy store-door delivery. In the winter of 1926 four of the six companies published Red Ball rates. By the following year, only Nelson and LASSCO were offering the special handling and both of these were operating the service at a loss. As a result, permission was obtained from the Railroad Commission to discontinue the Red Ball rates.[25]

The McCormick line strengthened its position by the absorption of the business formerly carried by the Los Angeles Dispatch Line. The weekly schedule of the *Rose City* and *Newport* increased the number of travelers sailing under the McCormick flag. But the McCormick Steamship Company did not confine its expansion to the coastwise trade. Within a period of a few months, it purchased the Pacific-Argentine-Brazil Line from the Shipping Board, started a weekly intercoastal service known as the Munson-McCormick Line, established a Pacific-Havana-Jacksonville service, and inaugurated sailings between the West Coast and the Caribbean Sea.[26]

STRUGGLE FOR SURVIVAL

The *Newport* rate war had forced the established steamship lines to work together against a common rival. When the danger was over, some cooperation continued. The most notable instance was the interchange agreement between LASSCO and the Admiral Line by which each firm honored the tickets of the other on their ships between San Diego, Los Angeles, and San Francisco. Under this agreement a passenger could use the same ticket on the *Harvard, Yale, H. F. Alexander, Emma, Ruth,* or other

25 California, Railroad Commission, *Decisions*, XXIX, 793-96.
26 Los Angeles *Times*, Aug. 13, 1926; *Railway and Marine News*, XXIII (Feb. 15, 1926), 12, XXIII (March 15, 1926), 13.

Admiral ships. The interchange arrangement provided practically a daily service between California points.[27] One of the reasons why the Admiral Line was willing to cooperate with LASSCO in the California trade was the stiff competition it was facing on the routes to the Northwest in which LASSCO had no part.

In order to attract patronage during the 1927-1928 winter season, the Admiral Line made sweeping reductions in its passenger fares. In the California trade, LASSCO made comparable cuts which provided a $4 saving on a one-way ticket between San Francisco and Los Angeles and a $5 saving on a ticket between San Francisco and San Diego.[28] The McCormick line was quick to follow the trend and announced reductions up to 25 percent on all fares on the *Rose City* and *Newport*. Publicly, the McCormick Steamship Company stated that the reductions had brought a 50 percent increase in passenger travel, although it implied that a contributing factor was the education of travelers to the "conveniences, punctuality and safety" of its water transportation.[29] Actually, however, the operations of the *Rose City* and *Newport* were not proving to be satisfactory. By the end of 1927 the *Newport* was returned to its owners and the *Rose City* was withdrawn from service. The *Newport* sailed from Portland for the last time on December 31, 1927.

By withdrawing the *Rose City* and *Newport,* the McCormick Steamship Company did not discontinue its coastwise passenger service. It concentrated instead on offering cheaper, if slower, transportation in connection with its freighters. In March 1928 the *Wabama* and *Celilo,*

27 *California Coast Sailings* (advertising folder of LASSCO) dated Dec. 5, 1932, LASSCO Mss, Maritime collection of John H. Kemble, Claremont, Calif.; *Railway and Marine News,* XXIV (May 1927), 25-26; San Francisco *Chronicle,* Feb. 5, 1930.

28 Los Angeles *Times,* Sept. 16, Oct. 23, 24, 1927; *Marine Digest,* VI (Oct. 1, 1927), 11.

29 Los Angeles *Times,* Nov. 4, 1927.

which could carry a limited number of passengers, were placed on a new schedule between the Puget Sound and California, providing a sailing every week. Passengers boarded the McCormick ship at Tacoma on Thursday afternoon and arrived at San Francisco the following Monday. Travelers from Seattle were taken to Tacoma on the 1:00 P.M. ferry. In contrast to the thirty-nine hour schedule maintained by the *H. F. Alexander,* these McCormick ships took over ninety hours for the journey. McCormick also provided service to fourteen coastwise points with the thirty vessels in its coastwise fleet.[30]

During the *Newport* rate war there were recurring rumors that the White Flyer Line was planning to build a new passenger and freight steamer at the cost of about one million dollars. No definite confirmation or denial came from the company until December 9, 1925, when it announced the purchase of the veteran steamer *San Juan* from the Panama Mail Steamship Company. At the time, the company denied rumors that it either planned to build a vessel or enter the Hawaiian trade. The *San Juan* was placed opposite the *Humboldt* on the route between San Francisco and Los Angeles. The White Flyer Line, as a result of this acquisition, began to offer sailings three times per week in place of the former schedule of one every four days.[31]

Since its inception in 1919, the White Flyer Line had been owned by several groups of people. By 1923, the control had passed to the firm of James K. Nelson, Inc., of San Francisco, which also controlled the Santa Cruz and Monterey Steamship Company. This latter company, organized in 1921, had purchased the little 521-ton steamer

---

[30] *Marine Digest,* VI (March 24, 1928), 3; *Railway and Marine News,* XXV (Feb. 1928), 1.

[31] Los Angeles *Times,* Nov. 6, Dec. 10, 17, 1925; *Pacific Marine Review,* XXII (Dec. 1925), 17 in advertising section, XXIII (Jan. 1926), 30; Los Angeles *Times,* Jan. 7, 1926.

Guarding a Wharf, San Francisco Maritime Strike, 1934. *Courtesy of the Cohen Collection, Bancroft Library, University of California, Berkeley*

Log Raft, Near San Diego. *Courtesy of the Historical Collection, Title Insurance and Trust Company, San Diego*

San Antonio which was operated between San Francisco and Monterey. In February 1925 the *San Antonio* inaugurated the only water freight service between San Francisco and Los Angeles that served local points. The James K. Nelson firm also directed the operations of the Mendocino Steamship Company whose one steamer, the *Cleone,* provided a weekly service from San Francisco northward to Fort Bragg and Caspar.[32]

During the *Newport* rate war the White Flyer Line forsook its original role as an independent and joined with its larger competitors to squeeze out the intruder. Following the acquisition of the *San Juan,* the White Flyer Line instituted, in February 1926, a store-door delivery plan to improve its competitive position.[33] Eight months later the company became the first steamship line to make Long Beach a regular port of call when the *San Juan* arrived at that port on Columbus Day 1926. She was greeted by crowds who lined the gaily decorated dock. At a luncheon held on board, the mayor of Long Beach reminded the one hundred and fifty guests that the arrival of the White Flyer Line "is the first break in the ranks of the shipping fraternity. Our conquest from now on will be easier. It is significant that this event occurs on the anniversary of Columbus' discovery, and I venture to prophesy the White Flyer Line will realize bigger results in a year from Long Beach than Columbus did during the rest of his life, from his new continent."[34]

But the rosy pictures painted by the Long Beach mayor

[32] "Annual Report of the White Flyer Line of San Francisco to the Railroad Commission of California" for 1919-1925 in ASF; "Annual Report of the Santa Cruz and Monterey Steamship Company of San Francisco to the Railroad Commission of California for the Year Ending December 31, 1922," p. 2 in ASF; San Francisco *Chronicle,* Jan. 17, 1922; Los Angeles *Times,* Feb. 7, 11, 1925; *Pacific Shipper,* I (March 1, 1926), 30.

[33] California, Railroad Commission, *Decisions,* XXIX, 795; *Pacific Shipper,* I (March 1, 1926), 30.

[34] Quoted in Los Angeles *Times,* Oct. 13, 1926.

and the White Flyer Line vanished in four short months. Because of financial difficulties the firm suspended operations on January 30, 1927, and its ships were tied up. James K. Nelson, president of the line, made efforts to refinance the concern. Three of the principal creditors became directors to put the company on a sound financial footing. Over the protests of the two remaining directors, the new group appointed a new manager who promptly reported that the financial condition of the line was deplorable. Another creditor filed a claim against the fleet which the new directors failed to contest. To satisfy the claim, the ships were sold at auction.[35]

Out of the financial tangle, a new company emerged which called itself the Los Angeles–San Francisco Navigation Company. It obtained the title to the *Humboldt* and *San Juan* and began to operate them on the same route. The original stockholders of the James K. Nelson company thereupon filed a suit which charged the three creditors with forming a conspiracy to wreck the company. It was pointed out that one of the new directors became a partner in the new Los Angeles–San Francisco Navigation Company. At the time of its suspension, the stockholders of the White Flyer Line claimed that, although it was short of ready cash, the company had assets of $400,000 and debts of $200,000. One result of this legal battle over the ownership of the fleet was the revelation that the White Flyer Line had, for some time prior to its bankruptcy, been illegally giving rebates to favored customers. This policy had been concealed through use of a private code whereby items on lists of alleged supplies for the ships were actually rebates made to certain shippers. The system of hiding these illegal refunds worked perfectly until the former manager revealed it in the bankruptcy

[35] *Marine Digest*, V (March 12, 1927), 11; *Shipping Register*, XI (Aug. 31, 1929), 6; San Francisco *Examiner*, March 26, 1927; San Francisco *Chronicle*, Jan. 31 and March 27, 1927.

proceedings. The White Flyer Line, born to a tradition of providing service for people of moderate means, ended its existence in disrepute.[36]

While the James K. Nelson company was having its difficulties, the Charles Nelson Company, through the Nelson Steamship line, was expanding at an amazing rate. The purchase of five steamships in 1925 from the Shipping Board was followed within a few months by the addition of four more from the same source. By February 1926 the company was averaging eight to ten sailings per week in the coastwise trade. When the rumor circulated that the Charles Nelson Company was trying to purchase seven more vessels from the government, shipping circles were amazed, for the Nelson firm had always been regarded as extremely conservative. In the middle of July 1926, the rumor proved correct when the Nelson Steamship Company purchased seven vessels of 3,545 gross tons each. As a result, the number of units in the Nelson fleet was raised to twenty-eight.[37] When the first of the new ships arrived in Los Angeles from the Atlantic Coast on October 14, 1926, a Nelson official observed that the seven ships would more than double the tonnage of the Nelson fleet. He added that it was a "big increase but freight offerings justify it."[38]

In the same year, the Nelson line won the right to establish through rates and bills of lading with the Union Pacific, Northern Pacific, and Milwaukee railroads. These railroads had previously refused to enter into joint rates

36 "Annual Report of the Los Angeles–San Francisco Navigation Company, Ltd. of San Francisco to the Railroad Commission of the State of California for the Year Ending December 31, 1929," p. 2 in ASF; San Francisco *Examiner*, March 26, 1927; San Francisco *Chronicle*, March 27, 29, 1927; *Marine Digest*, V (April 9, 1927), 9.

37 *Pacific Marine Review*, XXIII (Jan. 1926), 31, XXIII (Feb. 1926), 85; *Marine Digest*, V (Feb. 19, 1927), 3; *Railway and Marine News*, XXIII (Jan. 11, 1926), 11, XXIII (July 1926), 27; Los Angeles *Times*, July 10, 14, 1926.

38 Quoted in Los Angeles *Times*, Oct. 15, 1926.

because they claimed that the Nelson Steamship Company was not a common carrier, that the interline service then being rendered by the Admiral and McCormick lines was satisfactory, and that the granting of the right to a third line might impair the financial standing of the other two companies. The Nelson firm appealed to the Interstate Commerce Commission for relief. On March 31, 1926, that body ruled in favor of the Nelson Steamship Company. The commission found that the "anticipated curtailment or impairment of the service was mere speculation." The railroads were ordered to establish rates on the same basis and to the same extent as the rates maintained with the Admiral and McCormick lines. The Great Northern Railway was not one of the defendants as it had already established joint rates with the complainant.[39]

Shortly after this victory, the Nelson Steamship Company announced that it was going to convert thirteen of its steamers in order that each could carry seventy first-class passengers. As soon as the conversion could be accomplished, regular passenger sailings were to be maintained between Seattle, Portland, San Francisco, Los Angeles, and San Diego. In the spring of 1927 the new service was inaugurated when the *Doylestown* sailed from Seattle for California with a full passenger list. Nelson purchased three more ships in the summer and announced plans to enter the intercoastal service the following fall. Since the six ships used in the intercoastal trade each carried fifteen to twenty-five passengers, Seattle was linked for the first time with the East Coast by a passenger carrying line. In February 1928 Nelson again increased its combination passenger and freight service by offering three weekly sailings between Puget Sound and San

[39] *Decisions,* CIX (1926), 529-38; *Marine Digest,* IV (April 24, 1926), 7; *Railway and Marine News,* XXIII (April 1926), 34.

Francisco and two weekly between Puget Sound and Los
Angeles.

In August 1927 the Nelson company had advertised that
it operated the "Largest Coastwise Fleet on the Pacific,"
to which the Admiral Line countered that it had the
"Finest Fleet of Coastwise Vessels."[40] Although the Nelson
fleet may have been the largest on the coast, it was in fact
far from being the finest. It took eighty hours for its
fastest ships to go from Seattle to San Francisco and seven
days to go from Seattle to Los Angeles. But, within a few
short years the Nelson Steamship Company had grown
from a lumber concern to become the operator of a fleet
which surpassed that of the McCormick in size. Such
growth was looked upon as being the acme of American
enterprise and daring; the Nelson company had become
the largest, and there was something in the temper of the
times which confused size with quality.

Nelson continued to expand. In March 1929 the company opened its own offices in Portland to care for its
growing business. By the following month, it had done
the same in Cincinnati, Chicago, and Atlanta. If expenditures of money and rapid expansion meant success in the
maritime world, the Nelson Steamship Company was
destined to have a long life.[41]

In their struggle for existence, the marine transportation
companies were always vulnerable to new rivals and there
were constant rumors of moves by other groups. In 1925
Captain John F. Blain, who had formerly been the operating manager of the Dollar Steamship Company, purchased the steamer *Newport News* and announced his

[40] Los Angeles *Times,* Dec. 13, 1926; *Railway and Marine News,* XXIV
(March 1927), 27, XXIV (May 1927), 24, XXIV (Aug. 1927), 35, 36; *Marine
Digest,* V (March 19, 1927), 3, V (May 21, 1927), 3, VI (Aug. 9, 1928), 22;
Seattle *Times,* Aug. 9, 1927.
[41] *Marine Digest,* VI (Feb. 18, 1928), 3, 7; Portland *Oregonian,* March
27, 1929; *Railway and Marine News,* XXV (March 1928), 16.

intention of starting a passenger and freight service between Seattle and San Francisco.[42] After the initial announcement nothing further was heard of the project.
Two years later the Bayside Steamship Company, which
had been organized in 1923 by a group of San Francisco
lumber and shipping men, began to challenge the supremacy of the other lines. It placed five freighters on the route
between San Diego, Los Angeles, San Francisco, and Puget
Sound. Twice weekly sailings were maintained.[43] In 1927,
undisclosed Pacific Coast interests purchased four steamers
from the Shipping Board. This transaction brought forth
the rumor that a new coastwise line was about to begin.
In November of the same year a report circulated that the
company would have a fleet of six vessels, each capable of
carrying 200 passengers and 2,000 tons of freight.[44]

The ever-present threat that the Guggenheim interests
would place the liners of its Alaska Steamship Company
on the California route furnished another source of
speculation. The relations between the Guggenheim and
Alexander interests had not improved. In 1926, the Admiral Line decided to double the number of its sailings to
southwestern Alaska, thereby matching the weekly sailings
of the Alaska Steamship Company. Difficulty between the
two companies arose over the amicable arrangement of
sailing dates. H. F. Alexander bluntly declared, "As we
were the first steamship company to operate on this route,
we felt we had the perfect right to increase our service."
The Alaska Steamship Company finally agreed.[45] With
the exception of the Bayside Steamship Company, these

[42] Pacific Marine Review, XXII (June 1925), 21 in advertising section.
[43] Los Angeles Times, July 23, 1927; Pacific Marine Review, XX (Oct. 1923), 36b in advertising section.
[44] Los Angeles Times, Sept. 15, 1927; Railway and Marine News, XXIV (Nov. 1927), 22.
[45] Letter to Executive Committee, Jan. 27, 1927, and to directors, Dec. 12, 1926, in Admiral Mss, Honnold Library. See also Los Angeles Times, Oct. 3, 1927.

rumors of competition produced nothing more tangible
than the worry they caused officials of the established lines.

THE 1929 RATE WAR

While the rest of the country was enjoying the crest of
the Coolidge prosperity, the coastwise maritime industry
was being swamped by too many lines and too much
tonnage. In the scramble for business, the technique of
lowering rates to attract the customers of a rival line was
not overlooked. In 1919, the industry had been warned:
"Rate cutting is as old as the everlasting hills but it is a
question if the system ever did anyone a great amount of
good. Disorganization of trade and general uncertainty
are more apt to follow and while trade may be stimulated
in its movement, it is like any other stimulant, not lasting
in its effect."[46] But the warning was not heeded either in
1919, 1925, or 1929.

The Bayside Steamship Company led the procession by
announcing cuts in the winter of 1929. The Nelson line
shortly felt the pressure and met a dozen Bayside rates.
This action brought the Admiral and McCormick lines
into the fray. Differentials were claimed by the slower
lines but were denied by the rest. Rates were cut a second
time by some lines and again met by the others. By June,
the conflict was "getting snappier almost every day."[47] A
trade magazine concluded, "As a result of the free for all,
. . . the Coastwise Conference has gone on the rocks. It
has been dissolved."[48] Freight charges plunged to new
low levels.

In the chaotic scramble for business, operators carried

46 "Rate Cutting" (editorial), *Railway and Marine News*, XVII (March
1919), 19.
47 Portland *Oregonian*, June 14, 1929.
48 *Marine Digest*, VII (June 8, 1929), 7.

freight between San Francisco and Seattle for less money than between San Francisco and Portland, although the distance was over one hundred and fifty miles longer. The rate for salt fell from $3.75 to $2.00 per ton, that for tires slid from 55 cents to 30 cents per hundred pounds and that for canned goods tumbled from 34 cents to 20 cents per hundred pounds. One shipping man declared, "The participants apparently haven't been hurt enough yet."[49] By the end of June, the reductions were nearing 50 percent. Overtures for peace found little sympathy. Shippers took full advantage of the low rates and taxed coastwise steamers to capacity. The Nelson Steamship Company was even forced to use a barge to handle the cargo being offered for shipment.[50]

That the earnings of the companies would be adversely affected was obvious. As early as March the Admiral Line began to feel the effects. In June, its net freight earnings declined $43,440 over the previous year.[51] A $75,000 decrease was registered in July. H. F. Alexander stated that the "entire amount, with the exception of approximately $5,000 is attributable to the rate war."[52] To add to the confusion, two new companies entered the coastwise trade. One of these, the Sudden and Christenson Line, inaugurated a weekly freight service between the Columbia River and California on June 19, 1929. A month later, the frequency of the service was doubled. The other line was the Lewis Bean Company.[53]

The boom in the amount of cargo offerings was artificial. There was only a certain quantity of freight to

[49] Quoted in Los Angeles *Times*, June 29, 1929.

[50] Portland *Oregonian*, June 14, 29, 1929; San Francisco *Chronicle*, June 9, 1929.

[51] Letters to directors, April 22 and July 22, 1929, in Admiral Mss, Honnold Library.

[52] Letter to directors, Aug. 22, 1929, in Admiral Mss, Honnold Library.

[53] *Railway and Marine News*, XXVI (July 1929), 50; Portland *Oregonian*, July 6, 1929.

be moved and, while the low rates held, the shippers rushed to take advantage of them. The lines soon realized that their actions were merely producing large deficits and not materially changing their relative positions in the struggle for business. By the end of July, the average rate had dropped from $4.50 to $2.00 per ton. The lines decided to end the useless conflict effective August 1, 1929. Because a number of commitments had been made by the various companies rates could not be immediately raised. Attempts to cancel or adjust these agreements were finally successful and the Coastwise Conference was reestablished. On October 15, 1929, the Admiral Line issued a new freight schedule that raised rates. On the same date, the other lines took similar action and the hostilities were officially ended.[54]

The rate war proved disastrous for the Admiral Line. In place of the $140,000 profit earned in 1928, there was a loss of over $175,000 in 1929. The significance of the October stock market crash, which occurred a few days after the rate war was finally settled, was overlooked by shipping circles in their joy over peace. In March 1930 H. F. Alexander told a trade magazine that he was optimistic over the future because the rate differences had been amicably adjusted. No mention was made of the Wall Street debacle as a possible factor in future earnings.[55]

In the meantime, tragedy had again struck the coastwise steamship business. On August 29, 1929, the San Juan of the Los Angeles–San Francisco Navigation Company collided with the Standard Oil tanker S. C. T. Dodd. The accident occurred shortly after midnight while the

54 Letter to directors, Aug. 22, 1929, and letters to Executive Committee, Aug. 22, Sept. 20 and Oct. 22, 1929, in Admiral Mss, Honnold Library; Portland Oregonian, July 29, 1929.

55 Pacific Marine Review, XXVII (April 1930), 17 in advertising section; "Financial Statement" in Admiral Mss, Honnold Library.

ships were off Pigeon Point, south of San Francisco. The force of the collision virtually cut the *San Juan* in two. The little ship sank in three minutes. Out of the 115 on board, 75 were lost. It was one of the worst accidents in coastwise shipping. Blame for the mishap was placed on the third officer of the *San Juan* for his failure to call his captain when the lights of the tanker were first seen and for maintaining full speed in a fog. His license was revoked. In a lengthy decision, the supervising inspector disagreed with his assistants in that he felt that the *S. C. T. Dodd* was partly at fault. The first decision had been based to a large degree on the assumption that the *San Juan* was traveling at a greater speed; later investigation indicated that the tanker was making slightly more speed than the passenger vessel.[56] About the same hour that the *San Juan* was sunk, the other vessel of the Los Angeles–San Francisco Navigation Company, the *Humboldt*, rammed a fishing barge as she was coming into the wharf at Santa Barbara. The bow of the *Humboldt* penetrated more than eight feet into the side of the barge. Fortunately no lives were lost and only slight damage was sustained by the liner.[57]

Clouds were gathering on the horizon for the shipping industry. Competition, rate wars, and wrecks were to prove mild forerunners to the financial storm which broke over the entire country, sweeping all before it.

[56] *Annual Report* (1930), p. 15; Los Angeles *Times*, Aug. 31, 1929; San Francisco *Chronicle*, Dec. 13, 1929; *Pacific Marine Review*, XXVIII (Dec. 1931), 514.

[57] Los Angeles *Times*, Aug. 31, 1929.

SEVEN

Passenger Travel

FLOATING HOTELS

"PEOPLE PREFER something better than they are accustomed to. They cheerfully pay for the privilege of getting it. The business which sets about giving them something better, making them realize that it is available, and still holding the price within reason— that business is almost sure to prosper. . . . There in a paragraph is summed up the one outstanding fact from our experience." Thus H. F. Alexander summarized in 1925 the factors which had brought success to his companies.[1]

In line with that policy, thousands of dollars were spent in reconditioning the ships of the Admiral Line. The Alexander vessels became well known for their hotel-like accommodations. On the *H. F. Alexander,* there were thirteen de luxe suites which were finished in a variety of woods. Every stateroom had hot and cold running water, electric fan, telephone, and heater. Telephonic connections with shore were made by trunk lines as soon as the vessel was berthed. The public rooms included observation, music, writing, and smoking rooms. The boudoir for women was painted in old rose with furniture in ivory and was described as the "daintiest room imaginable." The observation room was finished in light gray with clouded ceiling effect. It had a mole carpet and satin draperies to match. There was a veranda palm garden, a colonial style dining room, and a glass-enclosed open air dancing pavilion. The *Ruth Alexander,* and *Emma Alexander* had comparable accommodations.[2]

There was some truth in the slogan that the *Harvard* and *Yale* provided "Royal Trips on Regal Ships." After their service in World War I, the two sisters were completely rebuilt. A veranda cafe and ballroom was provided on the after part of B deck. The entire space was enclosed with glass and covered with a dome ceiling. Decorative panels, between the windows, portrayed figures typifying the carnival spirit. During the day, the room served as a reading-observation lounge. While the passengers were at dinner, the oriental rugs and furniture were cleared to provide a spacious dance floor. Along the side, seats and small tables were arranged. A buffet, serving light lunches, was operated during the evening. This type of a veranda cafe and ballroom was advertised as the first of its kind on any ship. Each of the "White Comets" had twenty-six suites which were painted in a variety of colors. Most of the suites had twin beds and all had private baths. As a concession to superstition, there was no suite numbered thirteen. The great majority of the rooms, however, contained two standard berths. Prices for the de luxe accommodations ranged up to $50 one way as compared to $18 for the lowest cabin berth. To increase their smartness, the two ships were painted white. Lassco estimated that it cost $4,000 a year more to keep them white than if they were painted a darker color. The *Yale* was the first vessel on the Pacific Coast to be equipped with a loud-

1 H. F. Alexander, "Why We Made Money When Nearly Everybody Said We'd Fail," *System,* XLVII (April 1925), 449.
2 *Pacific Marine Review,* XIX (July 1922), 414; *Advertising Folder* and *Travel by Water* in Admiral Mss, Honnold Library.

speaker in order that her passengers could enjoy the programs being broadcast by the infant radio industry.[3]

The steamship operators tried to offer at sea services that were given by a first-class hotel on land. A library, special stationery, barber shop, bell-boy service, nursery, gymnasium, sea garage, and twenty-four hour switchboard service were usually provided. The nursery of the *Congress* had "mats to tumble on, 1,000 toys, and all kinds of indoor games."[4] On longer trips, a small printed or mimeographed newspaper was delivered each morning under the doors of the staterooms. For the convenience of mothers, bassinets were available. LASSCO announced that its cribs had been patterned after the furniture of the stateroom so that there would be no clashing of color schemes.

Everything was done to eliminate delays which were apt to attend the boarding of ships. Before the Hill companies withdrew from their maritime venture in 1917, they had adopted a system whereby each ticket purchaser was given a little flag, designed after the house flag of the Hill lines. When worn by the passenger, this emblem served as an identification badge at the gangplank and eliminated the necessity of producing a ticket.[5]

Sea garages, by means of which a passenger could take his car along with him, proved an incentive for sea travel. Most of the larger ships were equipped to take care of a number of automobiles. LASSCO advertised that cars could be driven directly onto the decks of the *Harvard* or *Yale*

3 Los Angeles *Times*, April 21, May 2, 1921, March 18, 29, 1922, June 18, 1924; *Passenger Schedule* and room plan for *Harvard* in LASSCO Mss, Maritime Collection of John H. Kemble, Claremont, Calif.

4 *Baby Bunting's Choice*, p. 2, in Pacific Coast Steamship Company Mss, Honnold Library.

5 *LASSCO Coastwise Log*, Sept. 29, 1931. By 1933, the name was changed to *LASSCO News* in LASSCO Mss, Maritime Collection of John H. Kemble, Claremont, Calif.; San Francisco *Chronicle*, March 2, 1922; *Railway and Marine News*, XIV (April 1916), 30.

from the dock without danger of rubbing or scratching. In 1927, H. F. Alexander estimated that "with every automobile checked there are two or more passengers" and added that the "accommodations we have to offer for the handling of a large number of automobiles has had a great deal to do with the increased business."[6] This feature of sea travel proved popular and the number of cars carried each year by the Admiral Line rose steadily. In 1922, 609 were handled; in 1935, the figure was 3,693. The number of cars followed the same seasonal pattern as the passenger business. LASSCO, the only other line furnishing this service, carried about a third as many as the Alexander company. Reasonable rates were charged and the motorist was urged to "take your car along— cheaper than driving!" In 1933, an automobile could be taken from San Francisco to Seattle for five dollars when accompanied by two adult passengers.[7]

Normally the coastwise lines included meals in the price of the ticket. In order to make this feature as attractive as possible, the traditional long, boarding-house tables were replaced by small, cozy tables. China, glassware, and silver replaced the old crockery which had been common on the older ships. A great variety of culinary offerings were available on the menus and the passenger was urged to eat as much or as little as he desired. It was not uncommon to have six choices of meat along with a great number of side dishes for a single meal. In addition to the three regular meals, between-meal "snacks" were customary.

6 Alexander to Executive Committee, Nov. 17, 1927 in Admiral Mss, Honnold Library.

7 Los Angeles *Times,* Aug. 2, 1921; "Statistics" in Admiral Mss, Honnold Library; "Annual Report of the Los Angeles Steamship Company to the Railroad Commission of California for the Year Ending December 31, 1934," pp. 500-501 in ASF; "Annual Report to Interstate Commerce Commission" (1934), in Admiral Mss, Honnold Library; *Travel by Water* in Admiral Mss, Honnold Library; *California Coast Sailings* in LASSCO Mss, Maritime Collection of John H. Kemble, Claremont, Calif.

The Admiral Line provided, at no additional charge, bouillon and crackers each morning at eleven, tea and cookies in the mid-afternoon, and a light lunch in the late evening, composed of coffee, fruit, and sandwiches. H. F. Alexander admitted, "No great amount of food is used in this way. But passengers get the idea that they are being well looked after—as they are."[8]

To expedite the serving of food, the *Harvard* and *Yale* were arranged in such a manner that the progress of the food from galley to dining saloon and the return of the dishes to the kitchen was in a continuous cycle without interference or reversals of flow. The excellence of the cuisine was a favorite topic with the publicity agents, who apparently believed that the traveling public, like an army, moved on its stomach. Al Levy, who was in charge of the food service for LASSCO, was termed the "Wizard of Gastronomy."[9]

In spite of the abundance of dishes offered and the policy that a passenger could eat as much as he pleased, the cost per meal to the steamship companies was surprisingly low. The Admiral Line paid, on the average, a little more than thirty cents for each meal served. Because of the depression, the average cost had declined by 1932 to 23.7 cents per meal.[10]

The development of first-class facilities aboard ship was reflected in the amount of money spent by each customer. Between 1917 and 1923, the average revenue per passenger rose from $16 to $29.33. That the public reacted favorably to the refinements is evident from the number which patronized the lines. The total number of miles traveled by passengers on Admiral ships increased from

8 H. F. Alexander, "Why We Made Money When Nearly Everybody Said We'd Fail," p. 498.
9 *Pacific Marine Review*, XVIII (June 1921), 330, XVIII (July 1921), 48 in advertising section.
10 "Statistics" in Admiral Mss, Honnold Library.

47,500,000 in 1921 to 83,500,000 in 1926, although this figure was not as high as the 128,500,000 passenger miles completed in 1917 when Alexander controlled the *Harvard* and *Yale* in addition to the regular vessels of the Admiral Line. The number of passengers using LASSCO ships increased from 92,235 in 1923 to 154,985 in 1929, but about 30 percent of these figures represented the Hawaiian trade in which LASSCO was also active. No breakdown of the San Diego to San Francisco figure is available.[11]

While most of the lines advertised their de luxe accommodations, there was a considerable amount of third-class or steerage passenger business. In furnishing this type of travel, the companies sacrificed speed and luxury for cheaper fares. In particular the Nelson and McCormick lines catered to that part of the traveling public who were willing to sleep in dormitories and eat in the crew's mess. Almost without exception, third-class was reserved for men. Between the de luxe facilities of the *H. F. Alexander, Harvard, Yale* and other Alexander ships and the slow lumber schooners which provided most of the third-class accommodations, were the independent lines which offered first-class service without embellishments. The *Humboldt* of the White Flyer Line was noted for her moderate fares which earned her the title of "The Family Boat of the Pacific." The *San Juan* of the Los Angeles Dispatch Line, during her short career as a coastwise vessel in 1925, attracted a similar clientele. A round trip on the *Humboldt* between San Francisco and Los Angeles was $20 whereas the lowest fare on the Admiral Line was $25 and on LASSCO was $35 for the same trip. Although some of the luxury ships carried third-class passengers, the *Harvard* and the *Yale* were one-class ships and the *H. F.*

11 "Statistics" in *ibid.,* "Annual Report of the Los Angeles Steamship Company to the Railroad Commission of California for the Year Ending December 31, 1923," p. 500; *ibid.,* for 1929, p. 501 in ASF.

The Queen. Courtesy of Allen T. Yost, Santa Barbara

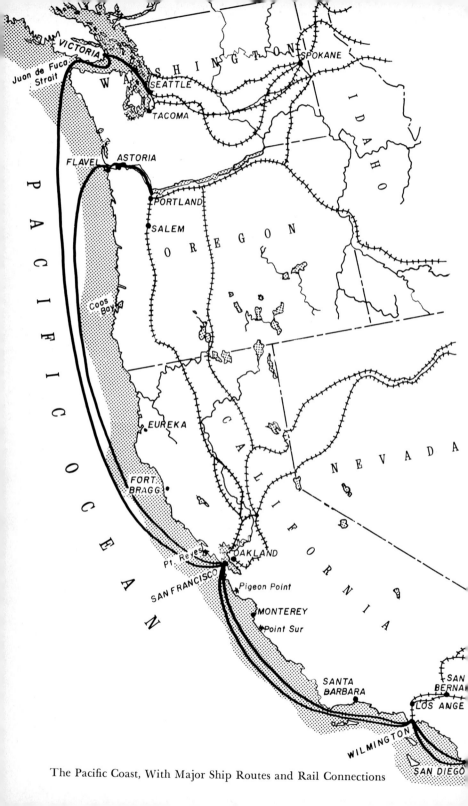

The Pacific Coast, With Major Ship Routes and Rail Connections

Alexander was not altered to accommodate third-class passengers until 1932.[12]

TECHNIQUES OF PUBLICITY

Efforts to persuade the public to travel by steamer rather than by some other mode of transportation were a constant problem for the passenger departments of the various lines. Adverse publicity, which always attended mishaps on the sea, had to be overcome. Not only did the people living in the West have to be educated to the advantages of sea travel, but tourists from other sections had to be attracted. H. F. Alexander once said, "From the standpoint of coastwise traffic the most important problem we have to face is to spread the fame of the Pacific Coast . . . , so that tourists . . . will come."[13]

All lines publicized the comfort, freedom of movement, fresh air, and relaxation of shipboard life. To increase patronage, a variety of schemes was employed. When a celebrity was aboard, the news was given to the daily press. In September 1921, for example, the San Francisco *Chronicle* noted the sailing of a well-known film star by reporting: "There was considerable cargo on the Los Angeles Steamship Company's liner Harvard—that is humanly speaking. Roscoe 'Fatty' Arbuckle, silver-sheet laugh producer, was a passenger sailing for Los Angeles." The public was informed of the elaborate arrangements which had been made for this "mirthful voyage" with "Fatty" as jester.[14] In the same month, LASSCO also gained

12 San Francisco *Chronicle*, Oct. 21, 1922; Los Angeles *Times*, March 17, 1922; *Shipping Register*, III (Dec. 31, 1921), 2; *Marine Digest*, X (April 16, 1932), 3.
13 H. F. Alexander, "Get Alaska Working," *Pacific Marine Review*, XXIII (Jan. 1926), 1.
14 San Francisco *Chronicle*, Sept. 7, 1921.

publicity by a press release describing an incident in which a mother planned to send her son on a coastwise trip in the hope that he would be enticed by the "vamps" in the ballroom of the ship to forget a girl he wanted to marry.[15] No follow-up report was given of the success or failure of the plan.

To counteract the idea that sea travel was tedious, LASSCO advertised that there was "something doing every hour" on its ships and furnished a schedule to prove it.[16] The Admiral Line proclaimed it furnished, "travel with the weariness all left out!" Because her spacious decks were often used by moving picture companies to shoot scenes of shipboard life, the *Emma Alexander* was called "Hollywood Afloat." As many as three companies had worked simultaneously as the vessel steamed along the coast. Their presence lent "glamour" to sea travel. To break the monotony of a long journey, many Admiral ships sponsored a "Morning Canter" in which the passengers, led by the orchestra, hiked around the ship for a "sea mile."[17]

The healthfulness of a sea journey was emphasized. LASSCO advertised, "Feel run down and all fagged out? As a tonic and pep-producer, you can't beat the salt-tang'd air of the Pacific." The Pacific Coast Steamship Company assured the public, "Ocean air is cleaner and, being free from germs, is more healthful than land air."[18] Rather paradoxically, the operators of the *Harvard* and *Yale* maintained, "Whether you are looking for rest or excitement, you'll find both on these floating playgrounds."

15 San Francisco *Journal,* Sept. 22, 1921.
16 San Francisco *Chronicle,* Feb. 9, 1922.
17 H. F. Alexander, "Why We Made Money When Nearly Everybody Said We'd Fail," pp. 451, 498; *Pacific Marine Review,* XXIII (Nov. 1926), 13, 20 in advertising section; San Francisco *Chronicle,* April 1, 1927.
18 *Pacific Marine Review,* XXI (Aug. 1924), 20 in advertising section; *Winter Outings,* an advertising pamphlet, p. 3 in Pacific Coast Steamship Company Mss, Honnold Library.

The *Congress* was claimed as "Baby Bunting's Choice" and mothers were told of the various conveniences available, which ranged from draught-proof staterooms to electric heaters for drying baby's clothes.[19] One LASSCO advertisement almost took the form of Imagist poetry:

> A Super-Express Ship! Splashing Waves! Salt
> Tang'd Breeze! Speed Ahead! Care Abandoned!
> Laughing Guests! Music! Spacious Decks! A
> View! A Thrill! Sensations! Rest! Recreation!
> Wonderful Meals! Spotless Ship, Lights and
> A C T I O N ! [20]

In addition to the ceremony of the formal inauguration of a new ship into service, every opportunity to attract attention to the favorable events in the life-history of a vessel was utilized. When the *Harvard* returned in 1922 to her regular run after an overhaul, she was received outside the Golden Gate by a salute from a battleship, was serenaded by the whistles of innumerable harbor craft, and was greeted at the dock by the mayor of San Francisco, James Rolph. When the *H. F. Alexander* resumed operations from Seattle in 1923 after her regular winter lay-up she carried "Miss Charmed Land," a University of Washington coed, as a passenger. The young lady had boarded the ship "attended by a bevy of University of Washington girls and gaily garbed young women ushers from the Liberty theatre." The jazz orchestra and the quartet of the university went along as part of the escorting party. Plans were made for the ship and "Miss Charmed Land" to be welcomed by the mayors of both San Francisco and Los Angeles when the two "guests" arrived in California.[21]

---

19 Los Angeles *Times*, March 17, 1922; *Baby Bunting's Choice*, p. 1 in Pacific Coast Steamship Company Mss, Honnold Library.

20 Los Angeles *Times*, July 15, 1924.

21 San Francisco *Chronicle*, May 31, 1922; *Marine Digest*, I (March 31, 1923), 3.

The regular sailings of the coastwise ships were made as colorful and enticing as possible. Thirty minutes before sailing time, the orchestra of the ship would begin to play. As the passengers lined the rails to wave farewells to friends and relatives, stewards passed out multicolored streamers which could be thrown shoreward as the ship pulled away from the dock. The traditions grew as the operators realized the publicity value which was inherent in the festivities. H. F. Alexander confessed that the four or five dollars spent on confetti per sailing provided excellent advertising.[22]

The companies learned that one of the best ways to advertise was to book excursions for clubs, lodges, and other organizations. In 1921, members of the Greeters, an association of hotel managers, were taken as guests of LASSCO for a moonlight cruise around Santa Catalina Island. The *Ruth Alexander* was chartered in 1924 by the Elks of San Francisco for a trip to their state convention in southern California.[23] When the *H. F. Alexander* arrived in Los Angeles Harbor on July 4, 1924, she flew from the main truck the flag of Potentate William Worden, Chief of Islam Temple, Ancient Nobles of the Mystic Shrine. The two hundred "Nobles" on board swelled the passenger list to 534, the largest number to arrive at the port of Los Angeles in one vessel up to that time. At Los Angeles, the Nobles were transferred to the *Emma Alexander,* which took them from "dry" America to the thirst-quenching beverages of Ensenada, Mexico. Sports events also provided excellent opportunities to fill the passenger lists and it became a regular custom for the *Harvard* or *Yale* to transport large numbers of football fans to the "big games."[24]

[22] H. F. Alexander, "Why We Made Money When Nearly Everybody Said We'd Fail," p. 454.

[23] Los Angeles *Times,* Sept. 8, 1921; *Pacific Marine Review,* XXI (Aug. 1924), 21 in advertising section.

The migration of students to and from colleges was a boon. One year, LASSCO mailed attractive dodgers to the students in the San Francisco Bay region, suggesting that they "start Christmas party-ing early" by joining the holiday crowds on the *Harvard* or *Yale*. Special student fares were quoted. Dancing, low fares, and the attractions of a sea voyage made these trips popular with college groups.[25]

An effective way of publicizing the advantages of sea travel was the slogan contest sponsored by LASSCO during the fall of 1921. The company offered $500 in prizes for slogans which could be used in advertising the *Yale* and *Harvard*. About one hundred and fifty thousand persons, from virtually every state of the Union and three foreign countries, submitted entries. The company estimated that had a man been employed to prepare that number, he would have worked steadily for more than four years. The five judges, who included the mayor of Los Angeles and a college president, awarded first prize to a San Francisco woman who submitted "Royal Trips on Regal Ships." Among other suggestions receiving awards were: "The Ships that put 'U' in Luxury," "Swells of the Pacific," and "The Sea Road of Raptures."[26]

The cost of the campaign to educate the public in sea travel rose perceptibly as competition became keener. The Admiral Line between 1917 and 1926 expended almost one million dollars and increased its annual advertising budget nearly four times.[27] All media were employed, but the greatest emphasis was placed on advertisements in newspapers and periodicals. The Admiral Line,

24 Los Angeles *Times*, July 5, 1924.
25 Printed dodger issued by LASSCO, Maritime Collection of John H. Kemble, Claremont, Calif.; Los Angeles *Times*, Jan. 11, 1928; San Francisco *Chronicle*, Feb. 6, 1924; *Pacific Marine Review*, XXII (Dec. 1925), 21 in advertising section.
26 See particularly Los Angeles *Times*, Oct. 9, 16, 28, Nov. 13, 27, 1921.
27 "Statistics" in Admiral Mss, Honnold Library.

for example, had advertising contracts with more than forty American publishing companies.[28]

THE SEASONAL NATURE OF WATER TRAVEL

In spite of the concentrated and expensive advertising methods, there was always a winter slump in the passenger business. The number of people riding Admiral ships in January was only about one-third of the number in August. This seasonal variation created difficulties, for the owners were faced with the problem of what to do with their large passenger vessels during the slack season. The cost of operating the express liners was much higher than the slower ships. To steam a mile, the *H. F. Alexander* consumed 161 gallons of fuel as compared to 20 gallons used by the *Admiral Watson*. The following table indicates how expensive the luxury ships were to operate:[29]

Ship	Average fuel consumption (gallons per mile)	Passenger capacity	Number in crew	Usual speed (knots)
H. F. Alexander	161.3	585	225	21.1
Harvard	102.0	466	135	21.0
Yale	98.0	466	135	21.0
Emma Alexander	68.7	442	153	14.3
Ruth Alexander	59.4	409	150	13.6
Dorothy Alexander	53.4	537	130	14.1
Admiral Dewey	20.7	162	36	11.7
Admiral Farragut	24.7	204	60	11.8
Admiral Fiske	21.8	187	30	10.8

[28] "Annual Report to the Interstate Commerce Commission" (1921). p. 504 in Admiral Mss, Honnold Library.

[29] The figures are for 1930. "Annual Report to Interstate Commerce Commission" (1930), pp. 402, 503 in Admiral Mss, Honnold Library; "Annual Report of the Los Angeles Steamship Company to the Railroad Commission of California for the Year Ending December 31, 1930," pp. 501-503 in ASF.

During the winter slump LASSCO officials withdrew the
the *Harvard* and *Yale* for their annual overhauls. Sailing
schedules were reduced while first one and then the other
of the "White Comets" was laid up. The Admiral Line
operated the *H. F. Alexander* for only about half a year;
and she showed a loss for about 60 percent of the time
she was in service. During the height of the summer
tourist season the big ship could make a large profit. On
one voyage in July 1926, she grossed approximately
seventy-six thousand dollars and earned over thirty-seven
thousand dollars in profits. But there were many sailings
that produced deficits.[30] The problem of what to do with
the big ship for the remainder of the year was constantly
before Admiral officials. One winter, five special cruises
to Honolulu were scheduled. Another year, the ship was
sent to the East Coast to compete in the New York to
Miami trade. Since two of the established lines had lost
five of their ships within an eighteen-month period, there
was room for another ship. Because of her deep draft, the
H. F. Alexander had to transfer her passengers to a tender
outside the harbor of Miami, but her speed more than
made up for this delay. Whereas the southbound trip
from New York took forty-six hours, the return voyage
could be made in four hours less because of the Gulf
Stream. During the time she was on the East Coast the
H. F. Alexander carried almost eighteen thousand passengers in thirty-seven round trips.[31]

The importance of the role that this ship played in the
life of the West was indicated by the enthusiastic reception
given the *H. F. Alexander* upon her return in 1926 from

30 "Statistics" and Alexander to directors, July 17, 1926 in Admiral
Mss, Honnold Library.
31 *Pacific Marine Review*, XX (Jan. 1923), 59, XXII (Nov. 1925), 498,
XXII (Dec. 1925), 574, XXIII (Feb. 1926), 56; U. S., Bureau of Navigation, *List of Merchant Vessels* (1924), p. 436; *ibid.* (1925), p. 834; *ibid.*
(1926), p. 853; *Railway and Marine News*, XXIII (June 1926), 28; "Statistics Working Papers, December 1926" in Admiral Mss, Honnold Library.

the Atlantic Coast. One paper observed, "The Pacific Coast can now sit back content once more in the assurance that the West again commands the tourist stage, the performers on which number myriads. For the return of the greyhound to home waters symbolizes, as little else can do, that Florida has yielded to California as an attraction to American pleasure-seekers."[32] The following autumn a second invasion of the Atlantic coastwise trade lanes was canceled because there was anticipation of an increase in winter travel on the West Coast. The decision "was received with great satisfaction in the Pacific Coast ports where the great speed queen is regarded as an asset to the whole Coast."[33] But the traffic did not measure up to expectations and the *H. F. Alexander* was laid up for the winter on December 3, 1926. In 1925, the *Dorothy Alexander* was also sent to the Atlantic Coast under a profitable charter to the Clyde Line.[34] The placing of these two Admiral ships on the Atlantic Ocean for the winter season proved to be merely a temporary solution to the problem, for the eastern lines soon obtained additional ships to replace their losses.

At times, special cruises were arranged for the Alexander ships. While prohibition lasted, trips to Mexico proved popular. On one of these "good will" cruises, the *Dorothy Alexander* spent twelve days visiting Ensenada, La Paz, Mazatlan, and Magdalena Bay, and provided her passengers with a "wine list designed" by a "connoisseur."[35] The

[32] Los Angeles *Times*, May 29, 1926.

[33] *Marine Digest*, V (Sept. 25, 1926), 7. For other comments see: Los Angeles *Times*, Sept. 25, 1926; *Railway and Marine News*, XXIII (Oct. 1926), 20.

[34] Alexander to directors, Nov. 18, 1926, Oct. 12, 1927, in Admiral Mss, Honnold Library.

[35] *Marine Digest*, IX (April 11, 1931), 3, IX (April 18, 1931), 7, IX (May 2, 1931), 14. For other accounts of Mexican cruises see: Los Angeles *Times*, July 19, Aug. 12, 1926; *Railway and Marine News*, XXIX (April 1932), 9; *Marine Digest*, XI (June 10, 1933), 3; Alexander to Executive Committee, May 23, 1929, in Admiral Mss, Honnold Library.

Mexicans did not always show as much good will in return. In 1929, H. F. Alexander regretfully reported, "There were no Ensenada excursions during March owing to the disturbed conditions in Mexico. It is hoped these excursions may be resumed again soon."[36] When the *President Adams* went aground outside the breakwater at Cristobal, the Dollar Line chartered the *Ruth Alexander* for one journey around the world in the winter of 1929. Since the Admiral Line received $1,100 per day for the ship, this mishap of the Dollar Line proved to be profitable to the Alexander Company.[37]

Occasionally the Admiral Line chartered one of its large ships to private parties. On October 19, 1922, the *Ruth Alexander* left San Francisco under such a charter. A newspaper reported, "With a jazz orchestra, hundreds of cocktail shakers and everybody carrying a pocket corkscrew it is rumored that a merry time is expected to be had by all." The three hundred passengers were ostensibly paying for a journey to Ensenada.[38]

When national prohibition went into effect in 1920, the steamship lines were confused by contradictory rulings. In 1920, the acting Attorney General decided that the "dry law" applied to all American ships. On June 13, 1922, the general counsel for the Shipping Board ruled that neither the Eighteenth Amendment nor the Volstead Act could be enforced on ships outside the three-mile limit. On October 6, 1922, the Attorney General submitted an opinion to the Secretary of the Treasury that the Eighteenth Amendment applied to United States ships wherever they might be. After this decision, the coastwise

36 Alexander to directors, April 22, 1929, in Admiral Mss, Honnold Library.
37 Alexander to directors, March 5, 1929, and Alexander to Executive Committee, May 23, 1929, in Admiral Mss, Honnold Library. *Pacific Marine Review*, XXVI (Feb. 1929), 14 in advertising section.
38 San Francisco *Examiner*, Oct. 20, 1922.

lines officially operated "dry" ships. There were many
passengers, however, who boarded the vessels with bulging
pockets and hopes that no federal agents would be
aboard.[39]

Charters, Mexican cruises, and invasions of other passenger lanes only partially solved the problem of what to
do with the large liners during the slack travel season,
but they served as excellent opportunities for keeping the
big ships in the news.

OVERCOMING PUBLIC DISTRUST

The steamship lines had to counteract constantly the
impression that sea travel was unsafe. Each wreck or
accident provided unfavorable publicity and caused the
passenger business to slump. Timid people who would
have otherwise enjoyed the freedom of ship travel were
discouraged by news of disasters. The national president
of the Propeller Club of the United States asserted, "There
is no question that the particularly poor cruise season of
the winter of 1934-1935 may be attributed directly to the
series of accidents to American vessels which occurred
last fall and winter."[40]

In discussing the problem one shipping publication
noted that marine wrecks attracted public attention to a
greater degree than land disasters. This condition tended
to create the supposition that water travel was more
hazardous than land transportation. But the magazine
concluded that official figures prove that the "chances for
longevity are 400 to 1 better on board government-

[39] *Pacific Marine Review*, XIX (Aug. 1922), 463-65. The opinion is
quoted in full in *ibid.*, XIX (Nov. 1922), 615-20.

[40] Arthur M. Tode, "United States Shows the Way to Safety at Sea,"
Pacific Marine Review, XXXII (Sept. 1935), 283.

inspected ships than they are dodging auto traffic."[41] Another periodical remarked that because of the way the newspapers "played up" the horrors of sea tragedies, the "idea of going on a sea voyage is becoming in the minds of too many Americans a rather gay way of courting a watery grave."[42] The secretary-treasurer of the Neptune Association, an organization of merchant marine officers, protested before a conference in Washington, D. C., against the efforts of the newspapers "to fix responsibility and blame" after a sea disaster and maintained that such endeavors were unjustified because experience proved that most cases were merely unavoidable accidents in which nobody was to blame. There might be some logic in this position but it provided little solace or comfort to friends and relatives of disaster victims.[43]

There was some justification for the feeling on the part of the marine transportation system that the newspapers overplayed the horrors of sea wrecks. In recording the sinking of the *San Juan,* one paper printed a four-column pen drawing, seventeen separate news stories, and twelve pictures, all of which appeared in a single issue. One of the pictures had the caption, "When Grinding Timbers and Rendering Iron Sang Dirge of Sixty-Eight." The "sickening whirlpool" that sucked down the victims to their watery grave was vividly described. Though probably unaware of the information at the time, the paper underestimated the fatalities. Seventy-five lost their lives instead of the reported sixty-eight.[44]

To counteract publicity of this sort, maritime publications and steamship lines attempted to prove how safe sea

41 "The Moro Castle Fire," *Railway and Marine News,* XXXI (Sept. 1934), 4.
42 "Safety in Ships" (editorial), *Pacific Marine Review,* XXXII (Jan. 1925), 1.
43 San Francisco *Chronicle,* Oct. 30, 1930.
44 Los Angeles *Times,* Aug. 31, 1929; *Annual Report* (1930), p. 15.

travel really was. Unfortunately the average person who
read about the sinking of the *San Juan* in the daily press
was rarely exposed to the rebuttal arguments. Each year
the trade publications would duly report the statistics,
furnished by the Steamboat Inspection Service of the
Department of Commerce, which usually showed that only
one passenger was lost to several million persons carried.
For the fiscal year ending in 1924, the ratio was one to
over six million.[45] The fact that the figures included
passengers carried on inland waters and those riding
ferries did not lessen the enthusiasm of the shipping
fraternity for drawing optimistic conclusions concerning
the safety of sea travel. One magazine declared that water
transportation "is almost safer, statistically, than sleeping
in your own bed at home." That sea travel was "safer
than walking" was asserted by the proponents but was
hardly believed by the public at large.[46]

When the burning of the *Congress* in 1916 was producing widespread criticism in the daily papers, the *Railway
and Marine News* maintained, "The whole official record
of the disaster brings out the heart, the soul, and the love
of humanity that is often held by such great corporations
[the Pacific Coast Steamship Company], although it frequently takes such disasters as this to bring forth credit
where credit is due." Such praise was based on the fact
that a special train had been rushed to the Oregon coast
to pick up the passengers.[47] Another technique, which
may have produced more results than the attempt to laud
the "soul" of a shipping company, was employed by the
Admiral Line. Each year a safety flag was awarded to the
ship in its fleet with the best record. The *Emma Alex-*

[45] *Annual Report* (1924), p. 14
[46] *Pacific Marine Review*, XXXII (Jan. 1935), 1; "Safer Than Walking"
(editorial), *ibid.*, XXI (March 1924), 161. See also: *Railway and Marine
News*, XXII (Jan. 1924), 30; *Pacific Marine Review*, XII (Feb. 1916), 62.
[47] *Railway and Marine News*, XIV (Nov. 1916), 37.

ander flew the flag from her masthead for a time in recognition of her record of carrying thousands of passengers and tons of cargo between Puget Sound and California during 1933 without an accident of any kind.[48]

To inspire confidence, all types of safety devices were installed. The *H. F. Alexander* was the first commercial carrier to have a Kolster radio compass and position finder, enabling her officers to determine the position of the ship from radio signals regardless of weather conditions. The new device proved practical in at least one instance. While proceeding in a heavy fog in 1923 the *H. F. Alexander* picked up the radio signals of a nearby ship. By taking radio bearings the captain of the *H. F. Alexander* discovered that the other ship was dead ahead on a collision course. After an exchange of radio messages each vessel hauled off slightly and passed the other in safety. In December 1923 the *Ruth Alexander* demonstrated her direction-finder equipment to a newspaper reporter. The favorable publicity which resulted included a picture of the ship, a map which showed how the equipment worked, and a column-long account of the trip. The Kolster radio compass proved so successful that by 1924 installations had been made on the *Rose City, Harvard, Yale,* and eight vessels of the Admiral Line.[49]

In addition to the Kolster radio compass, wide publicity was given the other safety equipment on board the *H. F. Alexander.* Although 810 persons were a capacity load, the lifeboats accommodated 926 persons. In addition, there were life preservers in every room, a number of unsinkable life rafts on the top deck, and a power lifeboat which was capable of taking other boats in tow. To control a fire, three separate fire alarm systems were provided. One

[48] *Marine Digest,* XII (March 10, 1934), 6.
[49] *Pacific Marine Review,* XX (July 1923), 331, XX (Dec. 1923), 585, XXI (Oct. 1924), 5 in advertising section; *Marine Digest,* I (Sept. 9, 1922), 6; San Francisco *Examiner,* Dec. 2, 1923.

of these instantly notified the officer on watch of a fire in any part of the ship. Another automatically isolated the affected area and poured steam into it. The vessel was built on the cellular system with a double bottom which was divided by numerous watertight bulkheads.[50]

Between 1916 and 1936, novel devices for assuring safety at sea were constantly being offered. To demonstrate a new life-saving suit, a marine sergeant jumped off the deck of the *H. F. Alexander* in 1922 and paddled around the water with apparent comfort and ease for half an hour while interested passengers observed the demonstration. In 1924, a self-bailing lifeboat was developed which could bail itself dry in twenty to twenty-four seconds. To warn navigators of approaching shoals, a sounding machine, called the fathometer, was commercially produced in 1925.[51] As an aid in picking up survivors of a wreck, a lighted life preserver was invented which would light automatically upon contact with salt water and burn for seventy-two hours. The voltaic cell was composed of carbon and zinc which produced electricity when immersed in sea water.[52]

The government kept abreast of safety developments. In 1935, it planned to install four new distance-finding stations along the Pacific Coast. These stations sent out synchronized radio beacons and audible blasts. By computing the time interval between the reception of these two signals and dividing by 5.5, a navigator could determine the distance of his ship from the station. Later in the same year, the first lighted gong buoy on the Pacific Coast was placed in operation. Unlike the weak, sobbing note of the time-honored whistles, this buoy had four

[50] *Pacific Marine Review*, XIX (July 1922), 414; *Railway and Marine News*, XV (April 1917), 36-37.

[51] San Francisco *Examiner*, Oct. 6, 1922; *Pacific Marine Review*, XXI (Aug. 1924), 23 in advertising section, XXII (April 1925), 182-83.

[52] *Log*, XXIX (May 1937), 18; *Pacific Marine Review*, XXXII (June 1935), 191.

separate-toned gongs which alternated in sending out long-range warnings. The first motor lifeboat provided with radio equipment was tested in December 1935.[53] In referring to the many modern aids to navigation which had developed during his long life, Captain Robert Dollar observed, "We all take these wonderful devices as a matter of course. This no doubt is due to the fact that inventions happen so often that only a signal from Mars would really excite us."[54]

In spite of the safety appliances mishaps on the sea continued to plague the steamship lines. In addition to the major wrecks which involved loss of life, there was a provoking series of minor catastrophes. In August 1922 the *H. F. Alexander* ran on the rock in a dense fog near Cape Flattery at the entrance to Puget Sound, but the ship was able to back off into deep water under her own power. A Coast Guard officer asserted, "It may be classed as a miracle of the sea that she is not there today—a broken hulk."[55] Nobody was injured but the passengers had to be transferred to a relief ship. The repairs kept the liner out of commission for several weeks at the height of the tourist season. At the same time, sea-going men did nothing to help inspire confidence when they labeled the *H. F. Alexander* a "jinx ship" because the vessel had been christened by a left-handed woman in 1914.[56]

In April 1924 the *Ruth Alexander* had to seek safe anchorage inside Trinidad Head, north of Eureka, when water was discovered in one of the holds. The pumps were unable to keep up with the incoming water and the next day the 350 passengers were transferred to the *H. F. Alexander,* which took them back to San Francisco.

53 Los Angeles *Times,* Jan. 3, June 12, 1935; *Log,* XXVI (Dec. 1935), 12.
54 Robert Dollar, *Memoirs,* IV, 48.
55 Lt. R. R. Waesche, "The Lair of the Pacific's Sea Monster," *Pacific Marine Review,* XX (July 1923), 322.
56 *Railway and Marine News,* XX (Sept. 1922), 26; San Francisco *Examiner,* Aug. 13, 1922.

After a canvas covering was thrown around the hull, the pumps were able to gain on the water and the *Ruth* proceeded to drydock.[57] Four years later, the *Ruth* ran into more difficulty when she collided with the battleship *Colorado* off Los Angeles and cut a fifteen-foot hole in the starboard bow of the naval ship. Fortunately the *Ruth* suffered only slight damage but the entire blame for the collision was placed on her captain, who admitted that he thought the *Colorado* was anchored when in fact the battleship was under way.[58] In December 1934 the *Ruth* collided with a ferry in San Francisco Bay. Both parties were adjudged at fault, the *Ruth* for excessive speed and the ferry for not blowing a danger signal. No one was injured.[59]

Faulty navigation added to the list of mishaps. At sundown on February 15, 1930, the *Admiral Benson*, while feeling her way into the mouth of the Columbia River in a heavy fog, grounded on Peacock Spit. An S.O.S. was sent out but help did not arrive until after midnight. The passengers and crew reached shore safely. The vessel, however, was abandoned to the underwriters. Charged with negligence, the captain explained that the reason he had not applied for a master's license for the Columbia River was, "I thought I did not have the necessary qualifications."[60] His license was suspended for six months. The wisdom of the Admiral Line in assigning an unqualified person to command one of its ships was as open to question as the inefficiency of the captain.[61]

These accidents, while not involving loss of life, created an unfavorable public opinion concerning the safety and

[57] San Francisco *Chronicle*, April 24, 25, 26, May 2, 6, 8, 1924; *Pacific Marine Review*, XXI (June 1924), 347.
[58] San Francisco *Chronicle*, March 17, 19, 1928, Jan. 26, Sept. 11, 1929.
[59] *Pacific Marine Review*, XXXII (Dec. 1935), 383.
[60] Quoted in San Francisco *Chronicle*, Feb. 26, 1930.
[61] *Marine Digest*, VIII (Feb. 22, 1930), 15, VIII (March 1, 1930), 3; San Francisco *Chronicle*, Feb. 16, 1930.

desirability of sea travel. In 1921 the *Queen* broke a crankshaft and drifted helplessly for several hours off Point Arena. She was towed back to San Francisco where the *Admiral Watson* had been held to take the passengers on their interrupted journey to Seattle; only 17 of the 130 passengers on board the *Queen* availed themselves of the privilege. A newspaper observed that the remainder were too happy to be on land to start right off to sea again. A few months later, when the main steam pipe line exploded on the *Admiral Farragut* while en route from San Francisco to Seattle, the ship had to be towed to port. Some of the passengers were not awakened and knew nothing about the accident until they found themselves back in San Francisco the next morning. Although the repairs were made within twenty-four hours, only a few of the original passengers decided to trust the ship again. A similar reluctance existed among the passengers who were taken off the *Ruth Alexander* in 1924 because of her leaky condition. A reported 140 of a possible 350 continued their journey northward on the *H. F. Alexander*.[62]

Accidents and human mistakes were not the only things which undid the work of the publicity agents. Storms and gales played havoc with schedules, as well as with the stomachs of the passengers. Only during a small portion of the year did the Pacific Ocean live up to the connotation of its name. Although heavy weather could occur any time, the worst storms were in the winter. In 1921 the captain of the *Rose City* encountered an electrical storm which he declared was like "the wrath of the gods." His description of it undoubtedly made landlubbers thankful that they had not ventured on the sea: "The first terrific fork lightning flashed through the darkness in the southeast, then the whole heavens were lighted up by sheet lighting so that one could read a newspaper on the bridge.

62 Los Angeles *Times,* April 27, 1924; San Francisco *Chronicle,* Jan. 11, July 23, 1921.

This lasted for ten minutes, and was followed by a terrific hail squall. The hailstones were as large as marbles, and similar to those which visit only the Polar regions."[63]

On a southbound journey in 1922 the *Yale* encountered mountainous seas that destroyed sixty feet of railing, tore the hatch cover off the forward companion scuttle, and flooded the observation saloon, drenching a number of the seventy-five passengers. The *Yale* arrived in Los Angeles Harbor seven hours late.[64] The next month, the *Dorothy Alexander* ran into a gale of such intensity that the attempt to pass through the Juan de Fuca Strait to the open sea had to be abandoned and shelter sought in Clallam Bay. She was twenty hours late in arriving at San Francisco.[65] For a twenty-four hour period in 1925, a fifty to sixty mile-an-hour wind stopped all shipping going in or out of the mouth of the Columbia River. The next year, the breakwater of the Los Angeles Harbor was awash. Delays were consequently encountered in docking the big ships because of the rough water. Ice floes at times prevented coastwise vessels from going up the Columbia River.[66]

Even the large *H. F. Alexander* was not immune to weather conditions. In October 1924 she encountered a gale which kicked up huge waves, one of which jumped completely over the first hold and came crashing down with full force on the lower bridge deck. The *H. F. Alexander,* carrying 300 excited passengers, arrived at San Francisco eight hours behind schedule. The only casualty was the fourth officer, who was knocked down by the force of the wave and broke his left arm. To allow time for repairs, the sailing to Los Angeles was canceled.[67]

---

[63] Quoted in Portland *Oregonian,* Jan. 14, 1921.
[64] Los Angeles *Times,* Dec. 11, 1922.
[65] San Francisco *Chronicle,* Jan. 2, 4, 1923.
[66] Portland *Oregonian,* Dec. 29, 1924, Feb. 2, 1925; Los Angeles *Times,* April 8, 1926; *Railway and Marine News,* XVIII (Jan. 1920), 34.

Delays caused by gales and fogs tended to decrease confidence in the dependability of sea travel. Though the Admiral Line advertised that it served the "Pacific Coast with Clocklike Regularity" and H. F. Alexander declared that during 1924 the *H. F. Alexander* had "been late docking only two times, for a total of 4 hours," the public remembered the exceptions.[68]

Fear of personal safety, as well as lack of punctuality, caused a loss of patronage. There were people who remembered some of the tragedies of coastwise navigation. In 1913 one passenger had been washed overboard and three crew members of the *President* drowned when they went to his rescue. The license of the first officer was suspended for eighteen months on the charge of negligence.[69] In 1907 three children had been swept off the same ship by a big wave and were lost. In this case, the officers were exonerated of all blame as the children had been warned against playing on deck.[70] In 1925 a passenger on the *Humboldt* disappeared between San Francisco and Los Angeles. No evidence was found to indicate either a suicide or an unfortunate accident.[71]

Less fatal, but just as serious from the standpoint of attracting patronage, was the effect of rough weather upon the health and comfort of the passengers. Many attempts were made to eliminate the roll to which all

---

67 San Francisco *Examiner*, Oct. 17, 1924; Los Angeles *Times*, Oct. 17, 1924. For other accounts of bad weather conditions along the coast see: *Pacific Marine Review*, XVII (Jan. 1920), 115; *Railway and Marine News*, XX (Dec. 1922), 27, XXII (Jan. 1924), 29; *Marine Digest*, I (Jan. 6, 1923), 4; *Pacific Marine Review*, XXI (Jan. 1924), 89; Alexander to directors, July 11, 1927, in Admiral Mss, Honnold Library; Los Angeles *Times*, April 8, 1926.

68 H. F. Alexander, "Why We Made Money When Nearly Everybody Said We'd Fail," p. 502; *Pacific Marine Review*, XXXII (April 1935), 4 in advertising section.

69 San Francisco *Examiner*, Nov. 28, Dec. 28, 1913.

70 San Francisco *Call*, Nov. 28, Dec. 7, 1907.

71 Los Angeles *Times*, Oct. 9, 1925.

ships were subject in restless seas. A foot of concrete was added to the keel of the *H. F. Alexander* to give her more stability, but even the concrete did not prevent the big ship from rolling, as many a person could testify who had spent a sleepless night on her. Naval architects had slight sympathy with the ship operator who wanted to narrow the beam in order to stiffen the ship. There was danger of the ship's capsizing if the metacentric height was too low. In a paper read before the annual meeting of the Society of Naval Architects and Marine Engineers in 1921, E. H. Rigg warned, "A live passenger is worth several dead ones, even if he were fractionally more seasick than the comfortably drowned ones."[72]

A partial solution to the problem of seasickness would have been the installation of gyrostabilizers, but no line on the coast was in the position to pay the cost. The companies did attempt to eliminate engine vibration wherever possible. In the reconditioning of the *Harvard* and *Yale*, the steel deck was extended for the entire length of the ship and 275 tons of structural steel were added. As late as 1929 the Admiral Line had the *Emma Alexander* reconditioned "in order to do away with the vibration which has always been objectionable."[73]

With the handicaps it had to face, sea travel did amazingly well to attract the thousands of persons who regularly used its facilities up and down the Pacific Coast. Freedom of movement, good food, and many diversions which did not exist on other types of transportation were the redeeming features of a service that was dependent in a large measure on the whims of nature in spite of the achievements of man.

[72] E. H. Rigg, "Passenger Liner Design," *Pacific Marine Review,* XIX (Jan. 1922), 63.
[73] Alexander to Executive Committee, Nov. 21, Dec. 20, 1929, in Admiral Mss, Honnold Library; *Pacific Marine Review,* XVIII (June 1926), 329-30.

EIGHT

The Last Struggle, 1930-1936

THE BEGINNING OF THE DEPRESSION

THE FINANCIAL CRASH in the fall of 1929 did not immediately affect the position of the steamship lines. Because of the disastrous rate war which had just been brought to a close, the financial condition of the steamship companies had been seriously weakened. As a result, a great deal of cargo had been moved by shippers which would have normally been spread over a longer period of time. In May 1929 the common stock of the Admiral Line had hit a record low of $24.27 as compared with the 1925 average of $62.46. Robert C. Hill, ship broker and former marine editor of the Seattle *Post-Intelligencer,* observed in August 1929 that "not in twenty years has North Pacific shipping experienced such a prolonged period of depressed freights"; and in November Hill declared that the "present depressed state of cargo offerings and freights cannot be attributed to the recent debacle in the stock market. Business has been bad with shipping since early this year and the collapse of securities prices caused scarcely any notice in maritime circles."[1] Although the stock market crash was not a cause of poor conditions in the shipping industry, it did accentuate them. By the second month in 1930 Hill noted, "There are those who assert that the present situation is the worst

since steel ships began to move the world's commerce."[2]
By February 1930 the common stock of the Admiral Line
was down to $6.70.

The effect upon magazines which dealt with marine
transportation was pronounced. The number of adver-
tisers in the *Pacific Marine Review* fell from 168 in 1926
to 44 in 1934. This magazine, which claimed to be the
"first established . . . marine paper published on the
Pacific Coast," was considered the leader of the field
because of its expensive format, thick issues, and slick
paper. The total number of pages it printed per year
dwindled from 658 in 1924 to 384 in 1933. The smaller
periodicals were also affected. The *Railway and Marine
News,* which was older than the *Pacific Marine Review*
but was not exclusively devoted to marine affairs, printed
only 256 pages in 1933 as compared to 600 in 1929. In the
same period, the weekly *Marine Digest* shrank to half its
former size. Among the other magazines which had similar
experiences, mention should be made of the *Shipping
Register, Pacific Shipper,* and *Log. Pacific Ports,* a Seattle
publication, had discontinued publication in 1924.[3]

The condition of the trade publications merely reflected
the general poor health of the industry. Water line rates
were down to approximately one-third of the levels in
1910, while the corporate surplus of ten steamship lines
which operated in the Pacific area declined from $5,042,159
in 1928 to $1,043,774 in 1932.[4] The temper of the times

[1] *Railway and Marine News,* XXVI (Sept. 1929), 29, XXVI (Dec. 1929),
15; "Statistics" in Admiral Mss, Honnold Library.

[2] *Railway and Marine News,* XXVII (March 1930), 14.

[3] *Pacific Marine Review,* XXIII (Nov. 1926), XXXI (Jan. 1934). These
figures exclude the advertising section which was numbered separately but
which did include news items. *Railway and Marine News,* XXX (1933),
XXVI (1929); *Marine Digest,* IV (1925), XI (1932). "Statistics" in Admiral Mss, Honnold Library.

[4] U. S., Senate, *Report of the Federal Coordinator,* 73d Cong., 2d sess.,
S. Doc. 152, pp. 138-40. For general discussions of shipping during the de-

was well expressed by the editor of the *Railway and Marine News* in December 1933: "As the year drags its weary way to a close, few tears will be shed in shipping circles when it passes into history. It has been a period of fervid hope and high expectation tempered by acute disappointment and deep anxiety."[5]

ATTEMPTS TO HELP THEMSELVES

During the depression, efforts were made by the lines to solve their own difficulties by strengthening the conference agreements which had been violated so flagrantly in the past. The development of the conference system in the maritime industry has been characterized as "a natural evolution—an attempt to better the cutthroat competition, slashing rates, and general chaos which prevail on the free seas under an individualistic economy."[6] However, there were objections to the system. Conferences often illegally paid deferred rebates and operated fighting ships which were vessels assigned to a particular trade lane for the express purpose of ruining a rival by rate cutting. The secrecy which was apt to surround the action of conferences was also attacked. In 1925 the chief of the Transportation Division of the Department of Commerce declared, "A steamship conference is, in essence, a monopoly, however brief its effective life may be," and observed that the "steamship conferences by their disregard of the

pression, see also: Hobart S. Perry, "The United States Shipping Industry," *Annals of the American Academy of Political and Social Science*, CXCIII (Sept. 1937), 88-98; Ronald A. Shadburne, "Coastwise and Intercoastal Shipping," *ibid.*, CCXXX (Nov. 1943), 29-36.

5 "Exit 1933–Enter 1934" (editorial), *Railway and Marine News*, XXX (Dec. 1933), 5.

6 Mears, *Maritime Trade*, p. 337; Grover G. Huebner, *Ocean Steamship Traffic Management* (New York, 1920), p. 68.

point of view of the shipper have brought criticism on themselves."[7]

In the coastwise trade, there had been little need for a conference as long as the Admiral Line held a practical monopoly; but as competitors, particularly LASSCO, McCormick, and Nelson, began to undermine its dominance, the advantage of some type of a cooperative control became apparent. The first organization, referred to as the Tariff Bureau, was established in 1925 as the result of the *Newport* rate war. Early in May 1928 this agency was reorganized and the three local sections—Puget Sound, Columbia River, and California—which formerly had issued separate tariffs were abolished. The members of the conference were LASSCO, Admiral, Nelson, McCormick, and the Los Angeles–San Francisco Navigation Company, the successor to the White Flyer Line. The conference employed a full-time secretary and issued for its members a single tariff which covered coastwise trade from San Diego to Puget Sound.[8]

The rate war of 1929 temporarily ended this joint effort, but by autumn the companies had again united in a solid front. Yet the life of the conference was destined to be brief. The temptation to offer the public lower rates in order to attract more business was too great for the Los Angeles—San Francisco Navigation Company. It withdrew from the conference on April 12, 1930, and immediately published rates below the prevailing levels. The conference lines protested to the Railroad Commission of California that the rates were too low and would demoralize the transportation industry if allowed to continue. After extensive hearings at which many shippers

---

[7] E. S. Gregg, "The Opportunity of Steamship Conferences," *Pacific Marine Review*, XXII (Sept. 1925), 408.

[8] California, Railroad Commission, *Decisions*, XXXVIII, 719; *Railway and Marine News*, XXV (May 1928), 33; Los Angeles *Times*, July 1, 1928.

appeared in support of the reductions, the commission found that the Navigation Company used slow, wooden vessels on irregular runs with high insurance rates which justified the lower rates. On June 16, 1930, it therefore approved the new schedule.[9]

Other non-conference lines began operations. On February 28, 1931, the Los Angeles–Long Beach Despatch Line, a new company, offered lower rates and was followed by several other newcomers to the field. In answer to this challenge, the established lines on April 7, 1931, cut charges up to 38 percent. But the independents continued to flourish. Because of this competition, the McCormick Steamship Company decided in December 1931 that it could no longer maintain conference rates. As a result, the conference ceased to exist. The previous January, the conference had narrowly escaped dissolution when all its members had submitted their resignations, but attempts to iron out the differences had been successful.[10]

The abundance of idle shipping, which was available at bareboat charter for as little as twenty dollars a day, provided the means by which new concerns could furnish ruinous competition to the companies that had invested large amounts of money in equipment. A bareboat charter was one by which a vessel was chartered from an owner without the crew, fuel, or provisions, which were furnished by the charterer.

No certificate of public convenience was required of an operator who desired to start in the shipping business. The Railroad Commission of California reported in 1932 that the "records of this Commission show that competing coastwise boat lines spring up over night, invariably

9 *Railway and Marine News*, XXVI (Oct. 1929), 21; California, Railroad Commission, *Decisions*, XXXIV, 753-61; Los Angeles *Times*, June 18, 1930.
10 California, Railroad Commission, *Decisions*, XXXVIII, 719; Los Angeles *Times*, April 7, Dec. 3, 1931; *Marine Digest*, IX (Jan. 31, 1931), 5.

offering rates lower than those of the established lines but without any knowledge of the cost of operations."[11] On its own initiative, the commission investigated freight conditions along the coast of California. During the first six months of 1932, it heard 241 witnesses testify at twenty-four hearings. Bluntly it was told by A. F. Haines, the traffic manager for the Admiral Line: "The Pacific Steamship Company's service is degenerating from good, substantial combination freight passenger steamers to a line of cheaply operated cargo boats, due to the lack of control of competitors. With large capital invested and the necessity of maintaining regular service, we are subject to attack by irresponsible operators using cheap, slow, antiquated tonnage, with practically no investment and insufficient responsibility to meet their liabilities in case of accident or disaster. . . . When the trade is poor these irresponsibles drop out and leave the companies with large investments to continue. Then when business revives the irresponsibles come out of their holes and attack again."[12]

These "irresponsibles" had a variety of backgrounds and corporate existences. The Christenson-Hammond Line, established on August 30, 1929, had no ships, assets, or liabilities but operated a freight service using steamers of several owners. At one time its fleet included six vessels from the Hammond Lumber Company, four from Nelson, two from Sudden and Christenson, and one from McCormick. Accounts were settled between the operator and the owners after each voyage. The amount of freight that the line handled rose from 2,075 tons in 1930 to 189,937 in 1935. By 1934, the name was changed to Hammond Shipping Company.[13] The Beadle Steamship Company,

[11] California, Railroad Commission, *Decisions*, XXXVIII, 119; Roland W. Charles, *Troopships of World War II* (Washington, D. C., 1947), p. 354.
[12] Case Number 3154, "Reporter's Transcript," III, 346 in ASF.
[13] "Annual Report of the Christenson-Hammond Line to the Railroad Commission of California," 1929-1935, in ASF.

which was organized on June 11, 1930, established a service between San Francisco and Oregon points. By 1933, it was operating five vessels principally in the lumber trade. The Sudden Steamship Company was a partnership which quadrupled the volume of its business between 1932 and 1934. Despite this increase, it experienced a loss of $46,524 in its brief existence of two years. The Schafer Brothers Steamship Lines began operations on November 18, 1932, with a capital stock of $50,000, which was owned by the lumber company of the same name. Its two vessels carried the lumber output of its parent company from Washington to California and general cargo on the return trip. In its first year it made a net profit of $52,936. The amount of freight carried by the line tripled in three years, from 49,733 tons in 1933 to 157,409 in 1935.[14] The Chamberlin Steamship Company was an outgrowth of the Western Steamship Company, which had been established by a former official of the Nelson Steamship Company. Its capital stock of $50 was somewhat out of proportion to the $6,480 loss which it suffered the first year. It maintained an irregular weekly service between the Northwest and California before operations were finally discontinued on March 31, 1936.[15] The rates of the Los Angeles–Long

14 *Pacific Marine Review*, XXX (July 1933), 16 in advertising section; "Annual Report of the Beadle Steamship Company to the Railroad Commission of California," 1933-1935, in ASF; "Annual Report of the Sudden Steamship Company to the Railroad Commission of California," 1932-1935, in ASF; "Annual Report of the Schafer Bros. Steamship Lines to the Railroad Commission of California," 1933-1936, in ASF; *Marine Digest*, XII (March 10, 1934), 2; *Railway and Marine News*, XXXI (March 1934), 10.

15 *Marine Digest*, IX (Sept. 6, 1930), 14; *Pacific Marine Review*, XXVII (Oct. 1930), 452; *Railway and Marine News*, XXVII (Oct. 1930), 17; "Annual Report of the Chamberlin Steamship Company to the Railroad Commission of California," 1931-1939, in ASF. An irregular weekly service was maintained between the Northwest and California before operations were finally discontinued on March 31, 1936. Letter from E. A. Chamberlin to Railroad Commission of California, Feb. 20, 1940, in ASF; *Marine Digest*, IX (Nov. 29, 1930), 13; *Railway and Marine News*, XXX (Sept. 1933), 12.

Beach Despatch Line, which operated a weekly schedule along the California coast with chartered wooden steamers, were so low that for the first four months of 1932, the line had a loss of $777 on an investment of $2,000. The South Coast Steamship Company for the same period lost $2,505 on an investment of $26,000. On August 8, 1932, both companies were ordered to increase their rates by the Railroad Commission of California.[16]

Although these various lines had little in common, they did sap the strength of the larger companies by cutting rates to attract as much of the business as they could. To control these "irresponsibles," the older lines decided to find the solution through the discredited conference. Accordingly, the conference rules were thoroughly revised, a manager was employed, and a new freight tariff published which increased rates on March 1, 1932, by about 30 percent. To insure faithful compliance with the rules, the members deposited bonds with the conference. In addition each company contributed to the operating expenses. Over $11,000 for this purpose was contributed by the Admiral Line in 1934.[17]

The revived conference was not able to attract into its membership all the "irresponsibles." Nine lines joined but the independents who did not join continued the policy of rate cutting.[18] A San Francisco bank official, speaking of the unhealthy financial condition of the coastwise steamship business, observed in 1933, "While this condition has been aggravated by the depression, it is not a direct result. While railroad and highway competition are responsible for the loss of a portion of the trade

[16] California, Railroad Commission, Decisions, XXXVII, 773-75.

[17] Los Angeles Times, Jan. 26, 29, Feb. 13, 29, 1932; "Annual Report of the Pacific Steamship Lines Ltd. to the Railroad Commission of California," (1934), p. 208; "Annual Report of the Los Angeles Steamship Company to the Railroad Commission of California," (1934), p. 208 in ASF.

[18] Los Angeles Times, Feb. 13, 1932; Mears, Maritime Trade, p. 358.

formerly coastwise, the real reason is ruinous competition and rate cutting by the carriers in coastwise trade."[19] The Interstate Commerce Commission reported to the United States Senate in 1934, "At the bottom of the troubles lies too much and uncontrolled competition. Within the industry itself competition has been particularly severe."[20]

As the toughest competition offered by the independents was along the California coast, the conference members requested the Railroad Commission of that state to stabilize rates. At the numerous hearings which resulted, the representative of the conference declared that if the lower charges were met by the established lines, there was no assurance that a new cut would not be made by the independents. The "irresponsibles" were accused of offering reductions to take business away from the major lines without considering whether the rates would provide a fair return. On their part, the independents claimed that they should be allowed to charge whatever they desired, that they did not want to be hampered by any agreement to maintain certain schedules, and that they felt they had a right to make further reductions should business conditions warrant such action. Incomplete figures presented to the commission showed that the conference lines had carried only 236,588 tons of freight in 1932 as compared to 428,313 in 1929. Part of the loss was due to the depression, but the wildcat lines were responsible for the rest. Because of the depressed conditions generally, the commission on May 22, 1933, authorized the established companies to reduce rates to the level of those maintained by the independents rather than forcing the independents to raise their rates. But it declared that no further

19 The banker was George A. Van Smith, vice president of the Anglo-California National Bank of San Francisco, who was quoted in Los Angeles *Times*, Feb. 17, 1935.

20 U. S., Senate, *Report of the Federal Coordinator*, 73d Cong., 2d sess., S. Doc. 152, p. 9.

reductions in rates could be made after July 1, 1933, without its approval and the commission stated, "It is not in the public interest to have permanent transportation agencies crippled or destroyed because new companies, by taking full advantage of temporary conditions, can for a time offer shippers reduced rates."[21]

In October 1933 the California Railroad Commission formally approved the lower tariffs presented by the conference lines and for the first time in three years, uniform rates existed along the coast. The new rate structure was mainly that of the independents and was considerably lower than the level desired by the established lines. One conference operator commented, "It isn't what we'd like, but at least we know where we stand."[22] The offensive against the "irresponsibles" had stabilized rates, but it had not raised them.

While the steamship lines were struggling against ruthless competition within the industry, a new threat developed from without. Under the fourth section of the Interstate Commerce Act and its amendments, the Interstate Commerce Commission could grant permission to the railroads to charge more for a short haul than for a long one. When, on April 17, 1931, the railroads were authorized to lower their rate differentials, the steamship lines protested. Since the railroads were permitted to lower the rates in the event that the water companies altered theirs, the industry claimed that the control of coastwise rates would be placed in the hands of the rail lines. The maritime leaders also declared that the traditional differential between water and rail routes had been

[21] California, Railroad Commission, *Decisions*, XXXVIII, 722. See also Los Angeles *Times*, Feb. 16, 17, May 25, 1933. In a personal interview on Dec. 31, 1948, in San Francisco, Mr. Hugh Brittan who served as general passenger agent for the Admiral Line stated that these decisions were the most important factor in the collapse of the coastwise industry.

[22] Quoted in Los Angeles *Times*, Oct. 6, 1933.

virtually wiped out by the blanket permission. The marine companies were joined by the Los Angeles Harbor Department in requesting a rehearing; but on October 6, 1931, the Interstate Commerce Commission refused to reopen the case. Maritime circles estimated that as much as one-sixth of the tonnage hauled each year on the sea lanes would be lost to the railroads by this decision.[23]

On December 15, 1932, the Interstate Commerce Commission allowed the rail lines to lower their rate on freight carried from San Francisco to Oregon and Washington. Since the new changes were only authorized on routes where water competition existed, the maritime industry charged that they were water-compelled. It was obvious that the new decision was a serious blow to the ship lines. One maritime man observed, "Now that the railroads can go still lower, steamship operators don't know where to turn for relief."[24]

The rate wars of 1925 and 1929 had weakened the financial standing of the water carriers so that few of them had sufficient reserves to face a prolonged period of business depression. In the face of problems created by the depression, ruinous competition within the industry, and the rate advantage gained by the railroads, the steamship lines were virtually powerless to resist the tide of adversity which was engulfing them.

THE ADMIRAL AND THE STORM

In common with its competitors on the seas, the Admiral Line by 1931 faced a bleak future. The value of its preferred stock had declined from a high point of $295.56

23 *Ibid.*, June 3, 28, Aug. 4, Oct. 7, 1931; *Decisions*, CLXV, 375-417; *ibid.*, CLXXIII, 577-83.
24 Quoted in Los Angeles *Times*, Jan. 4, 1933; *Decisions*, CXC (1933), 273-90. See also Los Angeles *Times*, June 7, Oct. 19, 1932.

in 1926 to $70.59 in August 1931. The decline had been rapid after the investing public learned that the regular quarterly dividend on the preferred stock, due February 1, 1930, was to be omitted. The $176,270 loss experienced by the company in 1929 rose to a staggering $734,332 deficit in 1930 and to $1,196,900 the following year. On January 1, 1931, the company defaulted on the marine equipment mortgage.[25]

In the midst of these reverses, H. F. Alexander, the steamship king of the Pacific Coast, resigned as president of the concern he had built largely on his own initiative. Defeat, which he had maintained in 1926 was impossible, was possible. His farewell statement resounded with a nostalgic note:

Having been actively engaged in the shipping business for the past thirty years, and having organized and built up the Pacific Steamship Company from a very modest beginning to its present importance and influential place in the maritime world, I am, effective August 1, withdrawing as president and active executive of that company to devote my time and attention to my private affairs. . . .

It is naturally with considerable regret that I take this step. I have had the confidence of and the delightful association with a wonderful board of directors and corps of employes, without whose loyalty and devoted cooperation the development of the Pacific Steamship Company could not have been achieved.

At the request of the board of directors I shall continue on the board of the company and shall retain my stock interests, and consequently the relationship with these good business friends, and associates shall not be severed.[26]

[25] "Financial Statement" in Admiral Mss, Honnold Library; *Railway and Marine News*, XXVII (Feb. 1930), 34; copy of the reports of the Admiral Line to the Interstate Commerce Commission for the years 1929 to 1931 in Admiral Mss, Honnold Library.
[26] Quoted in Seattle *Times*, July 31, 1930.

The resignation of H. F. Alexander was particularly regretted by the Seattle interests, for it marked the final triumph of the Dollars of San Francisco in their effort to gain control. Concerning H. F. Alexander, the Seattle trade journal, *Railway and Marine News,* observed, "Probably no man has done more for the Pacific Northwest in a maritime way than he"; and the *Marine Digest* declared that he "has laid aside the mantle of national leadership in the American merchant marine which he wore with honor to himself and the country over a long period of years."[27] A year earlier the same magazine had praised Alexander as "one of the ablest and most constructive men of the country. The importance of his labors is appreciated deeply by the generations of today. And yet it is doubtful whether this generation really grasps the full significance of all that Mr. Alexander has done. The historian of the future will study and analyze this man."[28]

The affairs of the Admiral Line were in a critical state and rumors of its complete collapse were circulated. A new blow to its prestige and earning power came when the Panama-Pacific Line announced that, after June 1, 1931, the Admiral Line would no longer be its operating and freight agent on the Pacific Coast. Since 1923 the two lines had interchanged freight on shipments going from one coast to the other by water. To add to the loss of prestige suffered by the Admiral Line, R. J. Ringwood, who had been the Admiral freight manager for fifteen years, was appointed the Pacific Coast freight traffic manager for the Panama–Pacific Line and the McCormick Steamship Company was designated as the transshipment party between California and the Northwest. Since the Dollar Line had just recently announced that its trans-

27 *Railway and Marine News,* XXVII (Aug. 1930), 45; *Marine Digest,* VIII (Aug. 9, 1930), 7.
28 *Marine Digest,* VII (Aug. 2, 1929), 28.

pacific liners would enter the intercoastal trade, shipping men felt that the action by the Panama–Pacific Line was somewhat retaliatory in view of the fact that the Admiral Line was now controlled by the Dollars.[29]

That the Dollars did not consider the Admiral Line moribund was soon evident. In March 1931 Stanley Dollar announced that reorganization plans would be completed as quickly as possible. This news was received with joy by the shipping fraternity along the coast. The *Railway and Marine News* asserted that the continuance of the Admiral Line "now is assured," and that its collapse would have been "nothing short of a calamity."[30] There were two principal reasons why the Dollars were willing to back the reorganization of a line which appeared to be a losing proposition. First they were anxious to safeguard the heavy financial interest they had in the company and, secondly, they desired to have a coastwise feeder line for their transpacific route. The fact that the Dollars, who had been noted for their business sagacity, were willing to rehabilitate the tottering Admiral Line appeared to maritime circles sufficient evidence that there was hope for its rebirth. Reports even circulated that, following the reorganization and refinancing of the concern, the Admiral Line planned to purchase the *Harvard* and *Yale*.[31]

The Dollars quickly utilized the Admiral fleet as a feeder line. In May 1931 the *H. F. Alexander* was ordered to Victoria, B. C., to meet the Dollar transpacific liner, *President Lincoln,* in order to carry a large shipment of raw silk to San Francisco for transshipment to the *Presi-*

[29] *Pacific Ports,* IX (Oct. 1923), 46; *Pacific Marine Review,* XXI (Sept. 1924), 11 in advertising section; *Railway and Marine News,* XXVIII (May 1931), 17; *Pacific Marine Review,* XXVIII (May 1931), 25 in advertising section.

[30] "Coast Needs Admiral Line" (editorial), *Railway and Marine News,* XXVIII (April 1931), 6.

[31] *Marine Digest,* IX (May 23, 1931), 9.

dent Grant, which would carry it to New York via the Panama Canal. Under this arrangement, the Dollar and Pacific Steamship Companies provided an all-water route of eighteen days from Seattle to New York. In addition to silk, it was hoped to attract other high-class cargo which required speed in delivery. A further development was announced in the summer of 1931 when a twenty-five day service from Seattle to London was offered which utilized the facilities of the Admiral Line from Seattle to California, the Dollar Line from California to New York, and the United States Lines from New York to London.[32]

To bolster sagging coastwise passenger patronage, excursion round-trip fares were offered in September that were only forty cents above the one-way rate between Seattle and San Francisco, and sixty cents above the Seattle to Los Angeles charge. As the direct result of this fare cut, a record passenger list of 575 sailed on the *H. F. Alexander* from Seattle on September 1. Instead of laying up the *H. F. Alexander* for the winter, the new operators announced plans for placing her on the San Francisco to Los Angeles run. Under the new arrangement, the Admiral Line provided six sailings weekly from each port, which compared favorably with the service offered previously by the company between those ports.[33] In October 1931 additional reductions were made in the regular fares. As an economy measure, Stanley Dollar, in 1932, consolidated the traffic and operating departments of the three Dollar companies: the American Mail Line, the Dollar Line, and the Admiral Line. Many changes in personnel were also made. To attract more freight, a store-door pick-up and delivery service was inaugurated in December

32 *Ibid.,* IX (May 16, 1931), 3; *Railway and Marine News,* XXVIII (July 1931), 23.
33 *Marine Digest,* X (Aug. 29, 1931), 10, X (Sept. 5, 1931), 10, X (Aug. 22, 1931), 5.

1932 between some three hundred towns in Southern California and the San Francisco region.[34]

Despite a loss in 1932 of $1,359,804, the highest deficit which the company had ever incurred, the Dollars vigorously pushed plans for reorganization. The last step in the lengthy process was the sale of the fleet at Seattle on January 23, 1933, by a trustee of the defaulted mortgage. Many of the bondholders had sold their holdings to the Dollar interests at 25 percent of par. At the time of the sale, about 94 percent of the bonds were owned or controlled by the Dollars. The Dollars offered the only bid and the fleet, which was valued at $4,159,500, passed to their control for $518,927. J. Harold Dollar became president and his brother, Stanley, became vice president of the reorganized company, which was called the Pacific Steamship Lines Ltd. The concern commenced operations on January 23, 1933. To the newspapers, Harold Dollar declared that the company was starting on a new era of progressive action unhampered by indebtedness.[35]

This optimism was shared by his brother, Stanley, who declared in the *Pacific Marine Review*, January 1933: "Conservative management and cheaper operation are two lessons which came out of the difficult period of the depression. Coupled with the upturn which is now seemingly assured these two elements will be invaluable aids in bringing back shipping to the position it once held."[36] There was truth in the statement that operating costs were lower. The cost for each meal per passenger declined from thirty-four cents in 1929 to less than twenty-four

[34] San Francisco *Chronicle*, July 18, 1924; *Marine Digest*, X (Oct. 10, 1931), 9; *Railway and Marine News*, XXIX (April 1932), 13-14; Los Angeles *Times*, Dec. 16, 1932; *Pacific Marine Review*, XXX (Jan. 1933), 4.

[35] San Francisco *Chronicle*, Feb. 24, 1933; "Annual Report" (1931) in Admiral Mss, Honnold Library; *Railway and Marine News*, XXX (Feb. 1933), 9.

[36] R. Stanley Dollar, "American Shipping During 1932," *Pacific Marine Review*, XXX (Jan. 1933), 7

cents in 1932. At the same time, payroll expenses dropped
from $4,340,023 to $2,858,567.[37] The new line appealed
to the past by retaining the Admiral trademark but made
it clear that there had been a complete divorce from the
Alexander management. The general passenger agent
issued the following statement in San Francisco:

Of course, we shall continue to carry the Admiral Line name
for the name is invaluable. As a matter of fact, in a way, this
is our real link with the past, for in every other way we are
a new company.

It is useless to deny that there have been rumors to the
effect that our line is moribund. The contrary is true. We
have a new, young line, unhampered by mortgages and
financial complications, and we are going ahead on a sure
course.

The Admiral Line is now definitely a Dollar concern. It is
one of a trio with the Dollar Line and the American Mail
Line. Passenger offices have been consolidated, and we all
feel a new zest and interest in the conduct of the affairs of the
company.

Fares are low, very low. In fact I was checking over our
schedule today and figures brought vague memories to me.
I looked back over some schedules of the Pacific Coast Company, before the consolidation in 1916, and found them
almost exactly the same.[38]

The fear of Seattle business men, that the control of
the line by the Dollars might be detrimental to the interests of the Northwest, proved groundless. In March 1933
the operating headquarters of the company were moved
back to Seattle from San Francisco where they had been
for a number of years. In June, the *H. F. Alexander* was
again placed on the Seattle to California run and, for the

37 "Annual Report of Interstate Commerce Commission" (1929, 1932),
p. 505 in Admiral Mss, Honnold Library.
38 Quoted in San Francisco *Chronicle*, Feb. 11, 1933.

first time, no extra fare was charged. One accident marred the 1933 summer season. While steaming in a heavy fog, the *H. F. Alexander* struck the shoals off Point Wilson in Puget Sound and the *City of Los Angeles* had to be chartered from LASSCO to replace her while repairs of $250,000 were made.[39]

The various Alexander subsidiaries continued their corporate existences under Dollar auspices. In 1931 the Portland California Steamship Company purchased, for $500,000, twenty-two vessels from the defunct Submarine Boat Corporation. The old Pacific Steamship Terminal Company, which had planned to build the three-pier terminal in Seattle, was reorganized. In June 1933, a sheriff's sale was held to satisfy the bondholders and a new Dollar company was organized, called the Pacific Terminals Inc. In November 1933 the Mexican Mail Steamship Company was formed as a subsidiary of the Admiral Line for the purpose of operating vessels between Los Angeles and the west coast of Mexico.[40]

In all this aggressive activity there was but a single retreat. In 1933 the Dollars entered into an agreement with the Alaska Steamship Company by which the Admiral Line withdrew from the Alaskan trade. In return, the Guggenheim company agreed to keep out of California. Each line consented to act as the general agent for the other in its own territory. This development set at rest two rumors: that the Admiral Line and the Alaska Steamship Company were to be consolidated, and that the Alaskan fleet of the Admiral Line was to be sold to its

[39] Seattle *Times,* March 19, July 27, 1933; *Railway and Marine News,* XXX (April 1933), 13, XXX (May 1933), 13; *Marine Digest,* XI (April 29, 1933), 3.

[40] Court order dated July 16, 1931, U. S. District Court, District of New Jersey, in Portland California Steamship Company Mss, Honnold Library; "Annual Report to Interstate Commerce Commission" (1933), pp. 106, 212 in Admiral Mss, Honnold Library; *Railway and Marine News,* XXIX (Nov. 1932), 12, XXX (June 1933), 14; *Pacific Marine Review,* XXX (Dec. 1933), 12.

rival. As a result, the Dollars were freed from the threat of Guggenheim competition and could concentrate on the coastwise service between Puget Sound and California. But the agreement did not eliminate all competition from the smaller Alaskan companies. For example, the Arctic Transportation Company placed its steamer, *Arthur J. Baldwin,* on a twenty-four day schedule between Puget Sound and California for the winter of 1933-1934.[41]

On February 1, 1933, the Admiral Line announced another reduction in fares which amounted to about 30 percent. The charges for carrying automobiles between any two points along the coast were reduced from $23 or more per car to $5, provided two passengers accompanied the vehicle. For the summer season, the Admiral Line and LASSCO jointly announced record low rates which represented a 20 percent cut over the previous summer tariffs. As a result, the one-way fare between San Francisco and Los Angeles was $10 and the round trip $14. In June, the one-way charge was reduced to $8.[42] Two new factors had entered the coastwise industry to make these drastic moves necessary. The first was the infiltration of the intercoastal lines into the coastwise business. The depression had forced the several lines offering service through the Panama Canal to seek trade elsewhere in order to keep their ships in operation. As early as 1931, the American–Hawaiian and Quaker lines began to provide service along the Pacific Coast. The Williams Line soon followed, and in April 1932 the Luckenbach Steamship Company inaugurated six sailings monthly between California and Puget Sound. Of all the intercoastal companies, the Grace Line became the most serious contender when, in 1933, it placed its four new "Santa" ships on the coast-

41 Board minutes of the Admiral Line dated March 1, 1933 in Robert Dollar Company Archives; Seattle *Times,* March 23, 1933; *Railway and Marine News,* XXX (April 1933), 5, XXX (Nov. 1933), 18.

42 Los Angeles *Times,* Jan. 28, April 27, June 15, 1933.

wise route. These vessels had excellent passenger accommodations. By 1934, the Grace company had developed sufficient patronage to increase its rates and to maintain weekly sailings between Seattle and San Francisco.[43]

The second factor was the renewal of foreign competition. In 1931, six foreign lines were providing passenger service between Los Angeles and British Columbia. Their sailings were proving popular with Americans because of the novelty of their "continental atmosphere." By 1933 the number of foreign companies had risen to nine. They operated fifty fast liners which provided sailings from Los Angeles and San Francisco to British Columbia. In the spring of 1933 these companies entered into an agreement by which a traveler could go north on one line and return on another. Sailings were so arranged that a vacation could be spent under four flags. An attractive folder, "International Vacations" disclosed that an American could sail under the flags of Denmark, France, England, Germany, the Netherlands, Sweden, and Italy.[44]

During the 1933 summer season there was a boom in sea travel. The low fares, a new tax on gasoline in Washington which retarded gasoline sales, and the desire of many people to get off the crowded highways were all given as explanations for the near capacity loads which the coasters were carrying. In Washington, it was estimated that gasoline sales had dropped at the rate of 3,000,000 gallons a month due to the new tax. For the entire year, the Admiral Line registered a gain of 5,647 in the number of passengers carried despite the fact that

[43] U. S., Senate, *Report of the Federal Coordinator*, 73d Cong., 2d sess., S. Doc. 152, pp. 138-39; *Railway and Marine News*, XXVIII (March 1931), 30, XXIX (March 1932), 21, XXIX (April 1932), 14; *Marine Digest*, XI (Nov. 26, 1932), 3, XI (Dec. 10, 1932), 3, XII (March 10, 1934), 4, XII (May 5, 1934), 3, XII (June 30, 1934), 3; Los Angeles *Times*, Jan. 26, 1932, April 22, 1933; Mears, *Maritime Trade*, p. 358.

[44] Los Angeles *Times*, July 9, 1931, April 22, 1933; *Marine Digest*, XI (April 29, 1933), 7.

the popular Alaskan cruises had been abandoned. To at-
tract more patronage, the Dollar Company offered "Around
America" tours by which a person could travel from
Seattle to San Francisco on the Admiral Line, from San
Francisco to New York via the Panama Canal on the
Dollar Line, and return home on one of the trans-
continental railroads. The price for this trip was $205
tourist or $285 first class.[45]

LASSCO, the California rival of the Admiral Line, also
encountered difficulties during the depression. In the
summer of 1930, LASSCO had announced plans for the
construction of two express liners as running mates of the
Harvard and *Yale*. With these new ships, which were to
have the same speed as the "White Comets," the company
proposed to increase the four weekly sailings from San
Diego, Los Angeles, and San Francisco to a daily schedule,
but plans for the new vessels were shelved when it became
apparent to the LASSCO officials that new ships would also
have to be provided for the Hawaiian trade if the company
was to maintain its share of that business. The Matson
Navigation Company had already placed in the Hawaiian
service the *Malolo* which, because of her speed, could
make as many round trips in a year as two of the LASSCO
ships combined. Representatives of LASSCO suggested to
the Matson Company that the two fleets be combined
under one management. On October 4, 1930, an agreement was signed whereby Matson purchased all the outstanding stock and assumed full control of LASSCO. The
announcement of this action to the public declared:
"Operations out of Los Angeles will continue under the
name of the Los Angeles Steamship Company and under
the direction of present officers of that company, with

45 Copy of reports to Interstate Commerce Commission by the Admiral
Line for 1932 and 1933 in Admiral Mss, Honnold Library; *Railway and
Marine News*, XXX (July 1933), 15, XXX (Dec. 1933), 5, 14; Portland
Oregonian, June 15, 1933; *Marine Digest*, XII (Dec. 2, 1933), 6.

increased frequency of sailings and capacities which will continue to grow. More efficient and economical operation as well as a further convenience for passenger travel and freight shipments will result from the consolidation."

Coastwise service was continued under the LASSCO flag. In April 1931 a new pick-up and delivery service between Los Angeles, San Francisco, and 125 other California cities was started. This service was in addition to the package express service which the company had offered for some time. Although the Los Angeles–San Francisco Navigation Company objected to this move before the Railroad Commission of California and asked that LASSCO be ordered to charge higher rates, the Commission decided in favor of LASSCO.[46]

As the clouds of the depression hung dark and low, LASSCO encountered a tragedy from a different facet of marine transportation. Steaming south "in a dense, blinding fog which had slowed the vessel down to half speed," the *Harvard* went aground off Point Arguello shortly after three o'clock on the morning of May 30, 1931. The 497 passengers were transferred to the freighter *San Anselmo* and later to the new cruiser *Louisville*, both of which had sped to the rescue. No one was lost, but the *Harvard*, her hull split by the relentless pounding of the sea, was abandoned a few days later.[47] The reaction of the passengers to their experience was varied. Some enjoyed

[46] *Pacific Marine Review*, XXVII (July 1930), 311; Seattle *Times*, Oct. 31, 1930; Los Angeles *Times*, Oct. 23, 31, 1930, April 18, 1931; "Annual Report of the Los Angeles Steamship Company to the Railroad Commission of California for the Year Ending December 31, 1931," p. 107 in ASF; Statement prepared for James M. Merrill by Mr. Herm Wilson of the Matson Navigation Company in May 1948, in possession of Mr. Merrill; California Railroad Commission, *Decisions*, XXXVI, 210-13.

[47] San Francisco *Chronicle*, May 31, June 6, 1931; *Marine Digest*, IX (June 6, 1931), 7. For a colorful account of the last hours of the famous coastwise liner see Captain John Johnson, "The Wreck of the Harvard," *Steamboat Bill of Facts*, XVII (Winter 1960), 107-108.

it thoroughly while others blamed the crew for drunken-
ness and inattention to duty. One lady maintained, "It
was a shipwreck de luxe. No one was hurt—it was a
genuine thrill and it earned us a ride on the navy's newest
cruiser."[48] But another woman passenger sued LASSCO for
$50,000.[49]

The exact cause of the grounding was obscure. In
direct contradiction to the earlier reports, the captain
declared that there was no fog when the *Harvard* struck.
After an investigation, the Steamboat Inspection Service
found that several waiters and one quartermaster had
been under the influence of liquor at the time of the
grounding. Two startling facts were also uncovered. In
order to conceal how close to shore the course had been
laid, the log of the *Harvard* had been falsified. It was
also revealed that thirty-two minutes before the *Harvard*
struck, the officer on watch had received a radio bearing
from the Point Arguello station which indicated that the
vessel was steaming directly towards shore. Had this
warning, and others which were received later, been
heeded, there would have been no wreck. The inspectors
suspended the licenses of three of the officers for varying
periods.[50] The confidence of the public was again shaken
in the safety of sea travel.

Temporarily, the *Calawaii* took the place of the *Harvard*
and later the *Iroquois* was chartered from the Clyde Line
at $1,000 per day as the running mate for the *Yale*. The
Iroquois had been built in 1927 for the Atlantic Coast
trade. She had excellent passenger accommodations, including a sea garage for eighty cars, but lacked the speed
of the *Yale*. The number of weekly sailings therefore had
to be reduced. Under the new schedule, there were six

48 Quoted in San Francisco *Chronicle*, May 31, 1931.
49 *Marine Digest*, IX (June 27, 1931), 11.
50 San Francisco *Chronicle*, June 6, 9, July 1, 3, 1931.

sailings weekly between San Francisco and Los Angeles but only two from Los Angeles to San Diego. The former schedule had provided four weekly sailings from each of the three ports. In December 1931 LASSCO returned the *Iroquois* to her owners and although there were rumors that the *H. F. Alexander* might be purchased or chartered as a running mate, the *Yale* continued to operate alone on a reduced schedule.[51] Since she was not able to maintain frequent enough sailings for a regular freight service, Matson formed a new coastwise subsidiary called the California Steamship Company to provide a freight service between San Diego, Los Angeles, and San Francisco.[52]

Within a space of three short years, the condition of LASSCO had changed radically. The depression, the merger, and the loss of the *Harvard* made the future uncertain.

THE NEW DEAL

The advent of the New Deal was looked upon with favor by most maritime groups. One magazine stated the position of shipping circles: "We are now beginning to have a 'new deal' in federal government. This new deal promises well in its beginnings. So far it has largely consisted in simple, direct, frank dealings by the executive, eliminating 'red tape.' "[53] When the National Industrial Recovery

[51] Testimony of R. J. Chandler, vice president of LASSCO before the Railroad Commission of California on Feb. 4, 1932 in Case Number 3154, "Reporter's Transcript," III, 329 in ASF; Los Angeles *Times*, June 1, 1931; San Francisco *Chronicle*, June 24, 1931; *Pacific Marine Review*, XXVIII (July 1931), 277, XXVIII (Oct. 1931), 17 in advertising section; *LASSCO Coastwise Log*, Sept. 29, 1931, in LASSCO Mss, Maritime Collection of John H. Kemble, Claremont, Calif.; *Railway and Marine News*, XXIX (Jan. 1932), 17.

[52] Los Angeles *Times*, Aug. 16, 1933; *Pacific Marine Review*, XXX (Sept. 1933), 288.

[53] "The New Deal and the Merchant Marine" (editorial), *Pacific Marine Review*, XXX (May 1933), 130.

Act was passed in 1933, steamship executives saw in it the means by which a conference could be administered with government backing. Rates could be stabilized, seasonal peaks in cargo handling could be flattened out, and standard business practices could be adopted which would eliminate the "irresponsible competitor." Charles L. Wheeler, vice president and general manager of McCormick Steamship Company, after a trip to Washington, D. C., asserted, "The NRA plan looks good to me now; it looks good for two years from now; it looks good, for the effect it will have, 10 years hence."[54]

This strong endorsement was influential, for the McCormick line was one of the few concerns which had not withdrawn any tonnage during the initial years of the depression. In fact, it had maintained a steady expansion. In March 1930, all northern railroads had established through rates with it via the Puget Sound gateway; previously such an arrangement had only been in force for the Columbia River trade. By November 1930 the McCormick company advertised that it had sent more ships through the Golden Gate than any other line. In 1931 it increased its sailings between San Francisco and Los Angeles to four weekly. In May of that same year it set a new port record at Oakland when it had seven ships dock within eight hours. Less than a week later, a similar record was made at San Francisco when ten of its steamers were berthed on the first of June.[55]

Not all operators, however, followed the lead of McCormick in endorsing the NRA. The opposition took the form of an attempt to exempt the industry from the provisions of the law. It was noted that the railroads,

54 Quoted in *Marine Digest*, XII (Aug. 19, 1933), 5.
55 Oklahoma *Tribune*, May 28, 1931; San Francisco *Examiner*, June 2, 1931; *Railway and Marine News*, XXVII (April 1930), 31, XXVII (Nov. 1930), 6, XXVII (Aug. 1930), 12, XXVIII (May 1931), 4; Seattle *Times*, March 20, 1930.

one of the greatest competitors to the domestic steamship lines, were not under NRA. On August 1, 1933, the American Steamship Owners Association and the Pacific American Steamship Association sent a telegram to General Hugh S. Johnson requesting that the powers of the NRA be delegated as far as shipping was concerned to the Shipping Board.[56] The request was denied and all branches of shipping were placed under the NRA when a New York lawyer, William H. Davis, was appointed administrator. After a discussion, the officers of the Admiral Line decided that it was in the interest of the company "to join the N.R.A. under the blanket Code, pending the completion of an industrial Code."[57] By September 1933 one trade periodical observed, "At this writing, the situation reveals the shipping industry willing and anxious to cooperate with the administration in a concerted effort to improve economic conditions."[58] Another publication noted, "This legislation, while entirely new in principle and utterly alien to the American individualistic type of capitalistic industrial economy, is not any hastily conceived plan prepared by theoretical demagogues. It seems to us that American industry, business, and commerce are being offered in the National Industrial Recovery Act a splendid opportunity. . . ."[59]

In 1934, a proposed code was drawn up by the industry and submitted to Washington for approval with the hope that it would prove to be a solution to the problem of depressed revenues. The *Pacific Marine Review* declared, "When we consider the chaotic cargo tariff conditions that have prevailed during the past few years . . . , it

[56] *Railway and Marine News*, XXX (Aug. 1933), 4-5.

[57] Board minutes of the Admiral Line dated Sept. 12, 1933 in Robert Dollar Company Archives.

[58] "American Shipping Included in New Deal" (editorial), *Railway and Marine News*, XXX (Sept. 1933), 7.

[59] *Pacific Marine Review*, XXX (July 1933), 193.

becomes evident that such a code as is here proposed should be welcome to all American ship operators."[60]

But these dreams of a prosperous future were shattered on May 9, 1934, when a strike of longshoremen tied up shipping along the coast. The union wanted a thirty-hour week, a wage increase, and the closed shop. Great issues also were at stake; one spokesman for the shipping industry summarized the situation with the assertion that the "shipping industry has reached a point where it must fight or die. Intimidation must be met with force. . . ."[61] Bitterness quickly developed on both sides and appeals were made to force. In San Francisco the controversy produced a brief general strike. The general strike ended shortly but the strike of longshoremen along the coast continued. Its violence was such that two months after its beginning, the San Francisco police reported 4 deaths, 266 injuries, and 40 cases of sabotage. For a brief period the National Guard was assembled in Portland to insure order. In Seattle on July 20, 1934, the police "routed hundreds of strikers by effectively using gas. Mayor Charles L. Smith standing firmly for law and order, personally supervised police operations."[62] As the result of the disorders, two men were killed in the Puget Sound city. Twice the employers and Joseph P. Ryan, the national head of the longshore workers, reached agreements which were rejected by the local organizations of the union. Appeals were made to the national government to solve the difficulty. One magazine observed, "Regardless of issues, regardless of either side, the Northwest crisis is a public crisis and President Roosevelt should have intervened.

60 "The Proposed Shipping Code" (editorial), *Pacific Marine Review*, XXXI (May 1934), 129. The text of the proposed code can be found in *ibid.*, 132-35, 142-44.

61 *Railway and Marine News*, XXXI (June 1934), 4; *Pacific Marine Review*, XXXI (Aug. 1934), 236-41; *Marine Digest*, XII (Aug. 4, 1934), 3.

62 *Railway and Marine News*, XXXI (July 1934), 4.

Such intervention would have been in full accord with his own philosophy of control and regulation of industry."[63]

The official journal of the shipowners recommended that the Fascist method of settling strikes be employed. "In Italy," it asserted, "Benito Mussolini and his advisors found a very practical method for insuring that the public cost of labor disputes be borne by the parties who initiated the primary cause of such cost. Since this method has been put into effect Italy has had neither a strike nor a lock out. We recommend to the N.R.A. that they study this method with a view to putting it or some similar scheme into effect for the stabilization of the national industry recovery."[64]

The strike came to an end on July 31, 1934, and the next week an agreement was signed between the contending parties whereby the questions were submitted to arbitration. On October 12, 1934, the arbitration board awarded the longshoremen an increase in wages and a thirty-hour week, but it placed the hiring halls under the joint operation of the employers and unions. Longshoremen were to be hired without regard to union affiliation. Labor Relations Committees were to be established at each port whose duties were to operate the hiring halls, to prepare lists of bona fide longshoremen, and to investigate grievances. Partly as a result of the award, the Pacific Coastwise Conference, in December 1934, raised freight rates 10 to 15 percent on certain commodities.[65]

Many operators blamed the New Deal for the strike and the several petty labor controversies that followed.

[63] *Marine Digest,* XII (June 23, 1934), 4.
[64] "Community vs Communism" (editorial), *Pacific Marine Review,* XXXI (Aug. 1934), 227.
[65] Mimeographed copy of the "Arbitrator's Award" dated Oct. 12, 1934 in Admiral Mss, Honnold Library. Intrastate and interline rates were not raised "for competitive reasons." H. C. Cantelow, "Traffic Problems of a Coastwise Steamship Service," *Railway and Marine News,* XXXII (Aug. 1935), 10; *Marine Digest,* XII (Aug. 4, 1934), 3, XIII (Dec. 15, 1934), 6; Seattle *Times,* July 22, 23, 30, 31, 1934.

The *Admiral Farragut*, 1931. Note the Scarcity of Passengers.
*Courtesy of the William T. Miller Collection, San Francisco Maritime
Museum*

The H. F. Alexander, Seattle. Courtesy of John H. Kemble, Claremont

These controversies made it difficult to maintain regular sailings. In 1935, the growing distrust of the Roosevelt regime was reflected in an editorial in one of the leading maritime magazines: "Theory, not practical reality, appears to be the guiding star of the administration. The program of the New Deal of adding thousands to the public payrolls and spending billions in public works, many of them entirely unnecessary, is being gradually unmasked as a delusion and snare." The editorial concluded, "We are standing up in the boat and blowing on our sails."[66] Before the annual meeting of the Pacific Coast Association of Port Authorities in 1935, H. C. Cantelow, who was the secretary-manager of the Pacific Coastwise Conference, declared that the NRA was used by militant labor leaders "as an invitation" to organize. The result, according to Cantelow, was the disastrous strike of 1934: "The Coastwise shipowner was able to survive the first few years of the depression only because he was reasonably free to manage his own business and free to exercise initiative in quickly adjusting his expenses to rapidly diminishing revenues. He entered the fourth year of the depression hopefully. . . . Then out of the depression there arose a new economic philosophy followed by a fear engendered manifestation of mass psychology which culminated in such unprecedented legislation as our National Recovery Act, the full significance of which was at first not understood by the shipowner."[67] At the same meeting an official of the Admiral Line stated, "I see little to be encouraged about. In fact, a bill known as the Wagner Labor Relations Bill, was signed by the President on July 5, and we shortly will be governed by the provisions of this Bill . . . [which] may

66 "A Will O' the Wisp" (editorial), *Railway and Marine News*, XXXII (March 1935), 3.
67 H. C. Cantelow, "Traffic Problems of a Coastwise Steamship Service," *Railway and Marine News*, XXXII (Aug. 1935), 10.

spell the death knell of private steamship operation."[68]
The attitude of the operators toward the New Deal had
changed from optimistic confidence to deep skepticism.

THE LAST OF THE SHIPS

The depression, strikes, lack of resources, and increasing
competition by other forms of transportation proved to
be the undoing of the steamship companies. The reorganization of the Admiral Line, brought about by the Dollars,
had done little to improve the finances of the company.
Deficits continued to pile up. By the end of 1936, the
reorganized Admiral Line had an accumulated loss of
$2,479,839, which represented almost half a million dollars
more than the value of its property. Under the circumstances, there was little choice. On September 12, 1935,
the Admiral Line announced the suspension of its passenger service for the winter. Continued operation of freight
vessels was promised.[69] The following statement was issued
by Hugh Brittan, the passenger traffic manager:

Rising costs of labor and operation, which have now become
prohibitive under the arbitration awards, and the continual
harassment of petty but costly strikes in violation of agreements, coupled with the general uncertainty over labor conditions, make it impossible for our company to continue its
passenger service for the present.

Our company's freight service will continue to operate as
usual.

It is not easy for me calmly to announce suspension of this
pioneer coastwise passenger service, whose record is written in

[68] H. T. Krull, "Traffic Problems" in Admiral Mss, Honnold Library.
[69] "Corporation Records" in Admiral Mss, Honnold Library; "Annual
Report of the Pacific Steamship Lines Ltd. to the Railroad Commission of
California for the Year Ending December 31, 1936" in ASF; San Francisco
Chronicle, Aug. 30, Sept. 13, 1935; California, Railroad Commission, De-
cisions, XXXIX, 884, 894.

the noblest traditions of the old West and which has endured
without interruption for over three-quarters of a century. . . .

I wish we could retain in other departments those whom
this necessary move will eliminate from service.

Freight schedules to and from all ports will be maintained
during the winter months with the same regularity as formerly.
If necessary, the fleet will be augmented to afford shippers
the same frequency of sailings that they have enjoyed for
many years past.[70]

In commenting on the suspension, the *Marine Digest*
stated succinctly, "In fact, no ship operator at the present
time knows just where in hell he is at."[71] On September
28, 1935, the *Ruth Alexander* left Seattle as the last Admiral passenger ship on the Puget Sound to California route.
Three days before, the Pacific Steamship Lines Ltd. had
sought permission in the federal courts to reorganize under
Section 77-B of the National Bankruptcy Act. The reasons
for this action were given:

Due to unforeseen labor difficulties entirely beyond the
control of the company . . . it is unable to meet its debts. . . .
These difficulties which are the sole cause of this current
financial condition are:

(a) The disastrous maritime strike of 1934 culminating in
the general strike at San Francisco, which effectively tied up
eighteen vessels, owned or chartered by this company, for a
three months period during the normally profitable summer
earning season of that year.

(b) The following fourteen months of continuous labor
inefficiency variously estimated as between 35 per cent to 50
per cent below normal.

(c) Constantly recurring walkouts during the past fourteen
months.

(d) The awards of the arbitration boards, making sub-

70 Quoted in *Pacific Marine Review*, XXXII (Oct. 1935), 12 in advertising section.
71 *Marine Digest*, XIV (Sept. 28, 1933), 3.

stantial increases in wages and costly working conditions which were retroactively effective.

(e) The Pacific Northwest lumber strike, materially curtailing shipments and reducing revenues to and from northern points.

(f) The continued threats of prospective strikes and the still unsettled demands for increased wages and changed working conditions.

To protect fully its creditors, the company necessarily decided that the only method of so doing was to avail itself of Section 77 (b).[72]

In January 1936 demands for shorter hours and more pay by the Sailors' Union resulted in the suspension of freight service also. An Admiral official declared, "This announcement is made most reluctantly. We have tried as hard as any humans could try to keep this service going. But we are faced with extraordinary conditions that render the costs of operation prohibitive."[73] The dilemma facing the shipping industry was presented by one of the trade journals, "It is a case with the coastwise operators of withdrawing their units or going into bankruptcy. They cannot raise rates to a level that will meet the demands of labor because they face the competition of trucks and railroads while foreign tonnage can be used from British Columbia ports to the United States markets." After forty-seven days, the strike was settled.[74]

On April 7, 1936, J. Harold Dollar, the president of the

[72] Quoted in Seattle *Times*, Sept. 26, 1935. See also San Francisco *Chronicle*, Sept. 26 and 27, 1935, and "Annual Report of the Pacific Steamship Lines Ltd. to the Railroad Commission of California for the Year Ending December 31, 1936," p. 100 in ASF.

[73] Quoted in Portland *Oregonian*, Jan. 23, 1936. In Oct. 3, 1935, the freight service had been temporarily abandoned but was resumed a week later when a truce was arranged between employers and union members. Seattle *Times*, Oct. 10, 1935; San Francisco *Chronicle*, Oct. 4, 10, 1935.

[74] "Business Lacks Confidence" (editorial), *Railway and Marine News*, XXXIII (Jan. 1936), 3; *Marine Digest*, XIV (Feb. 15, 1936), 3.

Admiral Line, died after an illness of more than a year, and Stanley was left as the only surviving son of Captain Robert Dollar. He became the active head of the line although the office of president remained vacant.[75] Passenger service was resumed at the close of May when the *H. F. Alexander, Dorothy Alexander,* and *Emma Alexander* were placed on a twice weekly schedule between Puget Sound and California. Although almost 34,000 passengers were transported during the summer season, a figure which compared favorably with other years, the passenger ships were tied up for the last time in September 1936.[76]

On October 29, 1936 the second prolonged strike since the depression began along the waterfront. For ninety-eight days shipping was brought to a standstill.[77] The controversy centered around the problem of how the hiring halls should be administered. The 1934 settlement, whereby the employers and unions were to share in the control, had satisfied neither party. Pessimistically one periodical stated, "Through six weeks of quiet desperation and frustration the issues at stake in the Pacific Coast maritime strike have become so involved, the negotiations so warped with sophistry, the proposals and counter-proposals so complex and the public attention so listless that the outlook for a just settlement seems almost obliterated."[78]

The year 1936 had been disastrous for the Admiral

75 *Pacific Marine Review,* XXXIII (May 1936), 147; *Marine Digest,* XIV (April 11, 1936), 3; "Corporation Records" in Admiral Mss, Honnold Library.

76 *Marine Digest,* XIV (Jan. 18, 1936), 5, XIV (May 30, 1936), 3; Copy of reports of the Admiral Line to Interstate Commerce Commission for 1934, 1935, and 1936 and "Statistics" in Admiral Mss, Honnold Library.

77 See: "All's Quiet on the Waterfront" (editorial), *Railway and Marine News,* XXXIII (Dec. 1936), 3, XXXIII (Nov. 1936), 6; *Marine Digest,* XV (Oct. 31, 1936), 3.

78 *Pacific Shipper,* XI (Dec. 14, 1936), 7.

Line. In addition to losing its president, it had incurred a deficit of more than half a million dollars. For eight consecutive years the Admiral Line had shown an annual loss which aggregated more than six million dollars (see Table 3). The enormity of this debt was accentuated by

Table 3.   NET EARNINGS OF THE ADMIRAL LINE*

Pacific Steamship Company	Loss	Profit
1916 (two months)	$ 72,603	
1917		$129,659
1918	554,102	
1919	1,025,066	
1920		47,230
1921	894,878	
1922	39,133	
1923		545,211
1924	455,791	
1925	230,681	
1926		4,088
1927	279,213	
1928		139,820
1929	176,270	
1930	734,332	
1931	1,196,900	
1932	1,359,804	
1933 (first 22 days)	114,699	
Pacific Steamship Lines Ltd.		
1933 (remainder)	338,897	
1934	950,874	
1935	668,772	
1936	521,346	

* Figures taken from copies of reports to the Interstate Commerce Commission in Admiral Mss, Honnold Library.

the fact that the par value of all its outstanding stock was only $3,495,675 in 1936. Following the end of the strike on February 5, 1937, irregular freight sailings were maintained, but in June 1938 all operations ceased.[79] Attempts were made to revive the line but none of them was successful. On January 20, 1939, a committee of stockholders decided that "the chance of recovery for stockholders is so remote that it does not seem advisable to levy an assessment on the stockholders for the purpose of trying to establish a higher appraisement" of the property of the company.[80] The low level to which the fortunes of the Dollar interests had fallen was illustrated by a remark of Joseph P. Kennedy, chairman of the Maritime Commission, who said in 1938, "There doesn't seem to be enough money [in the Dollar companies] to build a rowboat."[81]

The other lines that offered coastwise service also ceased operations. Lassco sought and obtained permission of the Railroad Commission of California to suspend the operation of the *Yale* on October 1, 1935. On May 16, 1936, lassco resumed passenger service with three weekly sailings between San Francisco and Los Angeles and one between Los Angeles and San Diego. No freight was carried. Less than two months later, the *Yale* was permanently withdrawn from service on July 6, 1936.[82] Rising operating costs were the main reason for the order to tie up the *Yale*. Since 1930 the company had not shown a profit and its officials saw little opportunity to change that

79 "General Financial Statement," in Admiral Mss, Honnold Library; *Pacific Shipper*, XI (Feb. 8, 1937), 3; *Marine Digest*, XV (Feb. 6, 1937), 3; California, Railroad Commission, *Decisions*, XLII, 907; *ibid.*, XL, 895, 899, 900, 901; "Annual Report of the Pacific Steamship Lines Ltd. to the Railroad Commission of California" for 1936 and 1937 in ASF.

80 Letter to stockholders, Jan. 20, 1939, from chairman of the stockholders' committee in Admiral Mss, Honnold Library; San Francisco *Chronicle*, Aug. 13, 1937; Seattle *Times*, Aug. 13, 1937, Oct. 26, 1938, Feb. 19, 1939.

81 Quoted in *Business Week*, Jan. 15, 1938, 41.

82 California, Railroad Commission, *Decisions*, XXXIX, 885, 892; *ibid.*, XL, 893; *Pacific Shipper*, X (Sept. 23, 1935), 7-8; *Marine Digest*, XIV (Sept. 21, 1935), 4, XIV (July 4, 1936), 2; *Railway and Marine News*, XXXIII (April 1936), 17; *Log*, XXVII (May 1936), 26, XXVII (Aug. 1936), 16.

condition. During 1936, the company spent $2.47 for every $1.00 of income.[83]

To meet the keen competition of the trucks, the Nelson Steamship Company had offered, in May 1931, a store-door delivery and pick-up service between San Francisco and Los Angeles, but deficits continued to occur each year. To reimburse its treasury and to provide working capital, the company was authorized in 1932 to issue $100,000 of common stock. Little could be done, however, to raise the revenues of the company. By June 1932 Nelson had reduced its intercoastal fleet from fifteen ships to four. In 1934, there was an operating loss of $227,233, which rose in 1935 to $443,962. In July 1936, the Nelson Steamship Company suspended operations and hauled down its house flag, which had waved for many years along the coast.[84] To satisfy the creditors, its ships were sold. There was one ray of sunshine in the storm which engulfed the Nelson company. In the spring of 1937, oil was discovered on some land owned by the company. This good fortune made it possible to pay off a larger percentage of the debt than was at first thought feasible.[85]

In 1934, the McCormick Steamship Company had been consolidated with the Pope and Talbot Lumber Company. Following the withdrawal of the Admiral ships from passenger service in 1936, it temporarily offered a limited passenger service between San Francisco and Puget Sound in connection with its freighters. On August 31, 1940,

[83] U. S., Bureau of Statistics, "Selected Financial and Operating Data from Annual Reports Carriers by Water" (mimeographed) 1931 through 1936, pp. 20-28, 40-43; "Annual Report of the Los Angeles Steamship Company to the Railroad Commission of California for the Year Ending December 31, 1936," p. 302 in ASF.

[84] Railway and Marine News, XXVIII (April 1931), 15; California, Railroad Commission, Decisions, XXXVI, 951; ibid., XL, 895, 908; Los Angeles Times, June 7, 1932; "Annual Report of the Nelson Steamship Company to the Railroad Commission of California" for 1935 and 1936 in ASF; Log, XXVII (Aug. 1936), 11.

[85] Pacific Ports and Marine News, XXXIV (July 1937), 13; San Francisco Chronicle, May 2, 1937.

the corporate existence of the McCormick Steamship Company came to an end and the activities of the line, which were then limited to an irregular freight service, were taken over by Pope and Talbot Inc. Coastwise sailings were discontinued in December 1941.[86]

In March 1937, the Los Angeles–San Francisco Navigation Company announced the indefinite suspension of its passenger service, which had been carried on between California ports by the two freighters *Wapama* and *Celilo*. On October 8, 1938, it withdrew completely from the transportation field. The other coastwise companies, which had struggled for booty in various rate wars, likewise ended their operations. By 1940, the Railroad Commission of California announced that the operative rights of all companies except four had been revoked because the carriers were unable or unwilling to render the services which they had undertaken. Of the four, only one, the McCormick Steamship Company, was operating and the next year, it withdrew.[87]

Coastwise shipping had reached a nadir from which its fortunes were not to rise. Appearing before the Senate Commerce Committee on February 2, 1938, Joseph P. Kennedy said of the coastwise trade, "Much as I oppose Government ownership, nevertheless, as a practical matter, to me it is inevitable, because of the impossible situation we have today. We have old ships; they are mostly in the hands of people who have no money."[88] In disaster, the Admiral Line was accompanied by the rivals it had tried to conquer.

[86] Letter from Pope and Talbot, Inc., July 6, 1948, in possession of the author; *Pacific Marine Review*, XXXI (Nov. 1934), 18 in advertising section; *Pacific Ports and Marine News*, XXXIV (April 1937), 19; "Annual Report of Pope and Talbot, Inc. to the Public Utilities Commission for the Year Ending December 31, 1946," p. 101 in ASF.

[87] San Francisco *Chronicle*, Oct. 3, 1940; Letter from the Los Angeles–San Francisco Navigation Company to the Railroad Commission of California, May 21, 1940 in ASF; *Log*, XXIX (April 1937), 20.

[88] Quoted in San Francisco *Chronicle*, Feb. 3, 1938.

NINE

The Passing
of an Era

CONTROL OF THE STEAMSHIP LINES

THE MEN who controlled the steamship lines were realists. Some effort was made to encourage the popular concept that people who followed the sea were living in a realm of dreamy adventure; and one marine journal, in 1917, declared that "commercialism is calling them, but it is a commercialism that is softened and chastened by the mysticism and romance of the great deep. It is a commercialism that possesses a soul."[1] Sober evidence suggests, however, that while their commercialism might be softened by mysticism, it was not overwhelmed.

The need to widen the basis of ownership in the industry was recognized. In order to prevent hostile legislation, the formation of shipping companies was suggested "whose stock is popularly subscribed in such a way that the majority of the voters in the United States will become actual shipowners and so be induced to put enough thought and study into the subject that they will compel their lawmakers to also be 'ship minded.' "[2] The problem confronting the shipping industry was stated clearly by magazine writer Andrew Farrell: "Many persons of the inland states, millions of them, must live and die without ever having gazed upon salt water; we must, therefore, take the ships to them. And that can be done only by disposing of stocks and bonds of shipping corporations in every city and every crossroads town of the country."[3] The theory of these suggestions was good, but it was seldom put in practice. In fact, the trend was toward a concentration rather than a dispersal of control. Between 1917 and 1926, the number of stockholders in the Admiral Line declined from 164 to 71.[4]

Who did control the steamship lines along the coast? Unlike coastwise shipping on the Atlantic where the railroads controlled 94 percent of the gross tonnage in 1914, West Coast companies were largely independent. On the Pacific Coast, only the Hill and Harriman steamship lines were tied to railroad empires and by 1924 both of these lines had discontinued operations. None of the new companies that contested the field with the Admiral Line had any connections with the various railroad systems.[5]

In his book, *Divided We Stand,* Walter Prescott Webb has ably presented the thesis that the economic life of the West was and is dominated by the financial "barons" of the East. He contends that with the admission of New Mexico and Arizona in 1912, the North had lost its political domination but that it had "forged the chain of economic control which enabled it to rule in a material way after its absolute political domination had passed."[6] Transportation has long been considered a means of economic control. The ownership of the steamship lines in

1 *Pacific Marine Review,* XIV (Jan. 1917), 72.

2 "Legislation Affecting Shipping" (editorial), *Pacific Marine Review,* XVI (Sept. 1919), 89. See also *Railway and Marine News,* XVII (Dec. 1919), 18.

3 Andrew Farrell, "Some Humble Suggestions," *Pacific Marine Review,* XVIII (Jan. 1921), xxxv.

4 "Statistics" in Admiral Mss, Honnold Library.

5 U. S., House of Representatives, *Steamship Agreements and Affiliations,* 63d Cong., 2d sess., H. Doc. 805, p. 403.

6 Walter Prescott Webb, *Divided We Stand* (New York, 1937), p. 12.

the West, therefore, furnishes one opportunity to test this thesis. In the following discussion, the geographical sections as defined by Webb have been used.

In 1911 H. F. Alexander had organized the Pacific Alaska Navigation Company as a holding company for his steamship lines. By 1917, the stock of this company was held by people in the following areas: West, 11,831 shares; East, 2,173 shares; and other regions, 971 shares. Four years later, the number of shares owned in the East had fallen to 130. In 1916, the Pacific Alaska Navigation Company had joined with the Pacific Coast Company to form the Pacific Steamship Company. The Pacific Coast Company was an eastern concern. Of the nine members on its board of directors, six lived in New York and three in Boston. As long as the Pacific Steamship Company was jointly controlled by these two organizations, it was directed by an East-West coalition. In 1918, the western interests became sufficiently strong to assume complete control. Between 1916 and 1927, the number of shares held in the West nearly doubled while the number in the East declined by more than 50 percent:[7]

Region	1916	1921	1927
West	22,420	24,736	44,630
East	3,204	3,780	2,408
South	....	....	....
Other	2,054	1,484	1,904

In 1925, the Admiral Line undertook a refinancing which required the raising of $8,750,000 in new capital. These three moves were largely supported by western money:

[7] Certified list of stockholders as of close of business, July 23, 1917, in Pacific Alaska Navigation Company Mss, Honnold Library; Confidential report to the U. S. Shipping Board, July 28, 1921, in Pacific Coast Steamship Mss, Honnold Library.

(1) Marine equipment mortgage bonds as of December 1927

Region	Amount
West	$4,232,500
East	473,000
South	20,000
Other	24,500

(2) Preferred stock as of December 1925

Region	Shares
West	20,469
East	716
South	126
Other	313

(3) Pacific Steamship Terminals bonds as of December 31, 1926

Region	Amount
West	$1,457,500
East	22,500
South	1,500
Other	18,500

During the corporate existence of the Pacific Steamship Company, the West increased its control of the company. By June 1932 the West controlled 45,538 of the 49,850 shares of common stock. The members of its board of directors, almost without exception, lived on the Pacific Coast.[8] Since both the Pacific Steamship Company and the Pacific Alaska Navigation Company were organized under the laws of the state of Maine, they could be considered eastern companies, but the actual management of both companies was in the hands of western men. When the Admiral Line was reorganized by the Dollars in 1933, it was incorporated under the laws of Nevada and thus even this superficial tie with the East was cut. That the

8 "Financial Records" in Admiral Mss, Honnold Library.

Admiral Line was directed, financed, and supported by the people of the West is patent.

The control of the other coastwise steamship lines was likewise centered in the West. LASSCO was organized by Los Angeles men, and throughout its life all of the directors were from southern California. Of the twenty largest stockholders in 1927, nineteen lived in Los Angeles and the other in nearby Riverside. When the Matson Navigation Company took over the company in 1931, no changes were made in the directorate. The White Flyer Line, the Nelson Steamship Company, and the McCormick Steamship Company were all controlled by men living in the West. In 1931, the *Pacific Marine Review* noted that the number of vessels owned and the number operated on the Pacific Coast were "practically identical."[9]

The West controlled its coastwise lines. The men who ran the ships, the money which was used, and the new capital which was raised, were western. The East, through the old Pacific Coast Steamship Company, the "Big 3," and the Hill line, had invaded the field, but the invasion was temporary. By 1924, eastern capital had retired and the West dominated its own maritime system.

ECONOMIC CAUSES

The plight of the steamship lines in the economic realm was described by A. F. Haines as the result of "unregulated carriers, steam schooners, irresponsible on one side; and the railroads and motor trucks, motor busses and the

[9] *Pacific Marine Review*, XXVIII (Jan. 1931), 1; "Annual Report of the Los Angeles Steamship Company to the Railroad Commission of California" for 1923 to 1931 in ASF; "Annual Report" of the White Flyer Line, Nelson Steamship Company, and McCormick Steamship Company to the Railroad Commission of California in ASF.

airplanes on the other side, which have gradually whittled us down."[10]

In considering the competition furnished by other types of transportation, it should be remembered that the steamship lines had some advantages over their rivals. When floods came, sea travel was seldom delayed. In 1916 floods interrupted train service for thirty-one days between San Diego and the rest of California. The Santa Fe Railroad had to request the steamship lines to handle its freight shipments to and from the isolated town.[11] Steamer business boomed. Nearly one thousand passengers arrived on the *Roanoke* and *President* in one day. The two ships also brought 2,200 tons of fresh vegetables, meat, general freight, mail, and express for the city, which was digging out after the flood. In 1922, storms halted railroad and highway transportation in the Northwest but "no great casualties were reported off shore by vessels."[12] During February 1927 floods in southern California made "travel by water a necessity" in that area and resulted in increased patronage for the Admiral Line.[13]

Another advantage the steamship industry enjoyed was its ability to adapt quickly to varying conditions. The steamer routes could be altered at will and schedules modified with ease. In order to accommodate passengers who wanted to attend the horse races at Tijuana, Mexico, the *Yale* served in December 1923 as an overnight hotel while tied up at a San Diego dock.[14]

But if the shipping industry had advantages of its own,

10 Case Number 3154, "Reporter's Transcript," III, 346 in ASF.
11 "An Inquiring Reader" in *San Diego Union*, February 1, 3, 12, 18, 19, 21 and 22, 1916.
12 "Storm Halts Transportation," *Railway and Marine News*, XX (Jan. 1922), 17.
13 Alexander to directors, March 16, 1928, in Admiral Mss, Honnold Library.
14 Los Angeles *Times*, Dec. 1, 1923.

it also had disadvantages. An accident in one part of the ship usually affected the entire vessel. On June 27, 1919, the *Rose City* was ready to pull away from her San Francisco dock on the return trip to Portland when a crack in one of her cylinders was discovered. A new cylinder was ordered but the ship was not ready to sail again for almost a month. The passengers, who were already on board, had to find other means of transportation. If a similar accident had occurred to a train locomotive, the rail line could have normally provided another engine within a few minutes. To establish a reserve to cover possible loss of earnings because of delays caused by such difficulties, the steamship lines took out "detention insurance." The owners of the *H. F. Alexander* had a policy which would pay $3,500 per day beginning with the eighth day of detention. The *Emma Alexander, Ruth Alexander,* and *Dorothy Alexander* were covered by similar policies which would pay $2,500 per day.[15]

The shipping companies never satisfactorily solved the problem of cargo handling. Stevedoring was the highest single expense in the budget of the water carriers, and in the case of the Admiral Line it represented about 19 percent of the expenses. The next largest item was 15 percent for wages. It was estimated that during 1925 to 1930 longshore labor absorbed up to 40 percent of the freight earnings of coastwise ships. The 1934 arbitration award increased this expense about 50 percent. Because of the poor rapport between employer and worker, pilferage and breakage were common. The resentment harbored by union labor as the result of the anti-union activities of the employers flamed openly along the waterfront between 1934 and 1936. Unlike railroad labor, the sailors

---

[15] *Pacific Marine Review,* XVI (Aug. 1919), 171; "Insurance Policies" in Admiral Mss, Honnold Library.

M E N U

On Board the S. S. Ruth Alexander

F. I. Nystrom, U. S. N. R., Commanding

Enroute Los Angeles *to* San Francisco

Friday, January 12, 1934

Sardine Canape

Celery en Branche   Salted Mixed Nuts   Queen Olives

Pearl Onions   Pickled Walnuts

Consomme Alphabet   Bisque of Oysters

Baked Red Snapper, Creole, Potatoes Barbant

Sweet Pickled Pork and Hominy

Salpicon of Baby Lobster, en Croustad

Sultana Fritters, Lemon Sauce

Prime Ribs of Beef au Jus, Browned Potatoes

Stuffed Leg of Veal, Brown Gravy

Steamed Potatoes   Snowflaked Potatoes

Brussel Sprouts   New Carrost, Vichy

Salmon Salad, Mayonnise

Steamed English Giger Pudding, Custard Sauce

Plum Pie   Assorted Pastry

Neapolitan Ice Cream   Season's Fruits

Candied Figs   Nabisco Wafers   Cluster Ruisins

McLaren's   Swiss Edam Roquefort

Toasted Crackers

After Dinner Mints

Cafe Noir

A. L. Bissell,, Chief Steward

Menu of the *Ruth Alexander. Courtesy of John H. Kemble, Clare-mont*

Promoting Steamship Travel

and longshoremen felt little loyalty to the companies which had nearly destroyed their labor organizations.[16]

Antiquated methods of handling cargo contributed to the high cost of loading and unloading vessels. The express liners *Harvard* and *Yale,* which provided every convenience for the comfort of the passengers, had to be loaded by hand trucks. An analysis of one voyage of a freighter in 1936 revealed that the stevedoring cost was equivalent to 87 percent of the freight earnings. One magazine observed, "From the viewpoint of the mechanical engineer and the material handling expert, present methods of handling commodities at seaport docks are very inefficient and extremely obsolete."[17]

That the shipping public was none too favorably impressed by the service rendered by the water carriers was shown by a questionnaire sent in 1932 to 1,722 shippers by the Railroad Commission of California. Only 4.7 percent of the shippers stated that they preferred coastwise water transportation while 61 percent preferred rail.[18]

Rivalry between rail and water carriers was keen. The steamship lines felt that the railroads were willing to take unfair advantage whenever the opportunity offered. In 1921 the Seattle Port Commission joined the Board of Engineers for Rivers and Harbors of the War Department in requesting the Interstate Commerce Commission to investigate the wharfage and storage charges on water terminals operated by the railroads. It was charged that the rates were less than half the operating costs with the result that it became impractical for private interests or public harbor boards to make improvements and compete

---

16 H. T. Krull, "Traffic Problems," p. 4, and "Statistics," in Admiral Mss, Honnold Library; "A Problem in Transportation Economics," *Pacific Marine Review,* XXXIII (Nov. 1936), 379.

17 *Pacific Marine Review,* XXXIII (Nov. 1936), 379; *Pacific Shipper,* X (Sept. 23, 1935), 7-8.

18 California, Railroad Commission, *Decisions,* XXXVIII, 103.

with the facilities offered by the rail lines. The Seattle
Port Commission felt that maritime progress was thus
retarded.[19] Nothing definite resulted from this request.

In a rate hearing before the Interstate Commerce
Commission the Admiral Line representative asked the
general freight agent of the Southern Pacific Company
concerning the proposed lower rates, "Primarily . . . you
have reduced rates where water competition appears to be
sharpest, and have transferred those rates to where the
competition is less, haven't you?" To that the reply was,
"Yes."[20]

When the railroads proposed that the Interstate Commerce Commission assume control over the rates of the
water carriers, a committee of the National Conference
on the Merchant Marine in 1932 called the plan "most
disastrous to our merchant marine. . . . The railroads alone
could benefit from the proposed change. The shipping
public will be denied the low rates by water which exist
today as the result of very keen competition."[21] By 1935,
the bitterness between the railroads and steamship companies had become so strong that one shipping man
charged that there was an "apparent effort of the . . . rail
lines to force us out of business." He also pointed out
that "rail lines must first increase their rates both as to
commodity and class, before we can do anything, otherwise
our rates are 'pegged' or 'frozen' at the moment."[22]

On their side, the railroad officials claimed that the
steamship lines were getting their share of the available
commerce and pointed out that during 1927 the steamship
lines between California and the Northwest handled more

[19] Seattle *Times,* June 17, 1921.

[20] Quoted in San Francisco *Chronicle,* April 27, 1922.

[21] The report of the committee was printed in *Pacific Marine Review,*
XXIX (March 1932), 98.

[22] H. T. Krull, "Traffic Problems," pp. 1-2 in Admiral Mss, Honnold
Library.

than twice the freight that was rail borne. The freight traffic manager of the Southern Pacific Company declared, "No railway anywhere faces competition so strong as that met by the Southern Pacific."[23]

On April 17, 1927, the Southern Pacific Company opened the Cascade Line through Oregon, cutting three and a half hours off the previous fastest schedule between Portland and San Francisco. The new rail line reduced the maximum grade from 174 to 95 feet per mile and eliminated over eighteen thousand degrees of curves or about fifty-one complete circles. As a result of this improvement, the trip from Seattle to Los Angeles could be made in forty-one hours and fifteen minutes by train as compared to sixty-five hours by the usual express steamer.[24] In 1931, a. second north-south rail line was established when the tracks of the Western Pacific and Great Northern railroads were joined at Bieber, California. During the controversy between the Southern Pacific and the Great Northern over this new rail route, which challenged the monopoly which the former company had enjoyed in this area, the board of the Admiral Line agreed that the steamship company should maintain a strict neutrality. Although it was agreed that the entrance of the new rail line to California would cause a considerable loss of business, it was also recognized that a similar loss would probably be sustained by antagonizing the Northern line.[25]

The activity of the railroads cut deeply into water travel. On April 22, 1929, H. F. Alexander wrote to the executive committee of the Admiral Line: "Competitive

23 Quoted in Portland *Oregonian*, June 16, 1929.
24 *Railway and Marine News*, XXIV (May 1927), 29, XXIII (Sept. 1926), 13; Los Angeles *Times*, Sept. 16, 1927.
25 The new route carried freight only. *Railway and Marine News*, XXVIII (Nov. 1930), 16.

conditions remain keen, especially from a passenger traffic standpoint, and we are just now advised that the Southern Pacific Company will, commencing May 1st, make their cheap coach fares good on three trains per day in each direction [between Seattle and California], as against one train per day in each direction theretofore [*sic*]. They have also announced that passengers taking advantage of these low rates will have the privilege of tourist sleeping cars, which formerly has not been the practice."[26]

In passenger travel, the train companies had an advantage in that they were able to maintain a lower crew-passenger ratio than the water carriers. Although a danger exists in generalizing from a comparison of two systems which are so unlike, the ratios are significant.[27] The *H. F. Alexander* and the *Emma Alexander* had crew-to-passenger ratios of 1–2.9 and the *Rose City* had a more favorable ratio of 1–3.7; on the other hand, the *Coaster* and the *Lark*, trains which operated between Los Angeles and San Francisco, boasted ratios of 1–14.3 and 1–6.2, respectively.

Not all relationships between the rail and water lines were hostile; though competition was the dominant tone, cooperation did exist in certain realms. For example, in 1916 the Pacific Coast Steamship Company provided a free side trip to San Diego on the Santa Fe railroad when a through ticket was purchased from some Eastern point to Los Angeles and the Pacific Northwest. In 1927 the Admiral Line was successful in getting the Southern Pacific Company to agree to interchange tickets between the two companies. The arrangement permitted a traveler to go one way by rail and the other by sea. H. F. Alex-

[26] Alexander to Executive Committee, April 22, 1929, in Admiral Mss, Honnold Library. See also similar letters dated March 16, Sept. 17, 1927, March 22, 1929.

[27] Letter from Southern Pacific Company to writer dated June 24, 1948; "Annual Report" of LASSCO and the "Big 3" in ASF; "Annual Report" in Admiral Mss, Honnold Library.

ander jubilantly wrote to his officers, "We believe we will be able to secure many additional passengers for our line."[28]

The interline business between the Admiral Line and the various railroads was a further evidence of cooperation. Under this system, a passenger could purchase a steamship ticket at any of the inland offices of the co-operating railroads. At the same time, the steamship line returned the courtesy. The number of tickets received by the Admiral Line from the railroads rose from about 2,600 in 1922 to over 6,000 in 1926 and the financial return from this source was almost three hundred thousand dollars by 1926. Freight was also exchanged. In 1925, the Admiral Line received 107,350 tons from the railroads for delivery to the various ports along the coast. In return, 72,235 tons were delivered to the rail lines which transported the freight to inland points.[29]

In other ways, the steamers and trains were complementary rather than competitive. Trains were faster and their fares were higher. Between San Francisco and Los Angeles, the Southern Pacific provided several daily trains which made the trip in less than fifteen hours. The fastest was the *Lark*, which in 1925 maintained a schedule of eleven hours, twenty-five minutes. By comparison, only three steamers on the coastwise trade lanes could negotiate the passage in less than eighteen hours. Most of the coasters required between twenty-five to thirty hours. Actual running times made in July 1925 by the various steamers were:[30]

28 Alexander to Executive Committee, Jan. 27, 1927, in Admiral Mss, Honnold Library; printed circular in Pacific Coast Steamship Company Mss, Honnold Library.
29 "Statistics" in Admiral Mss, Honnold Library.
30 San Francisco *Chronicle*, Feb. 11, 1925; Los Angeles *Times*, July 4, 5, 1925.

Company	Ship	Hours	Minutes
Los Angeles Dispatch Line	*Newport*	31	....
White Flyer Line	*Humboldt*	32	....
LASSCO	*Harvard*	18	....
Admiral Line	*Emma Alexander*	24	30
LASSCO	*Yale*	18	35
Admiral Line	*Admiral Dewey*	28	30
Admiral Line	*Admiral Farragut*	29	....
Admiral Line	*Admiral Fiske*	33	....
Admiral Line	*H. F. Alexander*	16	5

Steamer fares were low. In the winter of 1921, the Admiral Line charged $18 for a one-way fare between San Francisco and Los Angeles including berth and meals. At the same time, the Southern Pacific was charging $21.54 which included a berth but no meals. Fares on the slower steamers were even lower.[31]

The development of the truck and motor bus industry produced a new rival to the coastwise steamers. At first, shipping circles looked upon the newcomer with a tolerant interest. One maritime magazine in 1918 commended the low rates and the advantage of delivering freight directly to the customer and observed generously that for short runs the trucks were "here to stay."[32] When the truck operators refused to confine their activities to short runs, the attitude toward them changed appreciably. In 1921 a maritime magazine called them "transportation pirates," and concluded, "The motor bus never will produce state revenues, it never will give dependable service and it is doubtful if it will ever come within the law."[33]

Despite such caustic words the bus industry continued to expand. In 1922 a bus called the "Silver Fox" began

[31] San Francisco *Chronicle,* Feb. 4, 1921; *Railway and Marine News,* XVIII (Dec. 1920), 48.

[32] *Railway and Marine News,* XVI (Dec. 1918), 20.

[33] "Official Motor Bus Endorsement" in *ibid.,* XIX (Sept. 1921), 17.

to operate between Oakland and Los Angeles. It had upholstered seats, indirect lighting, and room for twenty passengers. In the same year the bus companies operated sixteen union depots in California and provided a coordinated service from Seattle to San Diego. Overnight stops were made at designated hotels along the way. By 1925 one bus line operating between San Francisco and Los Angeles advertised that its busses had a dining service, lavatory, and steward in attendance.[34]

The fares charged by the busses were lower than the steamer rate. At first the difference was slight. In July 1922, an "Auto Stage" company sold round trip tickets between San Francisco and Los Angeles for $20.00. The steamer fare on LASSCO and Admiral ships was $22.50. Since the bus fare did not include meals, the actual difference in price was very little. By 1931 bus fares had dropped considerably. In July of that year, the water lines were charging $22.75 whereas the bus fare was $16.[35] The use of private automobiles also cut deeply into steamer patronage. The passenger traffic manager of the Admiral Line told its board that the privately owned cars "are taking away more passenger business from the regular lines than anything else."[36]

Because of the greater distances and steep grades, bus and truck competition did not develop as rapidly between California and the Northwest as it did within California. The ship operators complained that this newest rival was not controlled by either state or federal laws, that uniform rates were not maintained, and that the trucking companies charged "whatever the traffic will bear, in order

---

[34] *Literary Digest*, LXXIII (May 20, 1922), 23, LXXIV (July 22, 1922), 21-22; *Railway and Marine News*, XX (Aug. 1922), 18; San Francisco *Chronicle*, July 20, 1926.

[35] San Francisco *Chronicle*, July 18, 1922, July 9, 1931.

[36] Board minutes of the Admiral Line dated March 27, 1929, in Robert Dollar Company Archives.

to secure tonnage away from the rail and water lines."
The competition furnished by the motor bus cut into the
passenger business of the Admiral Line. When a rate war
between the rail and bus lines developed in 1927, steamer
patronage was affected. To hold its share of the business,
the Admiral Line had to reduce fares. In order to overcome the advantage that the motor truck enjoyed in their
door-to-door service, most steamship lines were forced to
offer a store-door pick-up and delivery service.[37] Only in
a few instances was the new mode of transportation looked
upon as a friend. Lassco provided a special "motor coach
service" between Los Angeles and San Diego on the days
when its steamers were not scheduled to go to the southern
city, enabling the line to maintain a daily service.[38]

In marked contrast to the attitude toward the bus lines
was the reaction of marine circles to the airplane. From
the beginning, air travel was looked upon as an ally. As
early as 1920 the *Pacific Marine Review* was urging the
development of cargo planes which in war could be used
for military purposes. It also recommended the extension
of the air mail service to include parcel post, the development of necessary aids to aerial navigation, and the formation by the government of a separate department of aero-
nautics.[39] In 1928, the fifteenth annual convention of the
Association of Pacific and Far East Ports heard a speaker
declare, "It seems natural that air and sea transportation
should unite, and the seaport authority provide the airport

[37] H. T. Krull, "Traffic Problems," p. 2 and Alexander to directors,
March 15, 1927, and July 11, 1927, in Admiral Mss, Honnold Library;
California, Railroad Commission, *Report* (1931), p. 51; "Annual Report
of Lassco, Admiral and Los Angeles–San Francisco Navigation Company"
in ASF. See also "Wife with Bus Driver," *Railway and Marine News*, XX
(Nov. 1922), 16-17.

[38] Advertising folder in Lassco Mss, Maritime Collection of John H.
Kemble, Claremont, Calif.

[39] "Commercial Development of Aircraft" (editorial), *Pacific Marine
Review*, XVII (March 1920), 65.

facilities."[40] The strides made in air travel following World War I were spectacular. In May 1928 Western Air Express inaugurated a three-hour service between San Francisco and Los Angeles. The next year, the Union Air Lines and Pickwick Airways announced a new ten-hour service between Seattle and Los Angeles.[41]

The steamship lines realized the advantage of offering to their patrons a joint air-water service. In 1928 LASSCO announced a plan whereby a passenger could go "one way by water; one way by air." The Admiral Line quickly followed with an air connection of its own. In 1936 the Dollars negotiated an agreement with Pan-American Airways whereby the steamship company acted as general agents for the air line. Plans provided for constant radio communication between planes and ships in order to pool information concerning positions and weather conditions.[42]

The air lines never became the strong ally which the water carriers had envisioned. On the contrary, the speed provided by the new air service was another reason for the eclipse of the coastwise steamers. In addition, the agreements which existed between the rail and air lines tended to reduce passenger travel by water. For example, in 1930 the Great Northern and Northern Pacific railroads made arrangements with West Coast Air Transport by which a passenger reaching Portland by rail from the East could continue to California by air.[43] The potential ally had developed into another competitor.

40 James H. Polhemus, "Sea Ports and Air Ports," extract of the speech, ibid., XXV (Nov. 1928), 508.

41 Ibid., XXV (July 1928), 291; San Francisco Chronicle, Oct. 1, 1929.

42 Pacific Marine Review, XXV (Aug. 1928), 11 in advertising section. In 1930, the round-trip fare between San Francisco and Los Angeles was $34.50 if the joint service were used. The regular steamer fare was $18.00. San Francisco Chronicle, Feb. 5, 1930; Railway and Marine News, XXV (Oct. 1928), 32; Log, XXVII (Sept. 1936), 20.

43 Railway and Marine News, XXVII (March 1930), 26.

NAUTICAL HANDICAPS

Pacific coastwise navigation was made hazardous by three conditions: the necessity of traversing long courses, unpredictable variations in currents, and a great amount of fog. The chief of the Coast Pilot Section of the Coast and Geodetic Survey observed that the problem of navigation along California, Oregon, and Washington "is one of exceptional difficulty."[44] That coastwise navigation was more strenuous than offshore navigation was recognized by the steamship lines. Because of the nervous strain, the Admiral Line assigned two captains to the *H. F. Alexander* who alternated with each other.[45]

The disasters that occurred in coastwise navigation were generally considered no reflection on the navigators of the Pacific Coast, who were said to "rank with the best in the world."[46] Mishaps were apt to be attributed to coastal conditions rather than errors in human judgment. In the case of the wreck of the *Bear* in 1916, the Portland *Telegram* declared, "With such careful officers and so efficient a crew it is indeed hard to imagine that blunder could be committed. Thorough investigation of the condition of the compass should be made."[47]

Valid reasons existed for the feeling that human error played only a minor role in the spotty safety record of the steamships. The usual steamer track from Seattle to San Francisco contained one leg, from Umatilla Reef to Cape Mendocino, which was 464 miles long. At one end of this track, a navigator had to avoid Blunts Reef, a dangerous area of rocks and shoals off Cape Mendocino. At the same time, he needed to bring his ship within

[44] R. S. Patton, "Coastwise Navigation on the Pacific," *Pacific Marine Review*, XIV (Feb. 1917), 66.
[45] This policy was commended by an editorial "Coastwise Navigation Versus Deep-Sea," *ibid.*, XIX (Nov. 1922), 605.
[46] U. S., Coast and Geodetic Survey, *Annual Report* (1922), p. 14.
[47] "Fixing the Blame" (editorial), Portland *Telegram*, June 20, 1916.

hearing or seeing distance of the navigational signals on Blunts Reef light ship in order to plot the new leg of his journey. For the entire 464 miles, the ship was out of sight of land and being steered by dead reckoning. A slight current in either direction might be disastrous.

That currents existed was known. Some had actually been measured and been found to attain a speed of almost four knots.[48] In 1921, the Coast and Geodetic Survey reported that contrary to general belief, a wind creates a current not in its own direction but about twenty degrees to the right of the wind. A wind blowing parallel to the coast could, therefore, tend to set a vessel on shore.[49] The old theory that currents flowed along the curves of the shore had always been open to question. No one had adequately explained what would set a current back to land after it had once been started out to sea.

The 1921 hypothesis was challenged in the following statement in the *Coast Pilot* for 1943: "Current observations at lightships show that a wind-driven current usually sets in a direction somewhat to the right or left of the direction toward which the wind is blowing."[50] The fact that a wind-driven current might veer in either direction gave the mariner little opportunity to feel secure. But this hypothesis, too, was to be revised. Almost twenty years later a scientist at the Scripps Institution of Oceanography at La Jolla, California, after measuring the turbulent water, decided that the currents off California had a slow rotation, fluctuation, or "twist" which varied with the time of day and were associated with the movements and attraction of the moon.[51]

48 Jones, *Neglected Waters*, pp. 11, 12, 13.
49 U. S., Coast and Geodetic Survey, *Annual Report* (1921), pp. 8-9; *ibid.*, (1922), pp. 14-15.
50 U. S., Coast and Geodetic Survey, *United States Coast Pilot, Pacific Coast: California, Oregon, and Washington* (6th ed.; Washington, 1943), p. 38.
51 *Science News Letter*, LXXXII (Sept. 8, 1962), 161.

Between 1918 and 1923, there were forty-four collisions, strandings, and wrecks of vessels on the coast of California. These mishaps took the lives of forty persons and destroyed property valued at $8,000,000. In 95 percent of the cases, fog was reported to have been a major factor. When the *Alaska* stranded in 1921, one journal noted that two other vessels had gone ashore about the same time and in practically the same fog. On the Pacific Coast, fogs are apt to occur at all seasons but are particularly frequent during the summer. At Point Reyes the average number of days per year of dense fog is 148. During one thick fog the captain of the *Great Northern* remained on the bridge continuously for twenty-four hours. The development of the Kolster radio compass by which bearings could be received, regardless of visibility, helped to reduce the danger. But fogs remained one of the hazards of coastwise navigation.[52]

The lack of adequate water surveys also hampered safe navigation. In 1918, the Coast and Geodetic Survey reported that during the previous sixty-eight years, the percentage of water surveyed was: California, 27 percent; Oregon, 14 percent; Washington, 44 percent.. Because of the lack of adequate equipment, no systematic survey of Pacific water areas had been made for 21 years and it was estimated that at the rate the work was progressing, it would take 170 years to complete the surveys along the coast between Washington and California. The Superintendent of the Coast and Geodetic Survey concluded, "The fact that disasters to passenger-carrying vessels do not occur oftener than they do is not due to accurate charts based on complete surveys but rather to the knowledge, skill and vigilance of the men in command."[53] Because

[52] *Pacific Marine Review*, XX (Sept. 1923), 416; *Railway and Marine News*, XIX (Sept. 1921), 16; Jones, *Neglected Waters*, p. 7; *Pacific Marine Review*, XIV (Oct. 1917), 86.

of the publicity given this state of neglect, surveys were pushed more rapidly. By 1935, a belt eighty miles wide, which extended from the Canadian border to Mexico, was nearly completed.[54]

These nautical handicaps to Pacific coastwise navigation were reflected in the premiums which the ship operators had to pay for marine insurance. In 1933, the premiums indicated that Pacific coastwise shipping was about twice as dangerous as shipping along the Atlantic or Gulf Coasts.[55]

SHIPS THAT SAIL NO MORE

Early in September 1935 a fifty-three year old veteran of coastwise navigation pulled out of Seattle on her last journey. She flew a foreign flag, was manned by a foreign crew, and was destined for a scrap pile in a foreign land. She was the *Queen*. After fifty-three days, she arrived in Yokohama after having had "machinery and other troubles nearly all the way—the same kind of troubles that afflict any elderly person when a world that they have served faithfully and well for nearly two generations shunts them out onto the road over the hill to the poor house."[56] Her departure from the coast sea lanes was symbolic of the passing of the steamships. Factors largely beyond the control of the industry made profitable operations impos-

53 Jones, *Neglected Waters*, p. 13; *Railway and Marine News*, XVI (April 1918), 42-43.

54 Los Angeles *Times*, Jan. 3, 1935.

55 The average premium for each section was: Atlantic Coastwise, 2.676; Atlantic-Gulf, 2.421; Pacific Coastwise, 5.290; U.S., Senate, *Report of the Federal Coordinator*, 73d Cong., 2d sess., S. Doc. 152, p. 157.

56 R. J. Alexander, "Old Time Pacific Coast Steamships No. 2 S. S. Queen," *Pacific Marine Review*, XXXIII (March 1936), 84; San Francisco *Chronicle*, Sept. 20, 24, 1935; Seattle *Times*, Nov. 18, 1934; *Railway and Marine News*, XXXII (Oct. 1935), 5.

sible. To a generation which worshiped speed, the attractions of a leisurely sea journey held little appeal.

The remainder of the vessels that had sailed the coastwise trade lanes soon followed the *Queen* to oblivion. The *Rose City,* after serving for a short while as the gambling ship *Rose Isle* off southern California, was sold in 1935 to a salvage dealer who used "acetylene torches and 38,000 pound metal shears . . . to cut her up like so much paper."[57] A construction firm purchased the *Yale* and used her as a barracks for 600 workmen who were building a naval base in Alaska. In 1943, the *Yale* was recommissioned by the Navy for the war and served as a barracks ship in Alaskan waters. She was scrapped in 1949 but her shiny brass whistle was purchased by Mr. Robert McCormick of the Chicago *Tribune.*[58]

The *Dorothy Alexander,* known as the "honeymoon ship" of the coastwise trade, was purchased in 1937 by the Alaska Steamship Company and renamed the *Columbia.* In 1946 she was sold to a Portuguese company who took delivery of the ship on September 11, 1946, in Vancouver. Six years later she was scrapped in Spezia, Italy.[59] The *Ruth Alexander,* after having been sold to British interests, returned to sail under the American flag during the early days of World War II. On December 31, 1941, she was sunk by a Japanese bomber in the waters around the Dutch East Indies.[60] The *Emma Alexander,* renamed the *Empire Woodlark,* served in World War II and was deliberately scuttled in the Atlantic Ocean after the end of the war.[61]

[57] Portland *Oregonian,* Oct. 24, 1935.

[58] *Time,* LV (Jan. 23, 1950), 39.

[59] Seattle *Times,* Jan. 25, 27, 1937, Sept. 12, 1946; *Log,* XXVIII (Feb. 1937), 28; Charles, *Troopships of World War II,* p. 177; *Steamboat Bill of Facts,* No. 65 (March 1958), 7.

[60] San Francisco *Chronicle,* March 22, 1941, Jan. 10, March 23, 1942; Seattle *Times,* March 21, 1941, Jan. 9, 1942.

[61] *Steamboat Bill of Facts,* No. 22 (April 1947), 20. See also San Francisco *Chronicle,* March 14, 26, 1941; Seattle *Times,* March 13, 1941.

In 1938 a group of San Francisco men planned to convert the *H. F. Alexander* into a floating hotel to be anchored near Treasure Island for the convenience of Exposition visitors, but nothing further was heard of the plan. For a short time prior to World War II the ship was operated by the Canadian Pacific Steamship Lines. On July 26, 1942, the U. S. War Shipping Administration purchased her. She was altered to take care of 1,803 troop passengers and under the name *General George S. Simonds* took part in the Normandy landing as a troop transport for the Army. On March 5, 1946, she was redelivered to the War Shipping Administration and eventually sold for scrap.[62] The *Admiral Rogers,* formerly the *Spokane,* after fourteen years of inactivity, was sold in 1946 to Seattle men who planned to convert her into a resort hotel. Plans miscarried and the veteran ship was towed to the Puget Sound Bridge and Dredging Company in April 1948 for scrapping. In 1936 the *Admiral Rodman* was sold for scrap but fire destroyed her before she was broken up. Five of the "Admirals"—*Fiske, Schley, Farragut, Watson,* and *Dewey*—were acquired by Japanese interests in 1934 to be taken to Japan for scrapping.[63]

Since the days of the Gold Rush, the transportation pattern of the Far West had changed radically. Initially the economic life of the area depended almost entirely upon shipping as a means of safe, dependable transportation from the Mexican border to Oregon and Washington. By 1890, a north-south railroad was established which successfully challenged, but did not supplant, water travel.

[62] San Francisco *Chronicle,* Sept. 16, 1938; *Steamboat Bill of Facts,* No. 25 (March 1948), 15; Charles, *Troopships of World War II,* p. 30. For a lively and attractive biography of the *H. F. Alexander* see John Carrothers, " 'Hot Foot'—The Story of a Ship," *U. S. Naval Institute Proceedings,* Feb. 1956, pp. 170-79.
[63] Seattle *Post-Intelligencer,* April 30, 1948; *Log,* XXVII (July 1936), 12; San Francisco *Chronicle,* April 12, 1937; *Marine Digest,* XIII (Oct. 20, 1934), 3, XIII (Sept. 22, 1934), 3.

During the next forty years, rail and water companies paralleled and competed with each other between the major cities of the Pacific slope. For many a smaller community which had no rail connection, however, the steamer continued to serve as virtually the sole means of transportation to and from the outside world. Following World War I, water travel faced new competitors. Busses, trucks, and private automobiles, using public highways, were major factors in forcing the steamship companies to abandon at first the "narrow gauge" lines and then their major routes. This substitution of other forms of transportation for the coastwise vessel was gradual. By 1936 the rivals of water travel had captured the major proportion of the available trade. The result was that the breakdown of coastwise service caused little inconvenience to the people of the West.

The story of the collapse of maritime activity accentuates the fact that labor and the employer in the coastwise trade, instead of finding a community of interest, grew farther apart. The strike of 1921, which was so firmly suppressed by the operators, found its counterpart in the strike of 1934 in which labor won a Pyrrhic victory. Between these two violent controversies lay an undertone of distrust. The middle road between employer exploitation and labor dictation was never attained.

Fortunately for the United States, the failure to find a solution to the maritime collapse was not disastrous even though the passing of the ships made the economic structure of the West a little more rigid.

The indian summer of Pacific coastwise shipping which reached its zenith when the prows of the *H. F. Alexander, Harvard, Yale,* and other coasters cut the waters of the Pacific Ocean came to a close as depression and war cornered the headlines. Almost as an afterthought to an era, an older H. F. Alexander proposed in 1948 a revival

of a coastwise transportation system which would be
supported with a 50 percent subsidy from the federal
government.[64] His plan never materialized and today
there remains only a memory of the ships which maintained a transportation system of almost regal excellence.

[64] New York *Herald Tribune*, March 14, 1948. One West Coast paper
vigorously suported the proposal. See "Alexander's Plan" (editorial), San
Francisco *Call-Bulletin*, June 1, 1948.

Appendix

THE TONNAGE and hull dimensions given in this list are to be found in the *List of Merchant Vessels* prepared by the Bureau of Navigation. The tonnage figures refer to gross tonnage which is defined by the Bureau of Navigation as the capacity of the spaces within the frames or ceiling of the hull of a vessel and of the closed-in spaces above deck available for cargo, stores, passengers, or crew, with certain specified exemptions, expressed in tons of 100 cubic feet.

The hull dimensions appear immediately following the tonnage figure and represent the length, breadth, and depth of the ship. For the sake of simplicity, the words "length, breadth and depth" have been omitted. Other data given were derived from a variety of sources including contemporary newspapers and trade magazines. An attempt has been made to include all vessels which were operated by the various coastwise companies between 1910 and 1940 with the exception of tugs and barges. Passenger capacity, number in crew and other figures vary from year to year. In such cases, the most frequently used figure has been given. The name of the company which operated, but did not necessarily own, the vessel is given in parentheses following the name of the ship.

ADMIRAL BENSON (Admiral Line)
Steel steamer; 1 deck, 2 masts; 3,049 tons; 299.6 x 45 x 22.5 feet; 60 crew; 200 passengers; 11 knots.
Built in 1918; formerly called the *Tipton* and *Esther Weems;* launched at Wilmington, Delaware. Purchased by the Admiral Line in 1927 from the Baltimore and Caroline Steamship Company. Operated between Portland and California until February 15, 1930, when she stranded on Peacock Spit, near the mouth of the Columbia River.

ADMIRAL CHASE (Admiral Line)
Steel steamer; 1 deck, 2 masts; 3,285 tons; 324 x 46.2 x 25 feet; 28 crew; freighter; 9.7 knots.
Built in 1920 at Newark, New Jersey, as the *Sutransco.* Operated by the Admiral Line between 1929 and 1936 in the Ocean Falls, B. C., to California trade. By 1941, she was sold to British interests. Scrapped 1953.

ADMIRAL CLARK (Admiral Line)
Steel steamer; 2 decks, 2 masts; 2,437 tons; 242 x 43 x 26.5 feet; 26 crew; freighter.
Built in 1906 at Cleveland, Ohio, as the *Rutland.* Purchased by Pacific Alaska Navigation Company on January 24, 1916. Foundered in Caribbean Sea, August 16, 1916.

ADMIRAL COLE (Admiral Line)
Steel steamer; 1 deck, 2 masts; 3,285 tons; 324 x 46.2 x 25 feet; 28 crew; freighter; 9.7 knots.
Built in 1920 at Newark, New Jersey, as the *Surailco.* Operated by the Admiral Line in 1933 between Puget Sound, Columbia River, and California points. Owned by the Portland California Steamship Company. Operated by Admiral Line until 1936. Sold to USSR 1946.

ADMIRAL DAY (Admiral Line)
Steel steamer; 1 deck, 2 masts; 3,285 tons; 324 x 46.2 x 25 feet; 29 crew; freighter; 9.7 knots.
Built in 1920 at Newark, New Jersey, as the *Sutermco.* Operated by the Admiral Line between British Columbia and California, including way points. Sold to British company in 1940. Reported lost same year in mid-Pacific.

ADMIRAL DEWEY (Admiral Line)
Steel steamer; 2 decks, 2 masts; 2,104 tons; 280 x 36.1 x 22.7 feet; 36 crew; 160 passengers; 12 knots.

Built in 1898 at Philadelphia. Purchased by the Pacific Alaska Navigation Company on October 28, 1913, from the American Mail Steamship Company. Operated by the Admiral Line on the Seattle to California run between 1916 and 1925. Between 1926 and 1931 she operated usually from Portland to California. Sold to Japanese interests in 1934 for scrap.

ADMIRAL EVANS (Admiral Line)

Steel steamer; 2 decks, 2 masts; 2,393 tons; 253.1 x 38.4 x 22.8 feet; 45 crew; 194 passengers; 12 knots.

Built in 1901 at Toledo, Ohio. Purchased as the *Buckman* on October 5, 1905, by the Alaska Pacific Steamship Company. Name changed to *Admiral Evans*. Operated between 1916 and 1933 by the Admiral Line principally in the Alaskan trade, although between 1921 and 1923 she served on the Portland to San Diego route. Scrapped 1937.

ADMIRAL FARRAGUT (Admiral Line)

Steel steamer; 2 decks, 2 masts; 2,141 tons; 280 x 36.1 x 22.7 feet; 60 crew; 204 passengers; 12 knots.

Built in 1898 at Philadelphia. Purchased in 1912 by the Pacific Alaska Navigation Company from the American Mail Steamship Company. Between 1916 and 1933, she was usually operated in the Alaskan trade during the summer, the Portland to California route during the winter. Sold to Japanese interests in 1934 for scrap.

ADMIRAL FISKE (PCSC; Admiral Line)

Steel steamer; 3 decks, 2 masts; 2,432 tons; 280 x 38.1 x 19.6 feet; 30 crew; 187 passengers; 10.8 knots.

Built in 1898 at San Francisco as the *Senator*. In 1922, renamed the *Admiral Fiske*. Operated by the Pacific Coast Steamship Company prior to 1916. Assigned by the Admiral Line between 1916 and 1931 to a variety of routes including Alaskan, transpacific, Mexican, Portland to California, and Puget Sound to California. Sold to Japanese interests in 1934 for scrap.

ADMIRAL GOODRICH (Admiral Line)

Steel steamer; 1 deck, 1 mast; 1,419 tons; 224.4 x 41 x 16.6 feet; 28 crew; 135 passengers; 9.7 knots.

Built in 1913 at San Francisco as the *Aroline*. Acquired by H. F. Alexander on February 28, 1916, from the Independent Steamship Company (also called the Aroline Steamship Company). Operated by the Admiral Line between 1916 and 1922 on the Alaskan, transpacific, Portland to California, and Puget Sound to California routes. Withdrawn from service on September 13, 1923, and sold six days later to National Steamship Company. Stranded near Point Arena, California, 1935.

ADMIRAL GOVE (Admiral Line)

Steel steamer; 1 deck, 2 masts; 3,513 tons; 324 x 46.2 x 25 feet; 29 crew; freighter; 9.7 knots.

Built in 1920 at Newark, New Jersey, as the *Surico.* Operated by the Admiral Line between 1933 and 1936 from British Columbia to California. Sold to Panamanian company, 1940.

ADMIRAL HALSTEAD (Admiral Line)

Steel steamer; 1 deck, 2 masts; 3,285 tons; 324 x 46.2 x 25 feet; 36 crew; freighter; 9.7 knots.

Built in 1920 at Newark, New Jersey, as the *Suwordenco.* Purchased in 1930 from the Submarine Boat Corporation by the Portland California Steamship Company. Operated by the Admiral Line between 1930 and 1936 on the Puget Sound to California and Portland to California routes. Scrapped 1949.

ADMIRAL KNIGHT (Admiral Line)

Wood steamer; 1 deck, 2 masts; 630 tons; 142.2 x 35.7 x 12.3 feet; 24 crew; freighter.

Built in 1916 at Seattle as the *Portland.* Purchased by the Admiral Line in 1919 and renamed *Admiral Knight.* Burned in Straits of Georgia, British Columbia, July 27, 1919.

ADMIRAL LAWS (Admiral Line)

Steel steamer; 1 deck, 2 masts; 3,268 tons; 324 x 46.2 x 25 feet; 29 crew; freighter; 9.7 knots.

Built in 1920 at Newark, New Jersey, as the *Sunugentco.* Purchased by the Portland California Steamship Company and operated by the Admiral Line between 1933 and 1936 on the British Columbia to California route. Sold to Thai company in 1941.

ADMIRAL MAYO (Admiral Line)

Wood motorship; 2 decks, 4 masts; 1,934 tons; 248.6 x 44.6 x 21 feet; 25 crew; freighter; 6 knots.

Built in 1918 at Seattle. Purchased by the Admiral Line in 1918. Operated on transpacific line. Sold April 6, 1923, after having been laid up in Lake Union since December 1920.

ADMIRAL MOSER (Admiral Line)

Steel motorship; 1 deck, 2 masts; 2,063 tons; 250.5 x 43.5 x 20.4 feet; 24 crew; freighter; 8.8 knots.

Built in 1917 at Manitowoc, Wisconsin. Was formerly called

Ada, Lake Oneida, Astmahco IV, Glendarual, and *Willa Crosby* before being purchased by the Admiral Line in 1927. Renamed *Admiral Moser.* Operated between 1927 and 1932 on the Puget Sound to California route. By 1934, sold to Mexican interests.

ADMIRAL NICHOLSON (Admiral Line)

Steel steamer; 1 deck, 1 mast; 678 tons; 141 x 27.2 x 18.7 feet; 18 crew; freighter; 7.5 knots.

Built in 1908 at Seattle. Purchased in 1917 by the Admiral Line as the *Northland* and renamed *Admiral Nicholson.* Between 1918 and 1923, operated on the Alaskan, San Francisco to Hueneme "narrow gauge," and Bering Sea routes. Stranded near Umpqua River, Oregon, May 16, 1924.

ADMIRAL NULTON (Admiral Line)

Steel steamer; 1 deck, 2 masts; 3,250 tons; 324 x 46.2 x 25 feet; 29 crew; freighter; 9.7 knots.

Built in 1920 at Newark, New Jersey, as *Suscolanco.* Purchased by the Portland California Steamship Company. Operated by the Admiral Line between 1930 and 1936 on the British Columbia to California route. Scrapped 1949.

ADMIRAL PEARY (Admiral Line)

Steel motorship; 1 deck, 4 masts; 1,951 tons; 252 x 43.7 x 21.2 feet; 26 crew; freighter; 9.1 knots.

Built in 1916 at Toledo, Ohio, as the *Moonlite.* Purchased by the Admiral Line in 1922. In 1923, machinery and fittings of *Benowa* put in *Moonlite* and ship renamed *Admiral Peary.* Operated by Admiral Line between 1924 and 1933 on most coastwise routes. Sold to Mexican interests by 1934.

ADMIRAL PEOPLES (Admiral Line)

Steel steamer; 1 deck, 2 masts; 3,133 tons; 299.4 x 45 x 22.8 feet; 28 crew; 200 passengers; 11.3 knots.

Built in 1918 at Elizabeth, New Jersey. Formerly was the *Plainfield* and *Mary Weems.* Purchased by the Portland California Steamship Company in 1927 from the Baltimore and Carolina Steamship Company. Operated by Admiral Line on Portland to California route between 1927 and 1933. Sold to Northland Transportation Company in 1934 and renamed *North Sea.* Stranded on British Columbia coast, 1947.

ADMIRAL RODMAN (Admiral Line)

Wood steamer; 1 deck, 2 masts; 1,101 tons; 175 x 36 x 14 feet; 19 crew; 75 passengers; 8 knots.

Built in 1899 at Fairhaven, California, as *Despatch.* Purchased by Admiral Line in 1919. Operated between 1919 and 1930 in Alaskan trade. Burned at Seattle in 1937.

ADMIRAL ROGERS (PCSC; Admiral Line)

Steel steamer; 3 decks, 2 masts; 2,277 tons; 270.1 x 40.1 x 17.3 feet; 31 crew; 239 passengers; 12.4 knots.

Built in 1902 at San Francisco as the *Spokane*. Prior to 1916, operated by the Pacific Coast Steamship Company. In 1922, name changed to *Admiral Rogers*. Between 1916 and 1932, she usually operated in Alaskan waters. Sold in 1948 for scrap.

ADMIRAL SCHLEY (Admiral Line)

Steel steamer; 2 decks, 2 masts; 2,104 tons; 260 x 36.1 x 22.7 feet; 59 crew; 152 passengers; 12 knots.

Built in 1898 at Philadelphia. Purchased by the Pacific Alaska Navigation Company from the American Mail Steamship Company on October 2, 1913. Between 1916 and 1931, operated by the Admiral Line in the Puget Sound to California and Portland to California trade. Sold in 1934 to Japanese interests for scrap.

ADMIRAL SEBREE (Admiral Line)

Steel steamer; 2 decks, 2 masts; 2,446 tons; 242 x 43 x 26.5 feet; 28 crew; freighter; 9.3 knots.

Built in 1906 at Cleveland, Ohio, as *Ogdensburg*. Purchased by Pacific Alaska Navigation Company, January 24, 1916. Operated by the Admiral Line until 1932 on the Puget Sound to California route. Evidently scrapped.

ADMIRAL SENN (Admiral Line)

Steel steamer; 1 deck, 2 masts; 3,260 tons; 324 x 46.2 x 25 feet; 20 crew; freighter; 9.7 knots.

Built in 1920 at Newark, New Jersey, as *Sulanierco*. Purchased by Portland California Steamship Company and operated by the Admiral Line between 1933 and 1936 on the British Columbia to California route. Sold to Thailand in 1941.

ADMIRAL SIMS (Admiral Line)

Wood motorship; 2 decks, 4 masts; 1,929 tons; 249.2 x 44.6 x 21.1 feet; 30 crew; freighter; 6 knots.

Built in 1918 at Seattle and purchased by the Admiral Line in the same year. Employed in transpacific trade, 1918-1920. Stranded in Philippine Islands in 1920.

ADMIRAL WAINWRIGHT (Admiral Line)

Steel steamer; 2 decks, 2 masts; 1,783 tons; 221.5 x 40 x 22.5 feet; 27 crew; freighter; 8.5 knots.

Built in 1913 at Long Beach, California, as *Grace Dollar*. Purchased by the Admiral Line from the Robert Dollar Company in 1917. Operated in the Alaskan and transpacific trade. Sold in 1920. Stranded near Coquille River, Oregon, 1927.

ADMIRAL WATSON (Admiral Line)

Steel steamer; 2 decks, 2 masts; 2,009 tons; 253.1 x 38.4 x 22.8 feet; 63 crew; 285 passengers; 12 knots.

Built in 1902 at Toledo, Ohio, as *Watson*. Owned and operated by the Admiral Line between 1916 and 1933 in the Alaskan and Puget Sound to California trade as *Admiral Watson*. Sold in 1934 to Japanese interests for scrap.

ADMIRAL WILEY (Admiral Line)

Steel steamer; 1 deck, 2 masts; 3,253 tons; 324 x 46.2 x 25 feet; 35 crew; freighter; 9.7 knots.

Built in 1920 at Newark, New Jersey. Purchased by Portland California Steamship Company in 1930. Operated by Admiral Line between 1930 and 1936 on British Columbia to California route. Stranded latitude 3 degrees south, longitude 151 degrees east, June 13, 1940. Prior to 1930, called *Surichco*.

ADMIRAL WOOD (Admiral Line)

Steel steamer; 1 deck, 2 masts; 3,285 tons; 324 x 46.2 x 25 feet; 26 crew; freighter; 9.7 knots.

Built in 1920 at Newark, New Jersey, as the *Sugillenco*. Purchased by the Portland California Steamship Company in 1930. Operated by the Admiral Line between 1933 and 1936 as *Admiral Wood* on British Columbia to California route. Sold to Thai interests 1940.

ADMIRAL Y. S. WILLIAMS (Admiral Line)

Steel steamer; 1 deck, 2 masts; 3,252 tons; 324 x 46.2 x 25 feet; 32 crew; freighter; 9.7 knots.

Built in 1920 in Newark, New Jersey, as *Sunewco*. Purchased by the Portland California Steamship Company in 1930. Operated by the Admiral Line between 1934 and 1936 as *Admiral Y. S. Williams* on British Columbia to California route. Sold to American Trading & Shipping Company. Captured by Japanese in Hong Kong, December 1941.

ALASKA ("Big 3")

Iron steamer; 3 decks, 2 masts; 3,709 tons; 327 x 45 x 18.8 feet; 45 crew; 281 passengers; 15 knots.

Built in 1889 in Chester, Pennsylvania, as *Kansas City*. Chartered in September 1920 by the "Big 3" from the Alaska Steamship Company which had changed her name to *Alaska*. She was placed opposite the *Rose City*, serving Portland, San Francisco, and Los Angeles. Stranded off Blunts Reef, California, August 6, 1921. Out of 220 on board, 42 persons lost their lives.

AROLINE see ADMIRAL GOODRICH

AURELIA (PCSC; Admiral Line)

Wood steamer; 1 deck, 2 masts; 743 tons; 162.9 x 34.5 x 11.6 feet; 21 crew; freighter; 8 knots.

Built in 1902 at Prosper, Oregon. Prior to 1916, operated by Pacific Coast Steamship Company. Operated by the Admiral Line between 1916 and 1919 on the "narrow gauge" routes between San Francisco and Hueneme, and Portland and San Francisco. Sold to Peruvian company 1919.

BEAR ("Big 3")

Steel steamer; 3 decks, 2 masts; 4,507 tons; 357.5 x 47 x 26.4 feet; 79 crew; 545 passengers; 15 knots.

Built in 1910 at Newport News, Virginia. Operated by "Big 3" between 1910 and 1916 on Portland to California route. Grounded near mouth of Bear River, Mendocino County, California, June 13, 1916. Five persons lost their lives.

BEAVER ("Big 3")

Steel steamer; 3 decks, 2 masts; 4,507 tons; 357.5 x 47 x 26.4 feet; 80 crew; 571 passengers; 15 knots.

Built in 1910 at Newport News, Virginia. Began operating under the "Big 3" flag between Portland and California in 1910. Sold to the Navy in June 1918. Used as a submarine tender in World War I and World War II.

BENOWA (Admiral Line)

Wooden motorship; 1 deck, 2 masts; 3,093 tons; 268.1 x 48.4 x 24.6 feet; 28 crew; freighter; 8.8 knots.

Built in 1919 at Seattle. Was owned by British interests. Purchased by the Admiral Line, November 28, 1922. Her machinery and fittings were put in the *Moonlite* in 1923. The *Moonlite* was renamed *Admiral Peary*.

BOOBYALLA (Admiral Line)

Wooden motorship; 1 deck, 2 masts; 3,099 tons; 268.4 x 48.3 x 24.7 feet; 28 crew; freighter; 9 knots.

Built in 1919 at Seattle. Operated by the Admiral Line between

1924 and 1929 on Puget Sound to California route. Burned off Discovery Island, British Columbia, March 11, 1929.

BREAKWATER (North Pacific Steamship Company)

Iron steamer; 2 decks, 2 masts; 1,065 tons; 201 x 30 x 19.3 feet; 40 crew; passenger and freight.

Built in 1880 at Chester, Pennsylvania. Owned at one time by the Southern Pacific Company. Operated by North Pacific Steamship Company on Portland to San Francisco route in 1917. Sold to Mexican Fruit and Steamship Company in 1918.

BUCKMAN see ADMIRAL EVANS

CHALLAMBRA (Admiral Line)

Wooden motorship; 1 deck, 2 masts; 2,400 tons; 262.2 x 46.4 x 21.7 feet; 25 crew; freighter; 8.5 knots.

Built in 1918 at Olympia, Washington. Formerly owned by British interests. Chartered by the Admiral Line for Puget Sound to California route between 1925 and 1927. Stranded on White Cliff Island, British Columbia, June 17, 1927.

CHARLES see HARVARD

CITY OF SEATTLE (PCSC; Admiral Line)

Iron steamer; 3 decks, 2 masts; 1,957 tons; 244.6 x 40 x 15 feet; 59 crew; 234 passengers; 12.4 knots.

Built in 1890 at Philadelphia. Prior to 1916, operated by the Pacific Coast Steamship Company. Between 1916 and 1921, operated under the Admiral flag in the Alaskan trade. Sold in 1921 and operated on Atlantic coast. Scrapped 1937.

CITY OF TOPEKA (PCSC; Admiral Line; LASSCO)

Iron steamer; 2 decks, 2 masts; 1,057 tons; 198 x 35.2 x 18 feet; 54 crew; 161 passengers; 11 knots.

Built in 1864 at Chester, Pennsylvania. Prior to 1916, operated by Pacific Coast Steamship Company. Between 1916 and 1920, assigned by the Admiral Line to the "narrow gauge" route between San Francisco and Portland. Sold by Admiral Line in 1920. Returned to coastwise service when LASSCO purchased her from Inter-Island Steam Navigation Company in 1923. Operated by LASSCO between 1923 and 1931 on San Francisco–Los Angeles–San Diego route. Withdrawn from service and eventually sold. Under the LASSCO flag her name was *Waimea*. Scrapped 1933.

COLUMBIA see H. F. ALEXANDER and DOROTHY ALEXANDER

CONGRESS see EMMA ALEXANDER

CUBA (New Electra Line)

Steel turbo-electric driven vessel; 3 decks, 2 masts; 2,963 tons; 299.5 x 40 x 17 feet; 45 crew; 250 passengers; 17.28 knots.

Built in 1894 at Chester, Pennsylvania. Formerly known as *Resolute, Rawlins, Yorktown, Powhatan.* Brought to the West Coast and began operations between Portland and San Francisco, January 30, 1923, under flag of New Electra Line. Permanently withdrawn from that service in October 1924. She was reported to be the first turbo-electric driven vessel on Pacific coastwise routes.

CULBURRA (Admiral Line)

Wooden motorship; 1 deck, 2 masts; 2,353 tons; 261.7 x 46.6 x 21.7 feet; 24 crew; freighter; 8.5 knots.

Built in 1918 at Olympia, Washington. Formerly owned by British interests. Chartered by Admiral Line between 1925 and 1931 and operated in Puget Sound to California and Alaskan trades. Sold 1935.

CURACAO (PCSC; Admiral Line)

Steel steamer; 2 decks, 2 masts; 1,548 tons; 241.3 x 38 x 16.3 feet; 47 crew; 100 passengers; 9.5 knots.

Built in 1895 at Philadelphia. Prior to 1916, operated by Pacific Coast Steamship Company. Between 1916 and 1932, operated by Admiral Line on the Alaskan route with occasional assignments to the Mexican and Portland to California routes. Sold to Greek interests 1940. Sunk by explosion off Columbia River same year.

DAWNLITE (Admiral Line)

Steel motorship; 1 deck, 4 masts; 1,976 tons; 252 x 43.7 x 21.2 feet; 18 crew; freighter; 6 knots.

Built in 1916 at Toledo, Ohio. Purchased by Admiral Line from Standard Oil Company of New Jersey, March 31, 1922. She was laid up most of the time the Admiral Line owned her between 1922 and 1930.

DAYLITE (Admiral Line)

Steel motorship; 1 deck, 4 masts; 1,976 tons; 252 x 43.7 x 21.2 feet; 18 crew; freighter; 6 knots.

Built in 1916 at Toledo, Ohio. Purchased by Admiral Line from Standard Oil Company of New Jersey, March 31, 1922. She was laid up most of the time the Admiral Line owned her between 1922 and 1929.

DOROTHY ALEXANDER (PCSC; Admiral Line)

Steel steamer; 4 decks, 2 masts; 5,453 tons; 391.1 x 46.2 x 19.7 feet; 130 crew; 537 passengers; 16.3 knots.

Built in 1907 at Camden, New Jersey, as the *President*. Brought to the West Coast via the Strait of Magellan and operated by the Pacific Coast Steamship Company prior to 1916. Between 1916 and 1922, she sailed under the Admiral flag between Seattle and California. Renamed *Dorothy Alexander* in honor of the daughter of H. F. Alexander, July 12, 1922. Between 1922 and 1936 as the *Dorothy Alexander*, she continued to serve the Puget Sound to California route with occasional assignments to the Portland to California run. During the winter of 1925-1926, she was operated on the East Coast under charter to the Clyde-Mallory Line. During the summers of 1926 to 1932, she was the largest vessel to operate in Alaskan waters. Purchased by the Alaska Steamship Company in 1937 and renamed *Columbia*. Sold to Portuguese interests in 1946. Scrapped 1952.

EMMA ALEXANDER (PCSC; Admiral Line)

Steel steamer; 4 decks, 2 masts; 7,793 tons; 423.8 x 54.9 x 17.7 feet; 153 crew; 442 passengers; 14.3 knots.

Built in 1913 at Camden, New Jersey, by the New York Shipbuilding Company as the *Congress*. Operated by the Pacific Coast Steamship Company between Seattle and California until she caught fire off Coos Bay, Oregon, September 14, 1916. Sold to the China Mail Steamship Company which renamed her the *Nanking* and operated to the orient. Purchased by the Admiral Line, November 17, 1923. Renamed *Emma Alexander* and placed in service on the Seattle to California route in February 1924. Operated on that route until 1936. Sold to British by 1942. Sunk at sea 1946.

F. A. KILBURN (North Pacific Steamship Company)

Wooden steamer; 2 decks, 2 masts; 997 tons; 201.2 x 29.7 x 20 feet; 23 crew; passenger and freight.

Built in 1904 at Fairhaven, California. Operated prior to 1918 by North Pacific Steamship Company on Portland to California route. Sold to Mexican Fruit and Steamship Company, 1918. Burned off American Shoals Light, Florida, June 14, 1918.

GENERAL GEORGE S. SIMONDS see H. F. ALEXANDER

GEORGE W. ELDER (North Pacific Steamship Company)

Iron steamer; 2 decks, 2 masts; 1,709 tons; 250 x 36.5 x 21 feet; 49 crew; passenger and freight.

Built in 1874 at Chester, Pennsylvania. Operated by North
Pacific Steamship Company prior to 1917 on Portland to California
route. Chartered in offshore trade, 1917. Sold to Mexican Fruit
and Steamship Company in 1918.

GOVERNOR (PCSC; Admiral Line)

Steel steamer; 4 decks, 2 masts; 5,474 tons; 391.9 x 48.2 x 19.7
feet; 120 crew; 540 passengers; 15.4 knots.

Built in 1907 at Camden, New Jersey. Prior to 1916, operated
by the Pacific Coast Steamship Company. Operated by Admiral
Line on Seattle to California route from 1916 until April 1, 1921
when she collided with the *West Hartland* off Point Wilson, Puget
Sound, and sank.

GREAT NORTHERN see H. F. ALEXANDER

H. F. ALEXANDER (Great Northern Pacific Steamship Company;
 Admiral Line)

Steel steamer; 3 decks, 2 masts; 8,357 tons; 500.1 x 63.1 x 20.6
feet; 225 crew; 585 passengers; 23 knots.

Built in 1914 at Philadelphia as the *Great Northern*. Operated
between Portland and San Francisco by the Great Northern Pacific
Steamship Company from 1915 until 1917 when she was purchased
by the United States for war service. During World War I, she
made ten round trips between New York and Brest, and established
a world's record of fourteen days, four and a half hours for a round
trip to Europe. After her service as a troopship, she was renamed
the *Columbia* and commissioned the flagship of the Atlantic fleet
of the United States Navy. Purchased by the Admiral Line on
March 4, 1922, she was brought to the Pacific Coast and began
regular service between Seattle and California on July 11, 1922,
as the *H. F. Alexander*. Except for one winter (1925-1926) when
she was operated on the East Coast, she was laid up during the
winter season. Her 36-40 hour schedule between Seattle and San
Francisco, and her 16 hour schedule between San Francisco and
Los Angeles were the fastest times maintained by any vessel. She
was withdrawn from service by the Admiral Line in 1936. During
World War II, she served as a troop transport under the name
General George S. Simonds. She was sold for scrap in 1948.

HARVARD (Pacific Navigation Company; Admiral Line; LASSCO)

Steel steamer; 1 deck, 2 masts; 3,737 tons; 376 x 61.3 x 20.2
feet; 135 crew; 466 passengers; 21 knots.

Built in 1906 at Chester, Pennsylvania. Brought to the West
Coast and operated by Pacific Navigation Company in the Cali-

fornia trade from December 1910 to September 1, 1916, when she was leased by H. F. Alexander. Between 1916 and 1918, operated by the Admiral Line between San Francisco and San Diego. Purchased by the government for use as troopship in World War I. Renamed the *Charles*. Purchased in 1920 by group of Los Angeles men who later formed LASSCO. After extensive alterations, she was placed on her old run between California points as the *Harvard* in August 1921. Operated by LASSCO on this route until she grounded off Point Arguello, California, May 30, 1931. Ship given up as total loss.

HOMER (PCSC; Admiral Line)

Wooden steamer; 2 decks, 2 masts; 501 tons; 146 x 33.8 x 17 feet; 20 crew; freighter; 9 knots.

Built in 1891 at Bandon, Oregon. Prior to 1916, operated by Pacific Coast Steamship Company. Between 1916 and 1920, she served the San Francisco to Hueneme "narrow gauge" route under the Admiral flag. Sold in 1920. Scrapped 1937.

HUMBOLDT (White Flyer Line; Los Angeles–San Francisco Navigation Company)

Wooden steamer; 2 decks, 2 masts; 1,075 tons; 213.1 x 31 x 15.7 feet; 36 crew; 140 passengers; 14 knots.

Built in 1896 at Eureka, California. For years operated on the Alaskan route. Reportedly brought out five times more gold than any other ship from the Klondike. Her log showed $56,000,000. Purchased by White Flyer Line in 1919 and operated between San Francisco and Los Angeles until 1927 when the Los Angeles–San Francisco Navigation Company became her owner. She was operated on the same route until 1932 when she was withdrawn.

IROQUOIS (LASSCO)

Steel steamer; 6,209 tons; 394.7 x 62.2 x 19.4 feet; 177 crew.

Built in 1927 at Newport News, Virginia. Chartered by LASSCO in 1931 to replace the *Harvard*. She was returned to her owners, December 31, 1931.

MOONLITE see ADMIRAL PEARY

MOUNT CLAY (Admiral Line)

Steel steamer; 3 decks, 2 masts; 8,170 tons; 488.3 x 55.7 x 22.2 feet; 200 crew.

Built in 1904 at Stettin, Germany. Purchased by the Admiral Line in 1928. Plans to rebuild ship were never completed. Between 1928 and 1931, she was laid up at Baltimore, Maryland.

Her former German names had been *Prinz Eitel Friedrich* and *De Kalb*.

NEWPORT (Los Angeles Dispatch Line; McCormick Steamship Company)

Iron steamer; 2 decks, 2 masts; 2,643 tons; 325 x 38.2 x 23.9 feet; 49 crew; 125 passengers; 14 knots.

Built in 1880 at Chester, Pennsylvania. Purchased by C. L. Dimon from the Pacific Mail Steamship Company and placed on the San Francisco to Los Angeles route, January 9, 1925. Operated by the Los Angeles Dispatch Line, organized by Dimon, from that time until May 1926 when the vessel was chartered by the McCormick Steamship Company and placed opposite the *Rose City* on the Portland to California route. Returned to her owners, December 1928.

NORTHERN PACIFIC (Great Northern Pacific Steamship Company)

Steel steamer; 3 decks, 2 masts; 8,255 tons; 509.5 x 63.1 x 20.6 feet; 224 crew; 800 passengers; 23 knots.

Built in 1914 by William Cramp and Sons, Philadelphia. Between 1915 and 1917, operated by the Great Northern Pacific Steamship Company between Portland and San Francisco with her sister ship, *Great Northern*. Purchased by the government for war service as troopship, 1917. Purchased by Admiral Line, February 6, 1922, for Pacific coastwise service but burned off Cape May, New Jersey, February 8, 1922.

NORTHLAND see ADMIRAL NICHOLSON

PRESIDENT see DOROTHY ALEXANDER

QUEEN (PCSC; Admiral Line)

Iron steamer; 3 decks, 2 masts; 2,727 tons; 331.2 x 38.5 x 21.2 feet; 79 crew; 307 passengers; 13.7 knots.

Built in 1882 at Philadelphia. Prior to 1916, operated by Pacific Coast Steamship Company. Between 1916 and 1932, operated by the Admiral Line in the Alaskan trade with occasional trips between Seattle and California. Sold to Japanese interests and steamed across the Pacific Ocean under her own power for scrapping, 1935.

RAVALLI (PCSC; Admiral Line)

Wooden steamer; 1 deck, 2 masts; 998 tons; 186.2 x 38.1 x 14.8 feet; 20 crew; freighter; 8 knots.

Built in 1905 at Fairhaven, California. Prior to 1916, operated by the Pacific Coast Steamship Company. Between 1916 and 1918, operated by Admiral Line in Alaskan trade. Burned in Lowe Inlet, Alaska, June 14, 1918.

ROANOKE (North Pacific Steamship Company)

Iron steamer; 3 decks, 2 masts; 2,354 tons; 267 x 40.5 x 16.4 feet; 60 crew; passenger and freight.

Built in 1882 at Chester, Pennsylvania. Operated by North Pacific Steamship Company between Portland and southern California. Foundered off Port San Luis, California, May 9, 1916.

ROSE CITY ("Big 3"; McCormick Steamship Company)

Steel steamer; 3 decks, 2 masts; 3,468 tons; 336.2 x 43.2 x 22.3 feet; 68 crew; 389 passengers; 15 knots.

Built in 1889 at Chester, Pennsylvania. Formerly called the *Yumuri, Badger* and *Lawton*. Brought to the Pacific coastwise service by the "Big 3" in March 1908 and operated between Portland and Los Angeles until December 1918. After a lay up of over a year, she resumed service under the Harriman flag between Portland and San Francisco in May 1919. Purchased by McCormick Steamship Company, October 29, 1924. Placed on former Portland to Los Angeles run until January 1928, when she was withdrawn. Served as gambling ship, *Rose Isle*, off California coast. Sold to salvage dealer in 1935.

RUTH ALEXANDER (Admiral Line)

Steel steamer; 3 decks, 2 masts; 8,135 tons; 439.1 x 56 x 26.2 feet; 150 crew; 409 passengers; 14.1 knots.

Built in 1913 at Hamburg, Germany, for the South American trade as *Sierra Cordoba*. During World War I, interned by Peru and renamed *Callao*. Given to the United States under the reparation plan. Purchased by the Robert Dollar Company in December 1921. Chartered by the Admiral Line from 1922 until 1933 and operated on the Seattle to California route. In 1929, made one trip around the world in place of the *President Adams* of the Dollar Line. Sunk by a Japanese bomber in waters around Dutch East Indies, December 31, 1941, while flying the American flag. Previously she had been sold to British interests.

SAN JUAN (White Flyer Line; Los Angeles–San Francisco Navigation Company)

Iron steamer; 2 decks, 2 masts; 2,152 tons; 283 x 37 x 21 feet; 43 crew; 125 passengers; 12 knots.

Built in 1882 by J. Roach and Sons, Chester, Pennsylvania. Formerly operated by Pacific Mail Steamship Company and the Panama Mail Steamship Company. Purchased by White Flyer Line for San Francisco to Los Angeles route, December 9, 1925.

In 1927, the Los Angeles–San Francisco Navigation Company became her owner and continued to operate her on the same route. Collided with S. C. T. *Dodd*, off Pigeon Point, California, August 29, 1929, sinking within thirty minutes; 75 persons lost out of 115 on board.

SENATOR see ADMIRAL FISKE

SPOKANE see ADMIRAL ROGERS

SUNLITE (Admiral Line)

Steel motorship; 1 deck, 4 masts; 1,976 tons; 252 x 43.7 x 21.9 feet; 20 crew; freighter; 6 knots.

Built in 1916 at Toledo, Ohio. Purchased by Admiral Line from Standard Oil of New Jersey, March 21, 1922. Between 1922 and 1930, laid up most of the time at Baltimore, Maryland. Sold in 1930.

UMATILLA (PCSC; Admiral Line)

Iron steamer; 3 decks, 2 masts; 3,125 tons; 310 x 40.6 x 22.3 feet; 41 crew; 401 passengers; 11.5 knots.

Prior to 1916, operated by Pacific Coast Steamship Company. Operated by Admiral Line between 1916 and 1918 in Alaskan trade. Stranded off Japan, while in transpacific trade, March 5, 1918.

WAIMEA see CITY OF TOPEKA

WATSON see ADMIRAL WATSON

YALE (Pacific Navigation Company; Admiral Line; LASSCO)

Steel steamer; 1 deck, 2 masts; 3,731 tons; 376 x 61.3 x 20.2 feet; 135 crew; 466 passengers; 24 knots.

Built in 1906 at Chester, Pennsylvania. Brought to West Coast and operated by Pacific Navigation Company in the California trade from December 1910 to September 1, 1916, when she was leased by H. F. Alexander. Between 1916 and 1918, operated by Admiral Line on same route. Purchased by government for use as troopship in World War I. Purchased in 1920 by group of Los Angeles men who later formed LASSCO. After extensive alterations, placed on her old run May 2, 1921. Temporarily withdrawn October 1, 1935, to May 15, 1936. Permanently withdrawn from coastwise service, July 6, 1936. After serving as a barracks for construction workers on an Alaskan military base, she was recommissioned by the Navy during World War II and carried passengers between Aleutian Islands. Scrapped 1949.

Bibliographical Essay

A COMPREHENSIVE LISTING of the available materials for
Pacific maritime history is not intended here. Rather I have
noted those which were most useful for this study. One of
the problems in surveying these sources is the somewhat
paradoxical situation that there is both a dearth and an
abundance of materials—a dearth of reliable sources and
an abundance of printed information, mostly secondary,
which has been written with little or no documentation.
Exceptions do exist. Among them are Eliot Grinnell
Mears' *Maritime Trade of Western United States* (Stanford University, California: Stanford University Press,
1935), Paul S. Taylor's *The Sailors' Union of the Pacific*
(New York: Ronald Press Company, 1923), Hyman Weintraub's *Andrew Furuseth: Emancipator of the Seamen*
(Berkeley: University of California Press, 1959), and
Hobart S. Perry's "The United States Shipping Industry,"
*Annals of the American Academy of Political and Social
Sciences,* CXCIII (Sept. 1937), 88-98. Of the writers mentioned, Mr. Taylor had more than academic interest in
the subject since he had served at one time as an ordinary
seaman on board a coasting vessel. For the general reader,
an excellent brief biography of one of the companies is
"The Admiral Line, A Short History of the Pacific Steamship Company" by Glenn O. Roberts which appeared in
two issues of the journal of the Steamship Historical

Society of America, *Steamboat Bill of Facts,* **XIV** (Dec. 1957), 81-84, and **XV** (March 1958), 4-8.

The steamship society was established in 1935 "as a means of bringing together those amateur and professional historians interested in the history and development of steam navigation past and present" (*ibid.,* **XV**, June 1958, 55), and its quarterly journal, since June 1958 called *Steamboat Bill* and since 1961 published in New York, is useful to the historian as a source of articles, pictures, notes, and comments primarily on North American steam navigation. Another periodical of genuine value to the maritime historian is the *American Neptune,* a quarterly published in Salem, Massachusetts.

Newspapers serve as a fruitful, if somewhat erratic, source of information, and each of the five major ports along the coast had one or more aggressive dailies which covered the activities of the ship operators, the shippers, and the union men. These cities looked upon the maritime scene from different viewpoints and outright rivalries were not unknown. An example occurred in 1920 when the president of the Portland Chamber of Commerce, H. B. Van Duzer, claimed that Seattle was Portland's "most vindictive rival." He applauded the decision of the United States government to place Portland under the San Francisco office of the United States Shipping Board rather than the Seattle office and stated that Portland thereby had won "a long fight for the preservation of its prestige" (*Oregon Journal,* Oct. 5, 1920). This rivalry of the business groups was reflected in the pages of the newspapers, and the resulting tensions encouraged independent reporting of waterfront happenings. Although the usual care must be exercised in evaluating newspaper accounts, the rivalries, both active and latent, tend to strengthen the possibilities for accuracy by allowing the historian to check a great number of separate comments, judgments, and observations on almost any major event which affected the Pacific Coast. Of the papers published, special mention should be made of the San Diego *Union,* the Los Angeles *Times,* the San Francisco *Chronicle,* the San Francisco *Examiner,* the Portland *Oregonian,* and the Seattle *Post-Intelligencer.* The smaller ports along the "narrow gauge lines" were represented by the *Astorian* (Astoria, Oregon), the *Humboldt Standard* (Eureka, California), the Santa Barbara *News,* and the Tacoma *Ledger.* Each of these publications attempted to cover the waterfront of its particular area, and many of them accomplished the task with remarkable industry and voluminous results. It was traditional for the labor unions to feel that the coverage of the daily press was promanagement if not outright antilabor. The *Coast Seamen's Journal,* published in San Francisco, and its successor the *Seamen's Journal* were the official spokesmen for the International Seamen's Union of America. During its somewhat brief existence, the Seattle *Union Record* (1918-1928) attempted to cover "the doings of organized labor." Beyond these publications which were somewhat localized, the partisan side of labor was not represented.

The sheer amount of material printed by the newspapers over a thirty-year span is monumental and all but overwhelming. Fortunately some indexes and clipping files exist which can serve as partial guides through the labyrinth of news items, rumors, and reports. Since these may not be known generally, their names and locations might prove useful: the card index to the Portland *Oregonian,* the *Telegram,* and the *Oregon Journal* in the Library Association of Portland, Oregon; the card index and clipping files of the Los Angeles *Times;* the clipping file on shipping kept by the Society of California Pioneers Library, San Francisco; the newspaper index of the State Library of California, Sacramento; and the card file of the

Northwest Collection of the University of Washington Library, Seattle. The Seattle Public Library has a card file on shipping, a clipping file on shipping, and a special card file of ships. One, however, cannot completely depend on these bibliographical tools, since the comprehensiveness of any of them depends upon the accuracy and exactness of unnamed, and oftentimes forgotten, persons whose time and toil produced them. For the period of the study, therefore, all issues of the following newspapers were investigated: Los Angeles *Times,* San Diego *Union,* San Francisco *Chronicle, Seamen's Journal,* and Seattle *Union Record.* Those who have used newspaper materials well know the distracting and yet rewarding nature of this type of research.

Special note should be made of the so-called trade publications, since these magazines provide a wealth of knowledge which can be easily overlooked by scholarship. The *Pacific Marine Review,* modestly calling itself the "National Magazine of Shipping," was the official organ of both the Pacific American Steamship Association and the Shipowners Association of the Pacific Coast. This monthly, published in San Francisco, provides important information as selected by the operators. Unfortunately for clear reference, its advertising section is numbered separately from the main body of the magazine, and news items of interest are placed in both portions. The *Marine Digest,* a weekly published in Seattle, was established "to serve the maritime interests of Seattle and the other Northwest ports." As might be expected, it championed the cause of the farthest port north. In this geographical area it had a rival in the *Railway and Marine News,* whose monthly issues are jammed with facts and opinions on the twin realms of "sails" and "rails." The *Shipping Register* and the *Pacific Shipper* are both little known but worthy publications devoted to marine transportation. One started in 1919; the other in 1926. Both were weeklies, published in San Francisco, and for both the back files have to be used in the offices of the publishers. Almost without exception, all these periodicals represented the viewpoint of the owners and operators of the coastwise vessels.

Some of the difficulties in using government publications have previously been noted (see pages 152-54). Since there were many agencies, each concerned with certain phases of the maritime industry, inconsistencies, overlapping, and errors occur. Almost in despair, Eliot Grinnell Mears in his *Maritime Trade of Western United States* wrote "the searcher after information immediately encounters serious difficulties. He discovers that there are numerous bodies, official and otherwise, which regularly issue statistical reports, no two of which agree in classification of traffic or actual tabulated results" (page 147). For example, in the sinking of the *San Juan*, the *List of Merchant Vessels* for 1930 (page 917), published by the United States Bureau of Navigation, states that 71 lives were lost; yet the *Annual Report of the Supervising Inspector General Steamboat Inspection Service* for the same year (page 15) gives the figure as 75.

Despite these discouraging aspects, the publications by the various agencies of the federal government do provide a great deal of usable material. Particularly valuable are the *Annual Reports* of the Commission of Navigation, the *List of Merchant Vessels,* the *Annual Reports* of the Interstate Commerce Commission, and the *Port Series* published about the various harbors along the Pacific Coast by the Corps of Engineers of the Department of War and the United States Shipping Board. In addition to national governmental publications, the archives of the Public Utilities Commission of California, located in San Francisco, are rich in source material. Although they contain information only on those corporations which operated within the territorial limits of California, the files are surprisingly representative of the entire transportation industry along the Pacific Coast, since most coastwise lines served both San Francisco and Los Angeles. The *Decisions* and *Reports* of the Railroad Commission of California, which was later called the Public Utilities Commission of California, are important. In addition to the annual reports which the various steamship companies submitted and which contain many details about the operations of the lines, mention should be made of the twenty-one volumes of Case Number 3154. This typed manuscript of a special investigation made by the commission into the operations of the various transportation concerns doing business in California is comprehensive and helpful.

Each of the major cities along the coast compiled with varying degrees of completeness reports for the local docks. Typed or mimeographed annual reports were prepared for the port of San Diego by the Harbor Department of the city of San Diego. The port of Los Angeles published a *Monthly Report of Commerce* as well as an *Annual Report* issued by the Board of Harbor Commissioners. The Commission of Public Docks of Portland, Oregon, distributed a yearly *Report*. The Harbor Department of Seattle had a *Port Warden's Annual Report* and, since the harbor of San Francisco was under the control of a Board of State Harbor Commissioners, this agency produced a *Biennial Report* for San Francisco.

The maritime collection of the Honnold Library of the Claremont Colleges, California, is unique. Its several hundred items have been listed in a typed "Calendar of Archives and Records of Certain Pacific Coast Steamship Companies," which was compiled by R. C. Thompson in 1940-1941. This collection contains corporate records including ledger books, passenger schedules, reports of various officers, letter files, and miscellaneous material concerning the business relations of the various companies. The following companies are represented:

Alaska Coast Company
Alaska Pacific Steamship Company
Pacific Alaska Navigation Company
Pacific Coast Steamship Company
Pacific Lighterage Company
Pacific Steamship Company
Portland California Steamship Company
Olympic Steamship Company

The archives of the Robert Dollar Company in San Francisco have the important minute books of the Admiral Line and other corporate items not included in the Honnold collection. The maritime holdings of other libraries have proved useful including the public libraries in San Diego, Los Angeles, San Francisco, Portland (called the Library Association of Portland), and Seattle; the Mechanics-Mercantile Library in San Francisco; the San Francisco Maritime Museum with its oral history project and transcribed interviews; the Bancroft Library at Berkeley; the California State Library at Sacramento; the libraries of the California Historical Society in San Francisco and of the Oregon Historical Society in Portland; and the Northwest Collection of the University of Washington. All of these were visited and their holdings examined for information.

Finally, any person working in Pacific maritime history owes a real debt to Professor John Haskell Kemble of Pomona College, California, for his interest and concern in assembling material, much of it ephemeral, which might otherwise be lost. It was due to his efforts that the Honnold Library has its fine collection. In addition, his own private maritime collection is excellent and proved helpful.

A word might be said about the geography of the coastline that played such a prominent role in the coastwise transportation system. An attempt was made to visit every major harbor, headland, lighthouse, and straits that figured in coastwise shipping. The restless waves, the sandy beaches, and the jagged rocks that form the breaker line along so much of the coast are still the same as in the bygone days of the coasters. Today the sharp cries of the seagulls, the low moans of the foghorns and the brief flashes of the lighthouses may still be heard and seen. They serve as lonely reminders of ships that sail no more.

Index

Floods: gave steamships advantage over railroads, 223

Fogs: as contributor to marine disasters, 236

"Foolish laws": which affected steamship lines, 121

Ford, J. C.: president of Pacific Coast Steamship Company, 27

Foreign ships: competition of, 81-82; excluded from coastwise trade, 126-28; in Pacific coastwise service, 200

Fort Bragg, California, 145

Fort Ross, California, 1

Freight: importance of, 113-14; competition from contract and private shipping lines, 115; type of goods shipped by sea, 116-17; tonnage carried by three lines, 117; exchanged with rail lines, 229; ship and truck compared, 230-32

Frey, A. J.: 60

Fuel consumption by ships compared, 166

Furuseth, Andrew, president Sailors' Union of the Pacific: proposed use of German nationals as seamen during World War I, 48; described as "Agitating Andy," 103; mentioned, 66, 75, 79, 120

General George S. Simonds: took part in Normandy landing 1944, 239. *See also H. F. Alexander*

General strike: in San Francisco, 207

George W. Elder: history of 252-53; mentioned, 40

Geography of shoreline. *See* Pacific coastline

Germany: described as power behind passage of La Follette Seamen's Act, 119

Glendarual. See Admiral Moser

Glenwood Mission Inn, California: a tourist attraction, 2

Goliah: called "great grandmother" of Pacific coasters, 7

Golden Gate, California, 4, 205

Goodall, Charles: formed partnership which developed into Pacific Coast Steamship Company, 8

Goodall, Nelson and Perkins Steamship Company: established 1872, 8

Government action: desired by companies, 123-28

Government control: over steamship lines, 118-28; changed attitude by steamship lines, 129-30

Government reports: inaccuracies and inconsistencies, 122-23

Governor: rumored sale to H. F. Alexander, 27; placed on Honolulu run by Shipping Board 1917 but returned 1918, 45; rammed and sunk in Puget Sound 1921, 55; history of, 253; mentioned, 10, 62, 82, 83

Grace Dollar. See Admiral Wainwright

Grace Line: placed "Santa" Ships on Pacific Coast service 1933, 199-200

Great Northern: arrival on Pacific Coast, 13-14; construction of, 15n; sets Honolulu to San Francisco record 1916, 37; purchased by U.S. government for war service 1917, 44; purchased by H. F. Alexander 1922, 88; renamed *H. F. Alexander* 1922, 90; mentioned, 26, 62, 87, 94, 108, 233, 236. *See also H. F. Alexander*

Great Northern Pacific Steamship Company: created 1913, 13; ceased coastwise service 1917, 42-45

Great Northern Railway: organized Great Northern Pacific Steamship Company 1913, 13; joined Western Pacific at Bieber, California, 1931, 227; mentioned, 42, 148

Great Northern Steamship Company: operated *Dakota* and *Minnesota*, 13

Guggenheim Company, 64, 150, 199

Gyrostabilizers: installation too expensive, 180

McCormick Steamship Co. (*cont.*):
Pope and Talbot Lumber Company 1936, 216-17; controlled by Western men, 222; mentioned, 112, 128, 140, 148, 151, 184, 185, 186, 193

McCulloch, Coast Guard cutter: sunk by the *Governor* 1917, 55

Magdalena Bay, Mexico: *Dorothy Alexander* on "good will" cruise, 168

Mahony, Andrew: purchased North Pacific Steamship Company, 40

Mallory, Ward, and Clyde lines, 37

Malolo, 201

Manhattan: reported new vessel of "Big 3," 12

Manila, Philippines: Admiral Line established office 1919, 52

Marden, Captain H. H.: pilot of the *Governor* when it sank 1921, 55

Marine Digest, trade publication: hit by depression, 182; praised H. F. Alexander on leaving Admiral presidency, 193; commented on suspension of Admiral passenger service 1933, 211

Marine disasters: *Bear* grounded and *Congress* burned 1916, 30; *Governor* sunk 1921, 55; *Alaska* sunk, 79-81; *Northern Pacific* burned 1922, 87; *Roanoke* foundered 1916, 119-20; *San Juan* sunk 1928, 153-54; accidents discussed, 175-79; *Harvard* lost 1931, 202-203; hazardous conditions, 234-36

Marine Engineers' Beneficial Association: wanted 1921 wage level maintained, 66; employers sent appeal to all members, 69; accused of being at bottom of 1921 strike, 70; refused to agree to government plan to end strike, 72; San Francisco local defied national officers, 73; national president's resignation demanded, 74; withdrawal from American Federation of Labor 1923, 75;

Marine Engineers's Assn. (*cont.*):
operators demanded members resign, 76

Marine Service Bureau of Los Angeles, 103

Marine trade publications. *See* Trade publications

Maritime history: peculiarities of, 6

Maryland, 89

Mary Weems. See Admiral Peoples

Mary Winkelman, 123

Matson Navigation Company: purchased LASSCO 1930, 201; mentioned, 222

Mazatlan, Mexico, 168

Meals served on coastwise ships: variety and costs, 158-59; cost declined per passenger 1929-1932, 196-97

Mendocino Coast, 31

Mendocino Steamship Company, 145

Merchant Marine Act of 1920, 127

Metropolitan Steamship Company: enters coastwise trade 1910, 18; leases *Harvard* and *Yale* to H. F. Alexander 1916, 29

Mexican Fruit and Steamship Company: purchased vessels of Emerald Line 1918, 41

Mexican Mail Steamship Company, 198

Mexico, 198

Milwaukee railroad, 147

Minnesota, 13

Monterey, California, 8

Moonlite. See Admiral Peary

Morgan-Guggenheim Alaska syndicate, 36. *See also* Guggenheim Company

Morse, Charles Wyman: planned *Harvard* and *Yale*, 19

Moss Landing, California, 47

Motor trucks. *See* Trucks

Mount Clay, history of, 254-55

Mount Lowe, California, 2

Munson-McCormick Line, 142

Mussolini, Benito: methods praised by official publication of shipowners, 208

Nanking: burned hull of *Congress* rebuilt by China Mail Steamship Company and renamed *Nanking* later became *Emma Alexander*, 91-92. *See also Congress* and *Emma Alexander*

Narragansett: reported new vessel of "Big 3," 12

"Narrow gauge" lines, 240

National Bankruptcy Act, 211

National Conference on the Merchant Marine, 226

National Foreign Trade Convention, 123

National Guard: used in Portland strike, 207

National Industrial Recovery Act. *See* NRA

Nautical handicaps: necessity of traversing long courses, 234-35; unpredictable variations in currents, 235; great amount of fog, 236; higher insurance premiums resulted, 237

Navy Department: requested permission to examine "Big 3" vessels, 39; purchased *Harvard* and *Yale* 1918, 45; purchased *Beaver* 1918, 46; announced *Harvard* and *Yale* for sale 1920, 58

Nelson, Charles: began lumber operation 1858 which led to Nelson Steamship Company, 99

Nelson, Chris: formed partnership 1860 which developed eventually into Pacific Coast Steamship Company, 8

Nelson, James K., president of White Flyer Line, 146

Nelson Steamship Company: growth, 98-99; doubled tonnage 1925, 147; designated a common carrier by Interstate Commerce Commission, 1926, 148; operated in 1927 largest coastwise fleet, 149; suspended operation and ships sold 1936, 216; controlled by Western men, 222; mentioned, 114, 140, 151, 152, 184, 186, 187

Neptune Association: opposed La Follette Seamen's Act, 120; mentioned, 81, 171

New Deal: impact on shipping, 204-209; operator's attitude changed, 208-10; blamed for 1934 strike, 208-209. *See also* Labor, NRA, Wagner Labor Relations Bill

New Electra Line: inaugurated San Francisco to Portland service 1923, 93; suspended service, 94; mentioned, 138

New Mexico, 219

Newport: started as "rate cutter," 138-40; chartered by McCormick Line 1926, 141; withdrawn from service by McCormick Line 1927, 143; history of, 255

Newport News, 149

Newport Rate War of 1925, 138-41, 184

New York, New Haven and Hartford Railroad Company: instrumental in moving *Harvard* and *Yale* to Pacific Coast, 19

New York Shipbuilding Company, 9

Nome City, 37, 99, 102

Northern Pacific: construction of, 15n; purchased by U. S. government for war service 1917, 44; purchased by the Admiral Line 1922, 86; wrecked 1922, 87; history of, 255; mentioned 13, 94, 233

Northern Pacific railroad, 13, 147

Northland: salvaged and renamed *Admiral Nicholson* 1916-1918, 49. *See also Admiral Nicholson*

North Pacific Steamship Company: service of, 16; sold 1917, 40-41; mentioned, 25, 53

North Pacific Transportation Company, 8

Northwestern: chartered by "Big 3," 37; withdrawn from service by "Big 3," 38

NRA: endorsed by McCormick line, 205; attempts to exempt coastwise industry, 205-206; praised by *Pa-*

Point Wilson, Washington: *H. F. Alexander* struck shoals off, 198
Pope and Talbot, Inc.: discontinued coastwise sailings 1941, 217
Portland, Oregon: major seaport, 4, 5; Chamber of Commerce objected to Navy taking *Beaver* 1918, 46; through service to San Diego inaugurated 1921, 53; pleased "Big 3" resumed operations 1919, 63
Portland. See Admiral Knight
Portland California Steamship Company, 134, 198
Portland *Oregonian. See Oregonian*
Portland *Telegram:* objected to sale of Hill liners to Admiral Line, 43; mentioned, 94, 234
Port San Luis, California, 34
Port Series government publication, 122
Powhatan. See Cuba
President: rumored sale to H. F. Alexander 1916, 27; placed on Honolulu run by Shipping Board 1917 but returned 1918, 45; name changed to *Dorothy Alexander* 1922, 91; passenger lost 1913, 179; mentioned, 10, 86, 223. *See also Dorothy Alexander*
President Adams, 169
President Grant, 194-95
President Lincoln, 194
Prince George, 82
Prince Rupert, 82
Prinz Eitel Friedrich. See Mount Clay
Prohibition: enforcement, 108-109; effects on coastwise shipping, 168-70
Propeller Club, 170
Publicity: used as asset, 91; techniques, 161-65; cost, 165-66; problem of adverse news, 170-75
Puget Sound Bridge and Dredging Company, 239
Puget Sound, *passim*

Quaker Lines: provided Pacific coastal service 1931, 199

Quarantine: regulations, 121, 122
Queen (formerly *Queen of the Pacific*): praised by Sir Charles Russell, 9; reported sabotage but passengers unconvinced, 70-71; disabled 1921, 177; sailed to Japan for scrapping 1935, 237; history of, 255

Railroad Administration: supervised coastwise shipping and operated "Big 3" during World War I, 45; mentioned, 49
Railroad Commission of California: authorized rate increase because of war inflation 1918, 48; further rate increases 1919, 1920, 51-52; authorized LASSCO to issue stock 1920, 59; approved non-conference rates 1930 and investigated rates 1930, 184-85; investigated marine freight conditions, 185-86; ordered two independent companies to raise rates 1932, 188; requested by conference to stabilize rates, 189; permitted LASSCO to suspend operation 1935, 215; revoked operative rights of most coastwise companies, 217; mentioned, 52, 125, 129, 141, 190, 202, 225
Railroad competition: maritime industry wanted parity with railroads, 52; competition severe, 190-91, 224-30; H. F. Alexander noted stiff competition, 227-28
Railroads: controlled Atlantic shipping but not Pacific coastal shipping, 219, 220-22; cited as a cause for decline of shipping, 222; proposed ICC control over water carriers, 226; examples of cooperation with steamship lines, 228-29
Railway and Marine News: predicted more Alexander moves, 29; regretted loss of Hill liners, 44; praised Pacific Coast Steamship Company for its action in loss of *Congress* 1916, 172; hit by depression, 182; bleakness of ship-

Yale: brought to Pacific Coast 1910,
18-20; building of, 19; leased by
Admiral Line from Metropolitan
Steamship Company 1916, 29;
purchased by Navy Department
1918, 45; World War I service,
58; sold to LASSCO 1919, 59; arrived at Los Angeles under LASSCO
1920, 60-61; resumed coastwise
service 1921, 61; accommodations
under LASSCO, 156; steel deck extended entire length, 180; with-

Yale (continued):
drawn from service 1936, 215;
used as barracks in Alaska 1943,
scrapped, whistle purchased by
Robert McCormick 1949, 238; history of, 257; mentioned, 20, 83,
95, 173, 178, 194, 204, 223, 225,
240

Yokahama: Admiral Line opened
office 1919, 52; mentioned, 237

Yorktown. See Cuba

Yumuri. See Rose City, 256